Curriculum Development and Design

LEARNING CENTRE SERVICES
Bilston Campus   01902 821054
Wulfrun Campus   01902 317535

Curriculum Development and Design

Second Edition

MURRAY PRINT

ALLEN&UNWIN

*This book is dedicated to Karen, Mara, Kobi and Courtney;
and to my curriculum students over the years.*

First published in 1988
Second edition published 1993

Allen & Unwin
83 Alexander Street
Crows Nest NSW 2065
Australia
Phone: (61 2) 8425 0100
Fax: (61 2) 9906 2218
Email: info@allenandunwin.com
Web: www.allenandunwin.com

National Library of Australia
Cataloguing-in-Publication entry:

Print, M. (Murray).
Curriculum development and design.

2nd ed.
Includes index.
ISBN 1 86373 362 0.

1.   Curriculum planning–Australia. I. Title.

375.0010994

Set in 10/11 pt Times by DOCUPRO, Sydney
Printed by SRM Production Services Sdn Bhd, Malaysia.

20 19 18 17 16 15 14 13 12 11

Foreword

Curriculum, as an idea and as a practice, is and will continue to be contentious.

At one level, curriculum is an idea, a construct of society. It is a statement of what a society values: what it wants to continue, what it wants to change, what it wants to renew. Of course, even this conception of society as having an entity, a capacity to make choices, is contentious. In curriculum, our society makes choices in various ways: by legislation in parliament, by decisions by public examination bodies or groups of schools, by encouragement through public instrumentalities, such as the Department of Health, by expressions of view through parent groups, by statements from employer groups or trade unions, by contentions from special-interest groups. All these influences operate to varying effect in their own ways and there is rarely any comprehensive attempt to coordinate or link, or to assess the inputs. Nevertheless, this complex process operating in the many school systems in Australia, and in other countries, tends to produce very similar results.

At another level, curriculum is a practice. It is what we do intentionally in schools. It is the reality of interchange between teachers and students, students and students, students and learning materials and opportunities. It results from listening, speaking. thinking, reacting, responding, reading, writing, analysing, synthesising, evaluating. It emerges through changes in what students know, understand, believe and do. And in their enhanced capacity for all these. Our approach is similar—most schools in most places operate in familiar and customary patterns. Yet we are still unsure of the processes that will work best. Unsure of the ways in which the mind works. Unsure of the possibilities inherent in different human lives.

These contentions and struggles will continue. There is no easy end-point which we can reach. This is why books such as this one are helpful, in that they recognise the challenging relations with which all teachers and students deal. Murray Print has performed a valuable service by writing of a world which is familiar and not over-simplified, by recognising the impossibility of final answers but the necessity of finding day-by-day solutions. The welcome given by teachers to the first edition of *Curriculum Development and Design* was earned by this combination of practicality and vision. It comes from a writer who has continually tested his ideas against the judgments of practitioners as well as the findings of scholars. Thus, it is of value to both groups and so—and this may be the best test—it will be of value to students, even though they may never read it.

Professor Phillip Hughes

Contents

Abbreviations

ACER	Australian Council for Educational Research
ASEP	Australian Science Education Project
BOS	NSW Board of Studies
BSCS	Biological Sciences Curriculum Study
CAL	Computer Assisted Learning
CDC	Curriculum Development Centre
CHEM Study	Chemistry Study
DEET	Department of Employment, Education and Training
HSC	Higher School Certificate
HSGP	High School Geography Project
ISIS	Individualised Science Instruction System
KLAs	Key Learning Areas
K10	Kindergarten to Year 10
MACOS	Man A Course of Study
PEP	Participation and Equity Programme
SAC	Situational Analysis Checklist
SAT	Situational Analysis Techniques
SAT	Scholastic Aptitude Test
SBCD	School-Based Curriculum Development
SEMP	Social Education Materials Project
SMSG	School Mathematics Study Group
SRA	Science Research Associates
TAFE	Technical and Further Education
TEE	Tertiary Entrance Examination
USSR	Uninterrupted Sustained Silent Reading
VCAB	Victorian Curriculum and Assessment Board

Tables and figures

Preface to first edition

This book is the result of a decade of teaching curriculum at tertiary institutions and of undertaking curriculum research and writing. In this time it has become increasingly evident that a need exists for classroom teachers as well as school administrators and system level developers to be familiar with the skills and principles of curriculum development and design.

As we move towards the turn of the decade a message is becoming increasingly clear to our schools—more effective, more efficient and more appropriate curricula are required to meet the needs of our children and adolescents. To meet those needs we require people well prepared in curriculum development and design.

My intention in this book is quite deliberate. I want to provide classroom teachers, school administrators, systemic developers and all others concerned about education with a practical source of information about how curricula may be developed and designed. I hope this intention has been achieved.

I would like to acknowledge the support of my colleagues at WACAE and particularly the curriculum team within the School of Education. To those who gave constructive criticism I am indebted for their contribution. Finally I wish to acknowledge the many hundreds of students whom I have taught in numerous curriculum units. Their contribution has both inspired and provided the groundwork for this book. I hope their successors will find it valuable.

Murray Print
Perth, 1987

Preface to second edition

One of the most enjoyable features in preparing this second edition was the knowledge that the first edition had been a useful book that was well received. A small measure of that success was the five printings of the book before this second edition was prepared.

However, in the intervening period the study of curriculum has undergone some significant changes, and an updating has been necessary. Indeed the past few years have probably been the period of most profound educational and curriculum change in the past half century.

One of the most interesting and significant changes has been an attempt by governments to gain hegemony over the curriculum development process. Consequently educators need to be ever vigilant and address the major curriculum changes facing our schools. As part of this vigilance, educators must understand the process of curriculum development as well as understand the contemporary curriculum scene.

And as the study of curriculum has grown in sophistication so its very nature has become more problematic and less rigidly defined. This may present some difficulties to those learning about curriculum for the first time in a systematic manner such as the way presented in this book. Nevertheless as an understanding of curriculum grows within one, so the problematic nature of curriculum diminishes as a concern.

I wish to express my gratitude to numerous students who have studied curriculum with me over the years at both undergraduate and postgraduate levels. Together we have learnt much about curriculum processes.

I'd also like to thank the many colleagues who helped me with this book, either by providing direct feedback or through debating issues with me. The reviewers of my manuscript provided extremely useful feedback. Special mention must be made of the contribution of some who were most helpful: Professor Phillip Hughes at the University of Tasmania for his support and encouragement; at the University of Sydney, Drs Mike King and David Smith helped clarify my thoughts; and at Edith Cowan

University, John Woods and Mike Cullen provided me with excellent feedback. To all concerned I am most thankful.

Murray Print
Faculty of Education
University of Sydney
1993

Glossary of terms

adoption: the acceptance, and rate of acceptance, of an innovation within a system.

algorithm: a step-by-step procedure for solving a problem or accomplishing some end such as developing a curriculum.

architectonics: those principles responsible for ordering content into systematic categories for the purposes of study.

assessment: involves the interpretation of measurement data, usually in terms of whether or not an intended level of achievement has been attained.

behaviour: that which pupils do, from which thinking or feelings may be inferred, or which may be an end in itself.

behavioural objectives: precise statements of observable, measureable student behaviour. Behavioural objectives consist of three components: observable student behaviour, conditions for learning and acceptable standards of performance.

change: the process of transforming phenomena into something different. It has the dimensions of rate (speed), scale (size), degree (thoroughness), continuity (profoundness) and direction.

change agent: those individuals facilitating the process of change by establishing links between developers and clients.

cognitive: related to knowing or intellectual activity.

common curriculum: a program of learning undertaken by all students. This group of common or core learnings has been selected by curriculum developers as being of value to all students.

confluent education: is concerned with a 'total-life' orientation for students, that is, the integration of the affective and cognitive domains as a base for student learning. To accomplish this the programs presented have a balance of input from subject areas as well as values, attitudes, and feelings so as to make them meaningful to students. Emphasis is placed on the learner taking responsibility for recognising alternatives provided by the teacher and selecting from these alternatives those which increase the personal meaning of what is learned.

content: is the subject matter of the teaching–learning process and includes knowledge, processes and values.

core subjects: those subjects in a program which provide essential and required information or experiences, or teach essential skills for all students undertaking the program. Core subjects, within a curriculum, may be supplemented by elective subjects.

criteria-referenced: judged against a fixed standard of performance. Usually refers to criterion-referenced assessment which assesses student performance against predetermined criteria or standards.

criterion-referenced tests: are designed to measure student performance on objectives on which there is an established standard for acceptable performance.

curriculum: All the *planned* learning opportunities offered by the organisation to learners and the experiences learners encounter when the curriculum is implemented. This does *not* include the hidden curriculum.

curriculum conceptions: the way developers think and act about curriculum, particularly in terms of curriculum development.

curriculum decision-making: the process of making choices for curriculum action, requiring selection from a range of alternative curriculum directions.

curriculum design: the process of conceptualising and arranging the elements of curriculum into a coherent pattern.

curriculum development: the process of planning learning opportunities intended to bring about certain desired changes in pupils, and the assessment of the extent to which these changes have taken place.

curriculum dissemination: the process of ensuring that a curriculum reaches the target population, that is, the deliberate intention to inform clients of an innovation. The process includes such aspects as training those who will present the materials, sensitising those who will monitor it, and other goal-oriented activities to facilitate the adoption of the innovation.

curriculum elements: those distinct, yet related, parts of the whole curriculum including curriculum intent (aims, goals and objectives), content, learning activities and evaluation.

curriculum evaluation: the process of delineating, obtaining and providing information useful in making curriculum decisions and judgments.

curriculum foundations: those basic forces that influence and shape the content and organisation of the curriculum.

curriculum management: involves activities associated with planning, regulating, coordinating, developing, implementing and evaluating the curriculum.

curriculum outcomes: may be defined as the intended results of the teaching–learning process as identified in a curriculum document (usually called a syllabus) and expressed as a set of broad, comprehensive, assessable and observable indicators of student achievement. Taken together, a set of curriculum outcomes statements should cover not only the knowledge and skills domains of a subject syllabus but also the attitudes and values domain as well.

curriculum package: the presentation of materials covering all curriculum elements in a single framework. Commonly found with commercially produced products such as ASEP or SEMP but includes teacher-made materials as well.

curriculum planning: is the process whereby curriculum developers conceptualise and organise the features of the curriculum they wish to construct. This involves a broad analysis of the curriculum intent and context (what you wish to achieve), conceptualising the curriculum's design (what it will look like), organising the sequencing of developmental tasks (how to construct the curriculum) and arranging for the process of implementation and evaluation.

curriculum presage: those activities and forces that influence curriculum developers in their curriculum decision making tasks.

curriculum process: a continuous cycle of activities in which all elements of the curriculum are considered and interrelated.

diagnostic evaluation: involves the collection of appropriate data for two purposes:
1 To place students prior to the commencement of a program;
2 To determine the causes of deficiencies in student learning during the implementation of the instruction.

diffusion: the natural process concerned with the spread of new ideas, objects or practices from its origin to its adopters.

discrete: individually separate or distinct.

dissemination: the deliberate process to facilitate the spread of ideas, objects or practices from their source to clients.

elective subjects: those subjects in a program which, although not essential, supplement core subjects and are selected by students to complete the program. Most often they represent student interests.

evaluation: the systematic process of collecting data in order to make judgments of statements of worth. In education, data are collected and interpreted through measurement and assessment of student performance. Using these data, evaluative statements can be made about students usually in written forms such as reports.

formative evaluation: is directed towards determining how well students are progressing during the learning experience to determine if changes need to be made.

goals: are relatively specific, precisely worded statements of curriculum intent and are derived from aims.

heterogeneous groups: groups in which individuals display diversity in stated characteristics, for example, mixed ability classes are heterogeneous in aspects of student ability performance.

hidden curriculum: consists of those learnings unintentionally passed on to students during the presentation of the intended curriculum. These learnings were not intended by curriculum developers and are not stated as objectives in curricula. The hidden curriculum varies from situation to situation and is not recognised by the school personnel.

homogeneous groups: groups in which individuals display uniformity in stated characteristics, for example, an intellectually talented group is homogeneous in characteristics such as achievement or IQ.

horizontal organisation: is concerned with the arrangement of curriculum components at any one point in time. A latitudinal perspective that considers the issues of organising curriculum components so that they are arranged in such a way as to illuminate one another. Horizontal organisation is often used synonymously with the term 'scope', which more correctly refers to the organisation only of content.

humanistic education: is concerned with facilitating development of the self-actualising person. Emphasis is placed on the individual and in developing experiences which allow the individual to increase personal awareness and develop a positive self-concept. Learning experiences encourage the individual to 'discover' self rather than conforming to an externally determined mould.

inductive/deductive approaches: in reference to teaching–learning, inductive approaches are concerned with progressing from specific examples (facts) to generalisations or concepts. On the other hand, deductive approaches progress from the more abstract generalisations or concepts to specific facts.

innovation: an object, idea or practice which is perceived to be *new* and also the process by which that object, idea or practice is adopted.

institutionalisation: the process whereby an innovation becomes interwoven and formalised within an organisational structure. Seen as the final phase in a successful change process.

instruction: those activities that the teacher or instructor undertakes to enhance student learning. Instruction may take the form of a person (teacher, lecturer, tutor), an object (book, film) or a program (computer-assisted instruction, programmed learning).

learning activities: those activities offered to learners in the teaching–learning situation which enable them to acquire designated content and so achieve the stated objectives.

learning experiences: are those experiences through which the learner interacts with the learning environment to achieve the stated objectives. These experiences consist of teacher-initiated activities (learning opportunities) and learner-initiated activities.

learning opportunity: a planned and controlled relationship between pupils, teacher, materials, equipment and the environment, in which it is hoped that desired learning will take place.

measurement: the collection of descriptive data about student performance. Data are invariably represented in quantitative forms.

model: a simplified representation of reality, that depicts relationships between variables. Often depicted in a diagram.

national curriculum: a curriculum designed, through some central mechanism, to meet the needs of students across a nation.

needs assessment: an empirical and judgmental process for identifying human needs and establishing priorities among them.

norm-referenced: judged by comparison with the performance of others, for example, norm-referenced tests which compare a student's performance on a test with that of similar students on the same test.

objectives: statements of learner intent designed to bring out change within the learner. This change results from student interaction with the curriculum as the objectives are achieved.

outcomes: are observable, measureable and assessable statements of intended learner behaviour usually expressed in terms of specified levels of achievement.

phenomenology: a philosophical position which values what is perceived through the senses, for example, sight, touch. By gathering all of the possible perceptions of any phenomenon, true insight is gained. In schools, phenomenological studies may examine the realities of classroom life by focusing the senses on features such as student–student interaction.

planned change: the deliberate and collaborative process involving a change agent and a client system brought together to attain an improved state of functioning.

reliability: in measurement terms refers to the consistency with which a test or instrument measures any particular phenomenon, that is, the ability of the test to reproduce the same results over time. It is a significant factor affecting confidence in a particular test or instrument and instruments high in reliability are favoured for classroom measurement.

SBCD (School-Based Curriculum Development): is concerned with school-level creation and adaption of curricula as well as curriculum decision-making at that level.

schooling: the totality of student learnings associated with the school.

This includes both planned learnings (curriculum) and unplanned learnings (hidden curriculum).

scope: refers to the breadth and depth of *content* to be covered in a curriculum at any one time.

self-actualisation: the process of utilising one's talent, capacities and potentials to the full. Self-actualising persons think well of themselves and others, feel competent and are aware of their limitations.

sequence: refers to the *order* that content is presented to learners over time. Used in conjunction with scope to structure content within a curriculum.

simulation: a simplified representation under specific controlled conditions of phenomena or events in the real world. Used for the study of reality within an educational context.

situational analysis: the process of examining an educational context for which a curriculum is to be developed and the application of that analysis to curriculum planning.

social reconstructionalism: is the point of view which emphasises planning for and effecting social change. Reconstructionists argue that curriculum should be aimed at presenting social reality and developing the skills to change this reality for the betterment of future society.

standardised tests: these are tests which can be administered and scored consistently every time they are used because they have been 'normed' against a standard population. There are numerous standardised tests used in Australia, for example, ACER tests of learning ability for years 4 and 6, ACER cooperative reading comprehension test, ACER tests of intelligence.

summative evaluation: involves the collection of appropriate data at the end of a program to determine whether or not the objectives have been achieved.

syllabus: a list of content areas which are to be taught and assessed. Sometimes objectives and learning activities are included. A syllabus is subsumed within a curriculum.

teaching strategies: another term for learning activities and learning opportunities. All are methods by which teachers manipulate learners to achieve the desired objectives.

theory: a plausible or scientifically acceptable general principle or body of principles offered to explain phenomena.

transition education: is designed to facilitate entry into future employment. Developed for those people who are not able, because of a variety of reasons, to enter their chosen occupations immediately.

validity: in measurement terms validity is the degree to which a test or instrument measures what it is supposed to measure. If a test or instrument does what it purports to do, such as measure maths achievement, it is valid.

vertical organisation: is concerned with the relationship between curriculum components over the entire duration of the curriculum, that is, in what *order* they are presented to learners over time.

1 Introducing curriculum

. . . knowledge of curriculum is, by definition, central to . . .
the professional teacher and an essential orientation for all
'professionally responsible beginners'. (Karen Zumwalt, 1989: 174)

Curriculum is an area of vital importance to the professional teacher. Over the past two decades the study of curriculum has become an established part of teacher education programs in Australia and all pre-service teachers have become familiar with the concepts of curriculum in some way. Similarly, teachers undertaking postgraduate studies and professional development activities have been exposed to the concepts associated with curriculum. And in more recent years the term has become quite frequently used in the media and the community in general.

Such a development is highly appropriate for professional teachers. Curriculum is, after all, the very substance of schooling and the *raison d'être* for teachers in schools. Therefore teachers need to be knowledgeable about curriculum and understand the processes by which curricula may be developed. When teachers consider curriculum issues, for example, they tackle the substantive matter of schooling which may be expressed in terms of the fundamental questions of curriculum, namely:

What to teach?
How to teach?
When to teach?
What is the impact of teaching?

And from these general questions come a flood of well-recognised curriculum-directed questions for the teacher and curriculum developer to answer, such as:

What knowledge is of most worth to learners?
What activities are most effective in enabling learners to acquire
 this knowledge (information, facts, skills, values, attitudes, etc.)?
What is the most appropriate way to organise these activities?
How do I know if learners have acquired this knowledge?

These questions, and many others, will be addressed in subsequent chapters as we examine the processes involved with curriculum design and development. And underlying this examination will rest a fundamental premise—that the person best equipped to answer and implement the above questions is the professional teacher. To that end, the following chapters will hopefully assist the educational professional act more effectively with the curriculum. Karen Zumwalt has stated, in the context of ensuring that our teachers are professionals, that initial knowledge of curriculum should include an understanding of:

1 different views of curriculum and ensuing consequences for the role of teacher;
2 some conception of a curricular planning process and the knowledge necessary to carry it out;
3 the realities of curricular decision-making . . . (Zumwalt 1989: 174)

This book strongly supports Zumwalt's contentions and the ensuing chapters reflect that position.

The first chapter introduces you to important concepts associated with curriculum and, in so doing, will cover the nature of curriculum, definitions of curriculum, the hidden curriculum, curriculum as a manipulative strategy, school-level curriculum decision-making, school-based curriculum development and an introduction to curriculum development. In the process, numerous curriculum terms will be employed and it is recommended that you consult the glossary for definitions.

Finally, it is recommended that those involved with curriculum development consider the process of curriculum as a form of problem-solving activity. If the questions of what, when, how and so what of teaching are fundamental to schooling, then curriculum can be considered as providing answers to those 'problems'. Thus those teachers who design, develop and adapt curricula in schools are the frontline problem-solvers of schooling. As we shall see in later chapters this process requires one to take into account many aspects of teaching in resolving these 'problems'.

Smith and Lovat (1991) summarised this situation well when they characterised the curriculum process as:

> . . . a *problem-solving process*, in which the *teacher processes a complex variety of stimuli and information and uses this to make decisions and solve problems*: the teacher's key roles in this are those of *information processor, manager, decision-maker and problem-solver* (1991:xiv)(their emphasis)

In taking this position this book acknowledges the fundamental role that teachers play in the application of the curriculum process in their classrooms. Whether teachers are directly responsible for curriculum development, or whether they interpret, implement, modify existing curriculum documents, they require a sound, substantive understanding of the curriculum process with a consequential understanding of how it may affect them and their students.

The nature of curriculum

Many people find the term 'curriculum' rather confusing. After all, they contend, it is used in many different ways. For example, a common use of the term refers to 'the school curriculum'. This incorporates all the planned learnings offered by the school. However, an equally accepted use of the term is to talk about the 'lower-school curriculum' or the 'K10 curriculum'. One can also refer to the 'history curriculum', the 'maths curriculum' or the 'home economics curriculum'. The above are examples of the term 'curriculum' in practice and they can be placed in one of the following categories:

1 a systemic curriculum, for example, the Tasmanian primary school curriculum, New South Wales secondary school curriculum;
2 a subject curriculum, for example, the K10 social studies curriculum;
3 a school/institution curriculum, for example, the Kapinara Primary School curriculum; Neutral Bay Public School curriculum.

One could similarly refer to the flight-attendant curriculum, the real-estate-agent curriculum, the accounting curriculum and so forth. Indeed, any institution that offers an educational program to learners employs a curriculum of some form. For our purposes, however, we shall concentrate upon the use of curriculum in Australian schools.

Another way of conceptualising curriculum is to view it in terms of the perceptions people have of curricula. Different people perceive a school's curriculum in different ways and sometimes in multiple ways depending upon the context in which the concept is used. To complicate matters further, someone may perceive the curriculum in a particular way and use the term 'curriculum' to describe what they mean, while another uses the same term but means something different.

For example, a teacher may refer to the school curriculum and really mean the 'intended' or 'written' curriculum, while a parent may refer to the school curriculum and mean the 'entitlement' curriculum or the 'achieved' curriculum. Similarly a systemic curriculum developer may refer to the school curriculum and mean the 'ideal' or perhaps the 'intended' curriculum. Consequently it is important for us to be clear what perception we have of curriculum when we communicate with others. The most common perceptions of curriculum, expanded substantially from the types suggested by Glatthorn (1987), may be described as:

- *The ideal or recommended curriculum*: what is proposed by scholars as a solution to meet a need and consequently perceived as the most appropriate curriculum for learners.

- *The entitlement curriculum*: what society believes learners should expect to be exposed to as part of their learning to become effective members of that society.
- *The intended or written curriculum:* what organisations develop for the learners in their educational systems and what should be taught by the teachers in that system. This is often referred to as the syllabus by such organisations and systems.
- *The available or supported curriculum:* that curriculum which can be taught in schools through the provision of appropriate resources, both human and material.
- *The implemented curriculum*: what is actually taught by teachers in their classrooms as they and their students interact with the intended and available curricula.
- *The achieved curriculum:* what students actually learnt as a result of their interaction with the implemented curriculum.
- *The attained curriculum:* the measurement of student learning (usually through a testing process) which reveals those learnings acquired by students. Measurement is usually based upon the intended curriculum, particularly at systemic levels, though it may be based on the implemented curriculum at classroom level.

Thus in schools it is possible to talk about the intended modern history curriculum, Sydney Girls' High School's implemented curriculum, the attained physics curriculum and so forth. Similarly a university may refer to its achieved medical curriculum, its available teacher-education curriculum or its ideal architectural curriculum. In practice these different ways of conceptualising curriculum are usually blended into one term—'the curriculum', though when we discuss what we mean we invariably expose the subtle (and sometime not too subtle) variations as described above.

In professional parlance, therefore, the term 'curriculum' may be used in various situations to describe different, if related, things. While this may appear confusing, there is nevertheless widespread acceptance of these differing interpretations. The essential features common to curricula, however, are that all forms of curricula incorporate the following:

1 A formalised course of study designed for learners.
2 Conscious planning that attempts to determine learning outcomes.
3 Some form of structure to facilitate that learning.

In the following chapters we'll draw our examples of curriculum from the school environment although it is important to note that the same principles apply to any non-school institutions providing educational programs.

Characterisations of curriculum

William Schubert (1986) refers to many different images or characterisations of curriculum. He prefers these terms to that of 'definition' because '. . . they denote a broader conceptualisation than the label for a thing'. (1986:26) However, an image or characterisation can also mean a way of perceiving or viewing the concept concerned and hence facilitating understanding. I have chosen to examine a number of characterisations as a way of depicting the richness and comprehensiveness of the concept and as a means of understanding that breadth and depth of meaning. Further reading on this matter may be obtained from Schubert (1986), Gress & Purpel (1988), Saylor, Alexander & Lewis (1981), Marsh & Stafford (1988), Smith & Lovat (1991) and other references indicated in the reference list. Such characterisations may also facilitate an understanding of differing definitions. A selection of these characterisations includes:

Curriculum as subject matter: This is the most traditional image of curriculum which depicts it as the combining of subject matter to form a body of content to be taught. Such content is the product of accumulated wisdom, particularly acquired through the traditional academic disciplines. As a result of this content, one can predetermine the curriculum for learners. Most teachers, when asked to describe their school's curriculum, provide a litany of subjects or subject matter taught to students.

In earlier times this characterisation of curriculum saw students encounter the seven liberal arts, usually divided into the *trivium* (grammar, rhetoric and dialectic) and the *quadrivium* (arithmetic, geometry, astronomy and music). Today most school curricula in Australia have been developed as subjects (chapter 4) or from a subject base (see broad fields design, chapter 4). This characterisation of curriculum has become so deeply ingrained in people's understanding of curriculum that it has become axiomatic with the term itself.

Curriculum as experience: A more recent image sees curriculum as the set of experiences learners encounter in educational contexts. Most of these experiences have been purposively planned by means of the written curriculum but many more experiences are encountered by learners in educational contexts. Through experiencing the hidden curriculum learners acquire many forms of learning that were not planned yet which are usually highly significant (for more on the hidden curriculum see later in this chapter).

Experience is also seen from the perspective argued by John Dewey (1916), namely that in experiencing a curriculum one also reflects upon that experience and one consequently strives to monitor one's thoughts and actions in that curriculum context. In this characterisation of curriculum the teacher acts more as a facilitator to enhance the learner's personal growth.

Curriculum as intention: Early efforts to address curriculum planning saw educators make use of intentional strategies through the vehicles of aims, goals and objectives. This characterisation of curriculum argues that a comprehensive planning of learning experiences for students, predetermined before they commence that curriculum, is the best way to address learner needs.

This view of curriculum as a plan has two variations, first, curriculum consisting of a plan of predetermined statements of intent (aims, goals and objectives—what students *should* learn); and second, curriculum as statements of intended learning outcomes (what learners *must* acquire). The former argues for intention statements planned for students commencing a curriculum, while the latter emphasises statements of behaviour for students exiting the curriculum.

Curriculum as cultural reproduction: One characterisation of curriculum that receives support is the view that curriculum should reflect the culture of a particular society. The role of the school, it is argued, and hence the curriculum, is to pass on the salient knowledge and values used by one generation to the succeeding generation. The curriculum, particularly through the selection of learning experiences, provides a vehicle for that reproduction process.

However there is by no means consensus as to what knowledge and values are indeed worthwhile to be passed on from one generation to the next. Uncritical cultural reproduction has not occurred in our society and consequently this characterisation remains contentious.

Curriculum as 'currere': A more recent characterisation of curriculum views it as a process of providing continuous personal meaning to individuals. Coming from the Latin, *currere* may be interpreted not as a 'racecourse' but rather as the 'running of the race' (Pinar, 1975; Smith & Lovat, 1991). This emphasises the individual's capacity to participate and to reconceptualise upon one's experience of life. In essence, this characterisation emphasises an experiential perspective to learning and hence to the curriculum—the curriculum is the interpretation of lived experience (Schubert, 1986).

However this characterisation is also social in nature, in that a sharing of experiences and reconceptualisations is favoured. And through this social process of sharing, individuals come to a greater understanding of themselves as well as others and the world.

As you learn more about curriculum you will develop a clearer perspective of what you perceive is its nature. In that process you might reflect upon the above characterisations and see if they can assist with the clarification of your thinking.

Curriculum and syllabus

'Curriculum' as a term is often confused with 'syllabus'. A syllabus is typically a list of content areas which are to be assessed. Sometimes the list is extended to include a number of objectives and learning activities. However, in the literature syllabus is clearly intended to be a subsection of curriculum and as such is subsumed within the broader concept. However, those organisations involved with the construction of systemic-level curricula invariably produce syllabus documents, even if they emanate from a curriculum directorate or curriculum branch. Usually these bodies are departments or ministries of education as well as assessment and curriculum bodies such as the NSW Board of Studies, the WA Secondary Education Authority or the Senior Secondary Assessment Board of South Australia. A useful way to avoid confusion is to refer to syllabuses as curriculum documents.

By comparison, a curriculum includes not only content and a detailed statement of curriculum intent (aims, goals and objectives), but also the other curriculum elements including detailed learning activities and evaluation procedures. Similarly, the term 'instruction' refers to the set of activities employed by teachers to enhance student learning. Clearly this term is also subsumed within the broader context of curriculum.

Definitions

The search for an appropriate definition of the term 'curriculum' has become increasingly problematic over time. Rather than achieving consensus and thereby enhancing effective communication the literature reveals continued differentiation and disputation as to an acceptable definition. The result has meant that those writing and teaching about curriculum are well advised to preface their statements about curriculum by *their interpretation of the concept.*

Paradoxically the term 'curriculum' has a long history despite its apparently recent common usage. Curriculum was considered by writers on education such as Plato, Aristotle, J.A. Comenius and Friedrich Froebel, although the usage of the term has not been popularised until this century.

Educators define curriculum in different ways, in part because they bring to that task different perceptions of what curriculum should be. Some educators see the curriculum as a list of subjects to be studied, while others see it as an entire course content. Still others perceive curriculum as a set of planned learning experiences offered by teachers.

Another group state that the curriculum is a written plan of action, thereby distinguishing it from what actually happens in a school. As we have seen earlier, there are many ways to characterise the curriculum and this has enhanced a multiplicity of definitions.

Indeed, so many curriculum writers have participated in the debate (Doll, 1978; Eisner & Vallance, 1974; Hirst, 1968; Hughes, 1973; Lawton, 1978; Schubert, 1986; Gress & Purpel, 1988; Smith & Lovat, 1991; Pinar, 1975; Cohen & Harrison, 1982; Print, 1988; Zumwalt, 1989), that additional discussion of appropriate definitions may provide little illumination.

While agreeing with Robert Zais that '. . . a search for *the* correct definition of the term is not a very productive enterprise . . .' (1976:13), it is important that one has a feel for different definitions. It is within the context of these definitions that one can appreciate the problematic nature of curriculum and the definition that has been followed in subsequent chapters of this book. The following are some of the more well-known definitions that you might consider.

Ralph Tyler (1949):	'All of the learning of students which is planned by and directed by the school to attain its educational goals.'
D.K. Wheeler (1967):	'By "curriculum" we mean the planned experiences offered to the learner under the guidance of the school.'
E. Eisner (1979):	'The curriculum of a school, or a course, or a classroom can be conceived of as a series of planned events that are intended to have educational consequences for one or more students.'
G. Saylor, W. Alexander & A.J. Lewis (1981):	'We define curriculum as a plan for providing sets of learning opportunities for persons to be educated.'
M. Skilbeck (1984):	'The learning experiences of students, in so far as they are expressed or anticipated in goals and objectives, plans and designs for learning and the implementation of these plans and designs in school environments.'
A. Glatthorn (1987):	'The curriculum is the plans made for guiding learning in schools, usually represented in retrievable documents of several levels of generality, and the actualisation of those plans in the classroom, as experienced by the learners and as recorded by an observer; those

	experiences take place in a learning environment which also influences what is learned.'
J. Wiles & J. Bondi (1989):	'. . . the curriculum [is] a goal or set of values, which are activated through a development process culminating in classroom experiences for students. The degree to which those experiences are a true representation of the envisioned goal or goals is a direct function of the effectiveness of the curriculum development efforts.'

Definition: For the purposes of this book, curriculum is defined as all the planned learning opportunities offered to learners by the educational institution *and* the experiences learners encounter when the curriculum is implemented. This includes those activities that educators have devised for learners which are invariably represented in the form of a written document *and* the process whereby teachers make decisions to implement those activities given interaction with context variables such as learners, resources, teachers and the learning environment.

The above definition argues that a curriculum consists of:

1 Planned learning experiences;
2 offered within an educational institution/program;
3 represented as a document; and
4 includes experiences resulting from implementing that document.

This conceptualisation of the term goes beyond the notion of simply preparing a planned document to be applied later. When a curriculum document is implemented in an institution with an educational program (kindergarten, school, college, university and so forth), interaction takes place between the document, learners and instructors such that modification occurs and a 'curriculum' emerges. These notions are developed further in chapter 3 where a model of curriculum development is presented.

The hidden curriculum

Within the broader context of education, curriculum, as defined above, has a specified location. In stating this case, one can see more clearly exactly what is included within, and excluded from, the curriculum, or what is sometimes referred to as the planned or overt curriculum.

Figure 1.1 shows that *schooling* consists of the totality of student learnings associated with the school. Curriculum may be seen as all of

Figure 1.1   Schooling

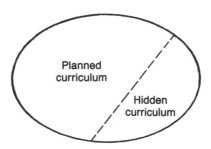

those planned learnings that students were deliberately exposed to by schools. Nevertheless, students acquired numerous learnings that were not planned and these have become subsequently known as the 'hidden curriculum'. The same phenomenon occurs in any institution offering an educational program, that is, that learners will acquire planned, intentional learning as well as unplanned, unintentional learnings.

'Hidden curriculum' has become an accepted and commonly used part of educational discourse in the past decade. Extensive research and writing have addressed multifarious aspects of the concept (Apple, 1983, 1990; Anyon, 1980; Giroux, 1981; Hewitson, 1982; Jackson, 1968; Seddon, 1983). But with what is the hidden curriculum concerned?

> . . . the hidden curriculum refers to the outcomes of education and/or the
> processes leading to those outcomes, which are *not explicitly intended by
> educators*. These outcomes are generally not explicitly intended because
> they are not stated by teachers in their oral or written lists of objectives,
> nor are they included in educational statements of intent such as
> syllabuses, school policy documents or curriculum projects. (Seddon,
> 1983:1–2; emphasis added)

The outcomes referred to above are invariably viewed as negative or as detrimental to the learner's development. But is this always so?

The following examples illustrate the pervasive nature of the hidden curriculum operating in our educational institutions in both positive and negative ways. See if you can determine which are the negative and the positive contributions of the hidden curriculum.

> A primary school teacher calls for volunteers to assist her with classroom
> duties. She selects boys to do the more physical tasks (clean the
> blackboard, move chairs) and girls to perform the gentler tasks (handing
> out paper, collecting pencils).

What message is the teacher passing on to students? What are students learning unconsciously? What values and attitudes are being transmitted to learners indirectly?

> A high school principal has formed a student council to assist with running the school. Students are elected by their peers, without teacher veto. When the council meets, representatives elect a leader, again without teacher interference. The principal accepts the advice of the student council and does her best to implement it.

What does this tell us about how students are regarded at this school? How does the principal treat students in this context? What values and attitudes do students acquire here?

> An English teacher has decided to moralise about truth and honesty in one of the novels being discussed in class. Reading a passage from a novel aloud, he is annoyed by some background noise. He requests the noisemakers to indicate themselves making reference to the message in the novel's content. One student admits talking and receives punishment, others do not.

What message do the students learn indirectly from this situation? Is the English teacher aware of his own dilemma? Which message is likely to have a more pervasive influence upon students?

> A kindergarten child brought two large stuffed dolls to school and sat them in her seat. During the first session of large group activity, the teacher referred to the dolls saying 'Raggedy Ann and Raggedy Andy are such good helpers! They haven't said a thing all morning.' (Apple, 1990:54)

How typical is Apple's example in relation to Australian preschools? What other forms of behaviour are learnt by students in this manner?

The hidden curriculum may be characterised as positive or negative, although which is which depends on one's point of view. Typically, all of the examples above, except the second, would be considered as negative examples of the hidden curriculum in operation. In the first example, the primary schoolteacher is reinforcing sex-type stereotypes by allocating certain tasks to girls. Unknowingly, students learn to associate certain tasks with sex type and this may well become the basis for a range of sex-stereotyping behaviour. Whether you consider this an example of positive or negative hidden curriculum depends upon your point of view and, perhaps, what you learnt through the hidden curriculum

The examples of hidden curriculum highlight the essential feature of the concept—its hiddenness. The messages passed on to students are essentially 'hidden' from them, at least in the sense that they have not been stated explicitly. Other researchers suggest that the hidden curriculum may also be hidden to teachers, as well as students, at least at a conscious level. In the first and fourth examples cited, it is quite possible that the teachers were quite unaware of what they were doing. The irony of the third example was probably not lost on the students and hopefully the teacher can find a way to overcome his dilemma.

In schools, Hewitson (1982) suggests that the hidden curriculum is acquired by students at three levels:

1 the school system as part of the society;
2 the operation of the school, and
3 the functioning of the classroom.

Most studies of the hidden curriculum have concentrated upon the latter two levels, while more recent studies examine the school in the broader societal context. The essential features of the hidden curriculum have been identified by Hewitson (1982:1).

> Learning the hidden curriculum is not the result of deliberate efforts on the part of learners, but is mainly inferred on their part. Such learning accrues over time as a seemingly inevitable consequence of continued exposure to delimited perceptions of reality. In this regard, it is something 'done to' learners, not something done with them or with their conscious assent.
>
> What is perceived or inferred by learners comes to be taken as the natural order of things, i.e. their social reality appears to have been ordained by nature rather than structured by man.
>
> At the societal level, the cause of the hidden curriculum lies in the way the school system is structured and resourced to achieve the functions for which it is established and maintained. Broadly speaking these functions have to do with preparing learners for future roles in society.
>
> At the school and classroom level, the hidden curriculum is learnt through structures and rules as well as through attitudes and values espoused by school staff, school text books, school syllabuses and the student peer group.

Learning the hidden curriculum

Students receive hidden messages from their participation in classroom activities, by attending school and by virtue of the context of school in society. In other words, they're *constantly* receiving information about which they are largely unaware from people who are often unaware of this transmission. Seddon (1983:2) states the situation succinctly:

> There seems to be general agreement that the hidden curriculum involves the learnings of attitudes, norms, beliefs, values and assumptions often expressed as rules, rituals and regulations. Taken as a whole these learnings can be termed the common-sense knowledge which we, as members of a given society, take for granted. As such, they are rarely questioned and often remain unarticulated . . . in educational institutions

learning associated with the hidden curriculum takes place in any situation involving two or more people: teacher teacher; teacher student; or student student.

As some of us are aware of, and indeed are able to study, the hidden curriculum it is obviously not hidden to everyone. Numerous researchers and writers (Apple, Seddon, Hewitson, Illich) have studied aspects of the hidden curriculum for many years. They have been concerned particularly about the influence the hidden curriculum is having upon learners. As well they have sought to determine how much of learning is obtained this way, how pervasive is this learning, how significant is this form of learning in the totality of school learning and the degree to which one can overcome the effects of the hidden curriculum.

One significant result of research and writing on the hidden curriculum and its effects has been the trend toward deliberately incorporating learnings, taken from the hidden curriculum, into the planned curriculum. Educators have argued successfully that if certain learnings from the hidden curriculum are so *pervasive* and so *powerful,* then they must be dealt with formally in classrooms. Here, in the overt curriculum, those learnings will be treated in the preferred manner and, hopefully, the desired effects will result.

In the earlier examples of the hidden curriculum several negative effects were witnessed. Educators have argued that children should, for example, acquire non-sexist approaches to the learning of values and attitudes in schools and that it is the curriculum's direct responsibility to enhance that learning. Consequently action must be taken in the overt curriculum to overcome the learnings acquired through the hidden curriculum. The result is that students will read non-sexist literature, perform tasks allocated on non-sexist grounds and study the same subjects. Other recent examples of learning deliberately moved into the school's overt curriculum include multicultural education, law education and changes to biased textbooks.

Figure 1.2 depicts how the situation may be resolved. The negatively learned effects derived from multiculturalism will hopefully be overcome by including multicultural education within the planned curriculum. Similarly, efforts to overcome gender bias can be found by incorporating aspects of gender equity within the overt curriculum.

The questions of how much can, and *should*, be transferred from the hidden to the overt curriculum are vexed. It would appear that the 1980s witnessed a trend towards expanding the overt curriculum by both transfers from the hidden curriculum and additional learnings from the ideal or perhaps the 'external' curriculum. The latter concept includes learnings that were formerly the domain of other institutions such as the family and the church.

In past generations, many of our values, attitudes and beliefs were

14   *Curriculum development and design*

Figure 1.2   Transformation of the hidden curriculum

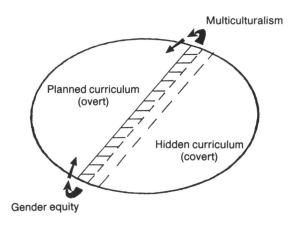

deliberately inculcated through interaction in these institutions. More recently, however, these institutions appear to be surrendering this role. Should the school curriculum take up this cloak of learning? Or, indeed, a more appropriate question may be—can the school avoid these additional responsibilities? The 1990s are witnessing the continuation of these curriculum issues, as pressure to add to the existing curriculum continues unabated.

The extent to which additional learnings can be added to the existing curriculum, without major reconceptualisation of the curriculum, has not yet been tested extensively. This phenomenon will undoubtedly become a major curriculum concern in future years. Later in this book the concept of a 'finite curriculum' is discussed, an indication that the problem has become acknowledged and is in need of attention. One thing is certain, though: the school curriculum simply cannot be added to like a limitless reservoir. It has finite dimensions and simply topping up, without reconceptualisation of the total curriculum, will produce significant pressures. The first signs of stress on the curriculum are evident already. Perhaps the national curriculum initiatives, should they become consolidated, will address and remedy the problem. More likely they will exacerbate it.

Curriculum: a cultural construct

Where do curriculum documents come from? In Australia they are generally produced by the curriculum directorate or branch within the department/ministry of education. This is a requirement of the department to meet its responsibilty to provide educational services. The curricula developed through this source usually relate only to the K10 years of schooling.

At the level of post-compulsory schooling, particularly tertiary entrance subjects, statutory authorities have responsibility for course development and assessment. Usually syllabus committees are created by the statutory authorities to construct curriculum documents in respective subject areas. These curriculum documents, usually referred to as syllabuses, have been developed only for the upper secondary years. One exception is the Board of Studies in New South Wales which has a complete K-12 curriculum mandate.

Yet all these documents have been constructed by groups of individuals who have differing views as to the nature of curriculum, the nature of their subject, what should be taught in schools, how their subject should be taught, and so forth. Thus those involved in the curriculum development task reflect a cultural background, more about which is discussed in chapter 2.

Similarly when these people construct their curriculum document they take into account the society in which we live, the nature of schools, the nature of learners and the resources available. In so doing they create a curriculum which is a *construct of that culture*. In other words, the curriculum that has been devised reflects the nature of that culture. And this is perfectly acceptable.

However, in our complex, democratically based, multicultural society, decisions will be made in the curriculum development process which reflect competing forces seeking to influence future generations. Pressure groups, for example, frequently seek to influence the school curriculum in order to further their own ends. In that sense they attempt to construct reality in schools along the lines of their own cultural perspective. Religious groups, environmentalists and political parties are but a few of the pressure groups which attempt to influence the nature of the school curriculum.

It is important educators realise, therefore, that curriculum development is essentially a manipulative strategy. When questions are posed about *what* students will learn, *when, how* and under *what conditions,* one is asking curriculum questions. However, these questions may be resolved in very different ways, and the results of the answers to those questions become the basis for the written curriculum. Therefore, in a broad sense, what students learn in schools is the result of what certain people want them to learn, that is, the answers to the questions above constructed in a way to meet predetermined needs.

If, for example, a group of curriculum decision-makers want students to develop heightened personal awareness through a knowledge of meditation and yoga, then these could become part of the written curriculum or what students should learn in schools. Similarly, if those decision-makers want students to learn mathematics, science, social studies and English, then those subjects will appear in the written document called the curriculum. Teachers then, in applying the written curriculum in schools, adapt and impart the content of those subjects to students in classrooms. Thus when curricula are devised, they are planned by certain people who have particular intentions in mind of what should be happening to learners, whether they be in schools, tertiary institutions or other organisations. Curriculum development must therefore be seen as a deliberate, purposeful, planning activity which seeks to achieve general and specific intentions (what we call aims and objectives).

If curriculum decision-makers have different purposes which they wish to achieve, these reflect the different conceptions or viewpoints of curriculum that people have. These conceptions will be elaborated substantially later in chapter 2. Meanwhile, imagine what a school curriculum would be like if it were devised by a group of people composed entirely from the following categories: state education department, unions, community and students. How different might the product be if it was devised by the department, universities and parent groups. In New South Wales, school curricula (syllabuses) are devised by the Board of Studies, a statutory authority representing a broad range of educational organisations, only one of whom is the Department of School Education.

The differences in the resulting curricula would be readily apparent. Each group would have in mind a particular type of curriculum that they would see as beneficial to students. And each group would be seeking to manipulate the minds of students to its own ends.

'Give me the child of today and I'll make you the adult of tomorrow', a well-established axiom of many political leaders and some religious groups, seems appropriate when discussing the manipulative aspect of curricula in schools. If one looked at prominent national leaders in the twentieth century, it could be said that many used the school, and the curriculum in schools, as a means to manipulate the young in their societies. The manipulation of curricula by Joseph Stalin, Adolf Hitler and Mao Ze Dong makes the point convincingly. And while we may deplore what they did to the students in their societies, it may be argued that we do much the same in manipulating the curriculum for our students. The major difference, we believe, is that the knowledge, skills and values associated with our curricula are designed for the betterment of our democratic society. Many disagree, frequently vigorously, that our school curricula strive to achieve this intention (Zumwalt, 1989; Apple, 1990, 1993; Smith & Lovat, 1991), and consequently the very nature of our constructed curriculum is problematic and contentious.

Teacher curriculum decision-making

Clearly teachers participate in a multiplicity of curriculum activities at a classroom level. These are the very substance of their daily teaching tasks and include such activities as selection of specific content, selection of teaching strategies, use of audio-visual aids and so forth. This classroom level of curriculum decision-making will not be covered in depth here.

In recent years teachers have become increasingly involved in a broader level of curriculum decision-making, namely that of the whole school level. A third level, that of regional/state/national curriculum decision-making (such as involvement in major curriculum projects), typically involves few teachers, although some teachers participate in syllabus committees. At the school level, however, staff are becoming more responsible for a vast array of curriculum decisions. The number and complexity of these decisions vary between states according to the degree of devolution of curriculum control. In essentially more 'centralised' states such as Queensland, Western Australia and New South Wales, curriculum control remains vested largely with the state authority. Schools and teachers in these states have been more concerned with adaption and implementation of centralised curricula rather than strong school-based curriculum development. The late 1980s saw a consolidation of that movement, particularly in New South Wales, and this is likely to continue well into this decade.

In Victoria, South Australia and Tasmania, where devolution of curriculum decision-making has been underway for some time, schools have considerably greater responsibility for curriculum development. In schools in these states teachers have become involved, willingly or unwillingly, in more school-level curriculum decision-making.

Regardless of the state in which one teaches, it has become obvious in recent years that all teachers are participating more in curriculum decision-making at the school level. The nature of this participation may be seen in the various roles that teachers adopt in the decision-making process. It is suggested that teachers may participate in any combination of four curriculum decision-making roles at the school level:

1 implementers
2 adapters
3 developers
4 researchers

As 'implementers' or 'receivers', the teacher's role is to apply curriculum developed elsewhere. In this role the teacher has a minimum of responsibility and involvement in the curriculum development phase of the curriculum process, though nevertheless a significant role in the application phase (as seen in the model of the curriculum process discussed in chapter 3). In this phase teachers play a vital part in implementing, monitoring and evaluating the curriculum. Indeed, most curriculum writers specialising in curriculum change would argue that teacher support is essential for the effective implementation of any curriculum innovation.

A typical example of the implementer role could be found with the implementation of a centrally devised curriculum such as the K10 social studies syllabus in Western Australia, or the numerous syllabus documents emanating from the NSW Board of Studies. Here the major curriculum decisions have been made by a centrally convened group and the teachers' role then is to 'pass' on to students what has been provided in the syllabus. In this minimal role played by teachers there is always some form of interpretation of the written curriculum and possibly greater variation as the curriculum is then applied in classrooms.

Alternatively, the teacher could adopt the role of adapter or modifier. Here an externally developed curriculum is interpreted and changed to meet the needs of a particular school population. This modification has occurred because teachers on the school's staff perceive that the curriculum concerned does not adequately meet the needs of their students. A health education curriculum, for example, may be appropriate in some schools but cause resistance in others. In the latter's case, staff may adapt the curriculum to meet local needs rather than reject it entirely or develop another. It is fair to say that most teachers, most of the time, adapt the written curriculum they receive in some ways. Indeed some centrally prepared curriculum documents are deliberately constructed in a way that provides teachers with options to adapt or modify the curriculum to the school's context.

The 'curriculum-developer' role involves the teacher in designing and developing, usually as a member of a group, a curriculum to meet student needs. Through the use of techniques such as situational analysis and needs assessment, teachers have been able to determine the nature of students' needs. Using this database they are then able to develop an appropriate curriculum to meet those needs. In recent years, for example, many teachers have developed curricula to meet the needs of non-tertiary-bound students staying on in upper secondary school. Existing curricula simply do not meet these students' needs. New, specifically created curricula were, and still are, required.

Finally, teachers may undertake the fourth role of 'curriculum researcher'. Here staff may be involved in improving one's own practice, testing curriculum materials, evaluating new curricula, testing teaching strategies and collecting data on student record needs. An example of this role was the numerous teachers involved with the testing of the SEMP packages in the late 1970s. Others have been involved in testing new techniques for languages, communications, mathematics and science.

In recent years an increasing number of teachers have become involved with action research, a role which has made them involved both with curriculum research and curriculum reflection. Smith & Lovat (1991:185) explain the concept of action research as:

> Action research is a *process of change aimed at the improvement of an individual's, or group's, OWN practice.* It is not engaged in because someone else is forcing you to change or because there is evidence provided by someone else that you should change. *It is a process entered into by us because we wish to improve our own practice, and understand in a more critical manner the reasons and basis for such practice, and the contexts in which it takes place.* (their emphasis)

In participating in one or more of these roles at a school level, teachers will find themselves inevitably questioning traditional curriculum practices and decision-making procedures. To stimulate this process, you might consider the following questions:

1 Who makes major curriculum decisions at the school level?
2 Who *should* make these decisions?
3 To what degree do teachers identify with or have 'ownership' over the curriculum in a school?
4 What curriculum decisions should be made at the school level? And what should be left to external organisations?
5 What should the curriculum include? What should it exclude?
6 What emphasis should be placed on specific subjects, or areas of learning, within a curriculum—such as a core?

In a major study on curriculum decision-making in Australian secondary schools, Cohen & Harrison (1982) found some surprising as well as some expected answers to these questions. It is beyond the scope of this chapter to delve into those results in depth, but they may be summarised by saying that teachers saw *themselves* as having little influence on school-level curriculum decision-making. Principals and senior masters/mistresses were perceived as powerful and the study also revealed considerable curriculum fragmentation within secondary schools. The *Curriculum Action Project* (Cohen & Harrison, 1982) is well worth reading for an insight into school-level curriculum decision-making.

School-based curriculum development

Within Australia in the 1970s and early 1980s the concept of school-based curriculum development (SBCD) gained considerable credence and support. This was not evenly distributed throughout the country and SBCD has been more in evidence in states such as Victoria, New South Wales and South Australia than in Queensland and Western Australia. In New South Wales the creation of OAS (Other Approved Subjects) courses, designed to meet the needs of increasing numbers of post-compulsory students who were not tertiary bound, reached some 10 000 in number (NSW Ministry of Education & Youth Affairs, 1989:24) before they were restructured by the then recently elected minister.

When the NSW Board of Studies was created in 1989 out of the Carrick Committee recommendations, all school subjects were required to be Board devised or Board approved. It was argued that this was an immediate need in order to rationalise and coordinate the proliferation of OAS courses which had mushroomed out of control. And while this has proceeded, and subsequently been largely overshadowed by developments with the Vocational Training Certificate (Carmichael, 1992), the intention was not to excise teachers completely from involvement in curriculum development. *Excellence and Equity* has stated the situation in a way which now reflects the prevailing attitude of most educational systems.

> Board determined courses should not be so prescriptive as to preclude significant input by teachers who wish to *adapt* them to particular local needs or in line with their individual interests and expertise. Teachers should *need to develop* separate school courses *only* in circumstances where there are particular local needs not otherwise met by Board determined courses. (NSW Ministry of Education & Youth Affairs, 1989: 23) (my emphasis)

Despite these and other initiatives against SBCD, over the past two decades there has been evidence of considerable support within all systemic organisations for some form of SBCD. The rise of alternative schools and alternative practices in the 1970s has provided further evidence of SBCD in practice. More recently, the rapidly increasing numbers of non-tertiary-bound Year 11 and 12 students has *demanded* greater SBCD expertise in schools.

In some states, particularly New South Wales, the government has allowed, and consequently tacitly approved of, parents participating in an educative process known as *home schooling*. This phenomenon has seen a variation in the curriculum development process in that parents have been required to become active curriculum developers. While most parents follow systemic syllabuses as a guide, they make considerable adaptations as well as more substantive developments.

Nature of SBCD

SBCD is the development of a curriculum, or an aspect of it, by one or more teachers in a school to meet the perceived needs of a school population, that is, an on-site resolution, in curriculum terms, of problems experienced with the existing curricula. This resolution is carried out by teachers, with or without outside advice, as they are considered to be those educators most aware of student needs. In effect, then, SBCD is the reverse of the bureaucratic, hierarchical, centralist approach to curriculum development.

Examples of SBCD could include multicultural experiences in a multi-ethnic school; an accelerated program for highly talented students; an agricultural unit in an outer urban secondary school; and an appropriate reading program for less able learners.

In 1977 the Curriculum Development Centre (CDC) devised an explanation of SBCD in the Australian context.

1 SBCD implies *teacher* participation. It may be only teachers or other groups as well, but teachers have a significant input.
2 It does not of necessity need to be a whole school exercise. The exercise in SBCD could apply to a few classes (for example, junior primary or upper primary) or to some aspect of content (for example, core subject or non-core subjects or psychomotor developing subjects) or some approaches to teaching (for example, competency-based education or behaviour modification) or finally, some particular developments in evaluation (for example, non-testing evaluation).
3 SBCD should not imply severance from the centre. It does, however, imply different development according to local needs. It also involves a shift of responsibility for curriculum decision-making.
4 Teachers and administrators will need to modify their present roles. They will need to become more concerned with the development of the total curriculum and with the sharing of decision-making power in curriculum areas.
5 SBCD may be selective, adaptive or creative, that is, teachers may concentrate upon the provision of appropriate resources; they may adapt existing materials to meet the needs of their students; or they may be involved in creating new curricula.
6 SBCD is a continuing and dynamic process. As well, support structures such as advisers, finances and materials, are necessary in order to keep the process ongoing.

If these, then, are the features of SBCD, at least as far as CDC was concerned, what impact has SBCD had upon schools? The answer to that question is largely self-evident in schools, although a more detailed explanation may be found in the *Curriculum Action Project* (Cohen & Harrison, 1982). The simple reality is that the problems listed below have outweighed the advantages to the point that little SBCD, of the essentially developmental variety, is now undertaken. In the context of increasingly centralised control over curriculum policy (see NSW Ministry of Education & Youth Affairs, *Excellence and Equity*, 1989 in NSW; *Common and Agreed National Goals for Schooling in Australia,* 1989) this situation will continue.

Advantages of SBCD

1 Those in the best position to appreciate the needs of a specific group of learners are the local teachers who can also determine the best use of the school's resources.
2 Those who implement the curriculum are those who have developed it. This gives a greater sense of identification with the learning tasks.
3 The needs of specific groups of students are met, which in turn has a powerful impact upon learners.
4 Greater accountability of curricula and teacher performance is noticed.
5 Parents and community members may be easily involved in meaningful curriculum planning.

Disadvantages of SBCD

1 Lack of support structures for administrators and teachers.
2 Conformity syndrome of administrators and teachers reduces creativity.
3 Lack of time for teachers to undertake SBCD.
4 Lack of teachers experienced or trained in the process of SBCD.
5 Movement of teachers between schools for promotion, country service and the like produces an unstable teacher base.
6 Requires significant changes in the roles of teachers and administrators, which are naturally resisted.
7 Schools can quickly become out of step with each other and overlapping may occur where students transfer between schools.

Nevertheless, the 1990s thus far have continued this change in the way educators address the issue of SBCD. Most fundamentally the term 'school-based curriculum development' is rarely found in the literature and certainly not in curriculum documents emanating from curriculum and assessment agencies, departments/ministries of education as well as other organisations responsible for curriculum development. Rather the emphasis is upon centrally constructed curriculum policy and policy directions associated with an acknowledgement of school-level curriculum interpretation and implementation. Teachers are perceived more in the role of refining and fine-tuning centralised curriculum initiatives in the specific contexts of their schools. Furthermore the national curriculum initiatives that have been underway for some years further consolidate the centralised direction of curriculum policy and decision-making.

It is not surprising, therefore, that recent initiatives in the area of post-compulsory schooling, such as Finn (1991), Mayer (1992), and Carmichael (1992), have attempted to provide central policy and direction for non-tertiary-bound curricula in schools at a time when the numbers of such students are increasing rapidly. A fundamental curriculum issue of the 1990s will be concerned with who should determine the curricula for these students and what impact this will have upon upper secondary school curricula now that these students are in the majority. At the moment the power lies with Carmichael (1992), DEET, TAFE and the proposed Vocational Training Certificate at the expense of the curriculum and assessment agencies, the state departments of education, the schools and those curriculum writers engaged in the debate. The early years of this decade portend an interesting and lively debate on this issue in the immediate future.

Curriculum development

As teachers become involved with school-level curriculum decision-making, they require a sound understanding of curriculum concepts and processes. To participate in any form of curriculum-related activity effectively, it is imperative that teachers acquire a basic familiarity with the principles of curriculum design and development. Chapter 4 will address the processes involved with curriculum design and planning. For the moment it is important to understand the meaning of the term 'curriculum development' as it is fundamental to the remainder of the book.

Planning, design and development in curriculum are closely related terms. Once a curriculum has been conceptualised, through the process of curriculum planning and incorporating a curriculum design, it may then be developed, usually to become a written document and finally to be implemented and evaluated. Within the literature a definition of curriculum development has gained some degree of consensus, unlike a definition of curriculum. For our purposes curriculum development is defined as the process of planning, constructing, implementing and evaluating learning opportunities intended to produce desired changes in learners.

In practice this means that curriculum developers take with them their conceptualisation of curriculum, construct a curriculum document from it, implement or monitor the implementation of that document and finally appraise the effectiveness of the entire curriculum. This is particularly the case at school levels where teachers are integrally involved in both curriculum design and development. Subsequent chapters will elaborate the concepts of curriculum development and curriculum design substantially.

Summary

- There are many ways of referring to curriculum and in schooling there are at least three levels—systemic, subject and institutional.
- Curriculum is defined as all the planned learning opportunities offered

to learners by the educational institution and the experiences learners encounter when that curriculum is implemented.

* Schooling consists of the (overt) curriculum together with all the unplanned learnings that students acquire. The latter are known as the hidden curriculum.
* While the essential feature of the hidden curriculum is that learnings are acquired unknowingly, there have been many recent examples of transferring such learning to the overt curriculum.
* The process of curriculum may be considered as a manipulative strategy, by answering the questions of what, when, how and under what conditions students will learn.
* Curriculum development must be seen as a deliberate, purposeful, planning activity that seeks to achieve general and specific intentions.
* Teachers have an important role in schools as curriculum developers as well as implementers, adapters and researchers of curricula.
* SBCD is the development of a curriculum, or an aspect of it, by one or more teachers in a school to meet the perceived needs of a school population.
* Curriculum development is defined as the process of planning, implementing and evaluating learning opportunities intended to produce desired changes in learners. Curriculum design is concerned with the arrangement of curriculum elements to produce a unified curriculum.

2 Curriculum presage

To be responsible, articulate professionals, teachers need to be conversant with the language of curriculum that will influence their professional practice and others' expectations of them. And, as professional teachers they are expected to develop or construct their own curriculum . . . (Karen Zumwalt, 1989: 176).

One of the most pressing problems confronting curriculum developers at the earliest stage of their work is simply—where to begin! At first glance this may seem barely a problem at all, but the more we delve into curriculum development the more we see the difficulties involved. This chapter will explore the issue of where and how to commence curriculum development and what factors need to be taken into account.

Where do curriculum developers begin when they commence their structural task? What conceptualisation is undertaken before the actual construction of the curriculum is initiated? These are important questions in the process of curriculum development and unfortunately there is little consensus amongst either writers or practitioners as to the answers. As seen in the previous chapter, the many theorists writing in the curriculum field have quite different approaches to the concept of curriculum and hence different interpretations of where to commence.

Similarly, many practitioners have quite different views, particularly from theorists, as to where the process of curriculum development should best begin. Many classroom teachers, for example, would argue that curriculum development begins with a statement of curriculum content— after all, they are familiar with content and know how it relates to student learning. This argument, and the problems that ensue from it, have been well documented in numerous research studies in Australia and other countries (CDC, 1977; Cohen & Harrison, 1982; Hughes, 1973; Brady, 1981; Print, 1986).

The answers to the questions posed above lie in the final model of curriculum development outlined in the next chapter. In the first phase (organisation), it is suggested that an effective commencement point for curriculum development is found with a concept called curriculum presage. Essentially this is a conceptualisation stage that precedes formal curriculum development, yet it is one that has profound influence throughout the curriculum development process.

Curriculum presage refers to those activities and forces which influ-

25

ence curriculum developers in their curriculum decision-making tasks. These activities and forces are brought with the developers when they come to the task of constructing a curriculum. As such they consist of the curriculum backgrounds (activities and experiences), curriculum conceptions, curriculum representations (organisations), curriculum foundations of the various curriculum developers and the curriculum context in which they work. This combination of past activities and current forces will have a profound effect upon the final curriculum through the nature of the input from the individuals involved.

We refer to this phenomenon as curriculum presage for two principal reasons. First, because everyone involved with curriculum development has been influenced by these factors as a result of their life's experiences. Consequently we cannot talk in absolute or definitive terms when discussing curriculum presage, rather we discuss the concept to explain why differences occur in curriculum processes and outcomes. Second, curriculum presage can best be explained as a set of experiences and understandings brought with curriculum developers to the curriculum development task. Thus this phenomenon is present prior to the actual construction of a curriculum document, though it will have a profound effect upon the final form that a written curriculum might take. Similarly this set of experiences and understandings affects the way teachers implement curricula in schools. Consequently the more we know about this phase in the curriculum process, the more we are able to explain, and perhaps adjust, subsequent developments.

When commencing curriculum development it is, therefore, useful to ask the following questions of the developers involved. Alternatively, it would be of considerable value if curriculum developers themselves were to reflect upon these very questions before they commenced their task.

1 Who are the individuals involved in this curriculum development task and what, if anything, do they represent?
2 What conceptions of curriculum do they bring with them and how will this factor influence the curriculum outcome?
3 What underlying forces have influenced their way of thinking about curriculum matters?

Curriculum developers

A famous question, long posed in the curriculum development process, asks 'What knowledge is of most worth?' Before we can ask that question we must pose, as Michael Apple (1992) suggests, an even more contentious question, '*Whose* knowledge is of most worth?' Such a question raises significant questions about how curriculum development might be considered, the role that curriculum developers might play in selecting knowledge and, more broadly, the influence of curriculum developers in the curriculum development process.

The starting point for any curriculum development is the selection/ participation of those individuals who compose what may be called the curriculum development team. This is a group of people who will devise the curriculum required and, in many situations, see it implemented into practice. The team may consist of a group of teachers undertaking a school-based curriculum initiative, a subject syllabus/curriculum committee constructing a tertiary entrance course, a group of teachers and consultants developing a Year 11 or 12 non-tertiary course, TAFE staff and industry representatives devising a trade course or even a group of tertiary staff constructing new units/courses for university students. In all these cases, and even in the instance where curriculum development is undertaken by an individual, the very nature of the persons concerned will have a significant effect upon the final curriculum outcome.

Why is it important to know who constitutes the curriculum development team? Simply because different people have different ideas about curriculum and the curricula needs of students and hence will produce different curricula to meet those ideas and perceptions. Take, for example, the development of curricula for Year 11 and 12 non-tertiary-bound students. A curriculum development team composed entirely of teachers in a school located in an area of very high youth unemployment would, it is suggested, produce a different curriculum product from a team composed of teachers and community members (perhaps from a school council) located in a low unemployment area or a team consisting of teachers and university staff consultants.

In these situations not only do individuals bring with them differing individual perspectives towards the curriculum development task but also differing contextual understandings and needs as well as the obligation to 'represent' what may be quite different perspectives and agendas from quite different organisations. In the above example, how significantly different would the final curriculum appear if representatives of teacher unions, parent organisations and state education departments were included?

And what role should outside bodies, which have minimal direct involvement with school curricula, play? For example, should a school curriculum being developed on environmental studies include representatives of the various environmental protection groups in its developmental team? If so, which ones should be included? And what of the more radical environmental action groups? And should the inclusion of such groups preclude representatives from the specific industries using that environmental curriculum to provide a 'balanced' point of view?

Let us examine briefly two specific cases where representational membership of an important review was a vitally important issue, particularly when certain groups and organisations found themselves excluded. This phenomenon and the resulting pressure on the state government to provide representative membership resulted in the Beazley Committee (1984) expanding to some 26 members and an executive staff of three, although the Carrick Committee (1989) saw a larger task completed by a group half that size.

In 1988 the newly elected Liberal government in New South Wales sought to stamp its imprimatur on schooling in New South Wales. It created the Committee of Inquiry into Schools in New South Wales under the chairmanship of John Carrick, a former Federal Minister for Education. The structure of that committee was such that it was designed to produce a general curriculum outcome consistent with the policy upon which the government had been recently elected. It is useful to compare the composition of that group with the composition of the Beazley Committee.

In 1983 the recently elected Western Australian Labor government initiated an inquiry into lower secondary education which concentrated upon the curriculum in Years 8–10. Subsequently the government also initiated an inquiry into upper secondary education. However the composition of the Beazley Committee was significantly different from the New South Wales experience. In undertaking these inquiries both state governments sought to address significant curriculum issues and hence the composition of those committees, analysed in table 2.1, was of vital importance.

Table 2.1 illustrates that individuals, when representing organisations, must be seen as potential power groups in any curriculum committee situation. Acting in unison, certain groups could sway final decisions in ways that would suit their organisation's or institution's purposes. Indeed that has become the very justification for representation sought by many groups on the decision-making group concerned. Similarly, decision-making leaders have increasingly become aware of the value of including representatives of the major client groups, if only minimally, in the composition of curriculum decision-making groups.

Table 2.1   Composition of review committees

	'Beazley' Committee	'Carrick' Committee
Education systems*	7	3
Schools*	7	3
Universities	5	2
Unions	3	1
Community (business/parent)	4	5
Total	26	14

* *categories include both government and non-government participants*
Source: Beazley, K. (1984); Carrick, J. (1989)

While the above compositions may be considered to be loose group-ings of people within these labels, it is nevertheless evident that they exist. As the main responsibility of the respective committees was to restructure a major part of the school curriculum (Years 8–10 in Western Australia; Years K–12 in New South Wales), it could be argued that:

1 Tertiary institutions did not require substantial representation in school curricula matters.
2 More classroom teachers were needed (the closest were a deputy principal and a union representative who was also a teacher).
3 Greater community representation was essential to reflect community needs, as argued in New South Wales (one was the 'independent' chairman in each committee).
4 Fewer union representatives were needed (in Western Australia) as this was an educational, not industrial, matter (as argued in New South Wales).

How different would the curriculum recommendations have been if the university representatives were not present? If more classroom teach-ers had been involved, would the final product have been significantly different? In what ways have community or trade union representatives made a difference? While these are highly speculative questions, they provide an insight into the extent of influence that the mere selection of participants can have upon the final curriculum product.

The issue of who should constitute the membership of curriculum reviews has come to the fore most recently in Queensland. The minister for education, perceiving that the state's curriculum needs were not being adequately met, established the Review of the Queensland School Cur-riculum in November 1992. The Review was given the brief to investigate and make recommendations with respect to curriculum development, management, assessment and accreditation in Queensland, with special consideration of the scope and sequence of the K–12 curriculum, and report by the end of 1993.

Interestingly the Review team was deliberately created without a curriculum expert and without representation of the Department of Edu-cation. The constitution of the three-member Review team represented public administration, education and environment, with the first two members from universities and the last a government department. These examples relate to the broader area of major curriculum decision-making, that level which creates general directions and trends. What of curriculum decision-making that affects classroom teachers more directly?

Syllabus committees

All states have curriculum and assessment agencies which have legal responsibility for constructing certain levels of school curriculum. These groups organise syllabus committees with the specific task of creating currricula, particularly at the upper secondary level. In most states these government statutory authorities share this curriculum responsibility with state departments of education, particularly when constructing curricula for lower secondary schools and primary schools. However, in all these cases, teams of curriculum developers work together to construct what we call systemic curricula, or what most teachers know as syllabus documents. In creating these curricula, the composition of the curriculum teams will make a substantial difference to the nature of the final product.

In New South Wales, this important task of curriculum development lies with the NSW Board of Studies. This statutory authority, similar in function to curriculum and assessment agencies in other states, has the legal responsibility for preparing system-wide curricula (what they call syllabuses) and presenting them for approval to the minister. In Western Australia, the Secondary Education Authority has direct reponsibility for curriculum development and assessment in the upper secondary years, particularly focused on the curriculum for the tertiary entrance examination. As well as it has substantial influence and control over curriculum development and assesment in the lower secondary years.

As with other states, the composition of the NSW Board of Studies and its numerous subject syllabus committees reflects the broader educational community and the community in general. However, the exact representation on these committees varies with the political persuasion of the government in power and with significant factors influencing education from time to time.

In recent years it has become more common practice in systemic curriculum development throughout Australia to ensure a relatively widely dispersed base for the construction and consultative processes. This enables curriculum development agencies not only to be broadly based in the collection and representation of information but it also forestalls possible problems that might arise through non-representation of significant groups. This is demonstrated in the example below where no single group has significantly large enough numbers to control the curriculum development process, though most groups have some representation.

In New South Wales, all syllabus committees, be they primary or secondary, come under the control of the Board of Studies. Table 2.2 shows the composition of a typical syllabus committee for Years K–6 and Years 7–12. As well, each syllabus committee is supported by a consultative network that the committee has created to assist it with its preparation of curriculum documents. In the New South Wales example, syllabus committees are responsible to more broadly based curriculum committees which cover a key learning area and are hence known as KLACCs (Key Learning Area Curriculum Committees). These committees

Table 2.2 Syllabus committee composition (New South Wales)

	(K–6)	(7–12)
University representatives	2	4
NSW Teachers Federation	2	4
Department of School Education	3	2
Catholic Education Commission	1	1
Independent Teachers Association	1	1
Joint Council of Professional Teachers Association	1	1
Assoc. Heads of Independent Schools	1	1
NSW Parents Council and P&C Associations	2	1
TAFE Commission	—	1
Others	3	—
Board of Studies officer	1	1
Additional members (specific expertise)		
Minimum total	17	17

also have reference panels to assist them with their deliberations and, together with their own broadly based composition, reflect the concept of a breadth of participation by those influenced by school curricula.

The consultative network consists of a group of organisations and individuals from whom a syllabus committee seeks advice during the curriculum development process. Broadly representative of all organisations and groups involved with the syllabus, as well as additional experts from that area and additional teachers involved in that subject in schools, the consultative network's advice generally takes the form of comments on the writing brief of the curriculum and upon draft syllabus documents. In the example of a syllabus such as history or chemistry, the consultative group is drawn largely from university staff and from practising teachers.

While this is an elaborate process of construction, advice and consultation in New South Wales, a similar process may be found in each state.

For those involved in the process of curriculum development, or in selecting these people, it is important to remember that the individuals selected to undertake curriculum construction will have a significant effect upon the curriculum outcome. This is extremely important in a situation such as a school where the pool of potential developers may be small, just as it is for systemic situations such as curriculum development for the Tasmanian or Queensland Departments of Education. You might reflect upon recent curriculum decisions, at systemic or school level, and consider the possible areas of influence of the individuals and groups involved in making those decisions.

Curriculum foundations

From where do curriculum developers obtain their basic understanding of education and curriculum? Developers' thinking does not exist in a vacuum, nor does the curriculum development of which they are an integral part. There exists a common pool of information from which people draw their requirements and this database then becomes the foundation upon which curriculum conceptualisation is built. Thus curriculum foundations may be defined as those basic forces that influence and shape the minds of curriculum developers and hence the content and structure of the subsequent curriculum.

The literature in this area of curriculum generally distinguishes three categories of sources for curriculum foundations (Tyler, 1949; Lawton, 1978; Tanner & Tanner, 1980; Taba, 1962; Saylor, Alexander & Lewis, 1981; Eisner, 1979; Brady, 1992).

1 Studies of learners and learning theory (psychology).
2 Studies of life (sociology and culture).
3 Studies of the nature and value of knowledge (philosophy).

In examining the role of these foundation disciplines in curriculum development, a modification of Dennis Lawton's model (1978) is a useful conceptual tool. When curriculum developers—whether at systemic, regional or classroom level—commence their task, they use curriculum foundations as indicated in figure 2.1.

The three sources of curriculum foundations constitute together the principal areas of influence on curriculum developers in their consideration of curricula. These influences affect developers' way of thinking about curricula and, in the process, produce conceptions of curricula. At some later time developers express these conceptions, both explicitly and implicitly, when devising curricula.

More specifically, in considering figure 2.1, you should reflect upon the following points in relation to curriculum development:

1 Curriculum developers have opinions about the nature of knowledge and what is worthwhile (philosophy).
2 These opinions are then set in the context of the developers' understanding of society and culture and future social needs (sociology and culture).
3 The contribution of psychology—the nature of students and how they learn—then acts to modify the previously assembled opinions and data (psychology).
4 Together these foundation sources provide a background of information upon which the curriculum developers rely to make future curriculum decisions.
5 When merged with the curriculum developers' past experiences in

Figure 2.1   The role of curriculum foundations

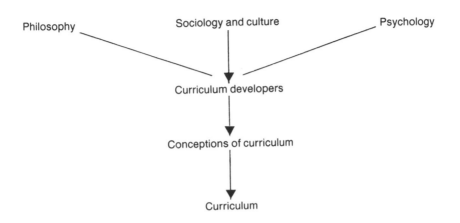

Source: After D. Lawton, 1978

curriculum, we can see how developers tend towards particular conceptions of the curriculum task.

6 When these foundation sources and curriculum conceptions are seen in relation to differing curricula contexts, we can explain why the final curriculum products are, and need to be, somewhat different.

The melding of these points in the early stage of the curriculum development process helps explain why educators, and even curriculum developers, have such different perceptions of curriculum and why those differences are maintained to achieve what are often very substantial differing curriculum outcomes.

Let us now examine these curriculum foundations in a little more depth. In so doing, it is not the intention to undertake an exhaustive study of the contributing disciplines as this has been achieved elsewhere (Hirst, 1968; Zais, 1976; Tanner & Tanner, 1980; Phenix, 1964; Lawton et al., 1978; Tyler, 1949; Habermas, 1972; Young, 1989; Kelly, 1977; Stenhouse, 1975), but rather to provide some sense of perspective to the influence of each foundation upon the process of curriculum development.

Philosophical sources

Philosophy and philosophical assumptions are basic to all curriculum foundations as they are concerned with making sense of what we encounter in our lives. To Paul Hirst (1968:39), philosophy is 'concerned with clarificatlon of concepts and propositions in which our experience and activities are intelligible'. For curriculum developers, then, an understanding of philosophy and a comprehension of one's own educational philosophy are essential in order to make useful and intelligible statements about experiences which are to be passed on to subsequent generations. Indeed, the principal area of philosophical influence in the curriculum is found in the way curriculum developers handled philosophical issues. The philosophical contribution to curriculum has been developed in far greater depth elsewhere and is well worth further investigation (Hirst, 1968; Hirst & Peters, 1970; Habermas, 1972; Zais, 1976; Young, 1989; Smith & Lovat, 1991).

How curriculum developers perceive the world, and hence education, may be determined by posing three philosophical questions: What is real? What is good? What is true? Individuals will perceive and answer these questions in different ways and hence individual philosophies emerge. In turn, differing philosophies will affect how individuals perceive and relate to the curriculum.

Let us take an example from history to illustrate how one's philosophical position may influence the development and implementation of a school curriculum. The subject is social studies as taught in both Australian primary and secondary schools and the topic deals with the activities of what has become known as 'bushrangers'. The commonly accepted version of events is as follows:

> In the 1870s a group of bushrangers led by Ned Kelly committed a number of major crimes in northeastern Victoria. These were mainly armed robbery and murder and included the significant events of:
>
> Stringybark Creek (October 1878)
> Euroa (December 1878)
> Jerilderie (February 1879)
> Glenrowan (June 1880)
>
> These crimes, perpetrated in the so-called 'Kelly Country', finally led to the destruction of the gang and Kelly's subsequent death in Pentridge Prison. While Kelly may have been a colourful and brave character who gained much popular support, especially through his 'Jerilderie letters', he was little more than a common criminal and murderer. His hanging was appropriate justice for the murders he committed.

That is how the 'standard' version of this piece of history has been generally portrayed. The events of these years relating to the Kelly Gang have long been consolidated within curriculum documents and taught in schools for many years, much as described above. But is this really how such a piece of history should be written into a social studies/history/human society curriculum for subsequent generations of students to learn? In answering this question one should pose the three questions mentioned earlier: What is real?, What is good? and What is true?

Before answering the questions above, consider three alternative interpretations to the 'accepted' first version described above.

1 The Kelly Gang were murderous, depraved and wretched bushrangers who preyed on innocent people and deserved all they got.
2 The Kellys were symbols of working-class resistance to capitalist (squatters) and government oppression. This helps explain why they received so much popular support and defied the police for so long.
3 The Kellys, particularly Ned, were an expression of Irish opposition to the tyrannical English rule. The Irish, as labourers or selectors, barely survived against the English, the squatters and the controllers of the government, military and police.

Which interpretation do you support? Why not pose the three philosophical questions to yourself before making up your mind? In so doing, you may have to challenge information you've accepted in the past and restate your position. Let us examine these three fundamnetal questions in a little more depth and see how they can significantly influence curriculum developers and subsequent curriculum development.

Ontology

Ontology is concerned with the nature of reality and it asks the question: What is real? While this question may appear obvious at first glance, it deserves greater consideration. Different societies, for example, perceive reality in quite different ways as do the individuals who constitute those societies. In medieval society, for example, it was accepted as real that the earth was flat, yet today we would regard that as nonsense. Similarly, one society may regard the use of chemical fertilisers as essential, while to another the reality consists of the waste products of animals.

Thus what is real to a society is very important when constructing a curriculum that will perpetuate that sense of reality. Indeed, it may well be that some curriculum developers see their role as re-creating reality in society by using the school curriculum as a vehicle for change. Thus a new social studies curriculum may depict the Kelly Gang as a symbol of working-class resistance to authoritative oppression and so re-create reality for a new generation of school students. Indeed, some recent curriculum developments—multiculturalism, gender equity, environmental education—have sought to achieve just that.

Epistemology

The philosophical problem that deals with the nature of knowledge and the nature of knowing is called epistemology. For Walker & Evers (1988), 'Epistemology is the study of the nature, scope and applicability of knowledge.' In curriculum, where what we advocate becomes the basis for student learning, we are centrally concerned with the nature of knowledge, how we know and how we know what we know.

When posing epistemological questions in curriculum we ask: What is true? How do we know the truth? How do we *know* that we know? These are obviously vital questions for curriculum developers to consider, particularly in a society which purportedly values truth and seeks to pass on truth to subsequent generations.

Let us again consider the example of the Kelly Gang. Given the differing interpretations, we can ask: What is true? How do we know if that is true? And how do we know that we know? On a re-examination of the historical evidence available, particularly in our modern context, we may reassess the Kellys as a symbol of anti-English sentiment and Irish unity. But how do we know if that is true? And how do we know that we know?

Ultimately our position becomes a statement of faith—a stand on those questions which we believe, and are prepared to accept, as true. As such we rely heavily upon our fundamental ontological beliefs (what is real). In this way the close relationship between epistemology and ontology is consolidated.

Thus in any curriculum development activity, but particularly in that related to schools, the epistemological stance taken by those developers involved is of vital importance. Will they include the accepted truth? What does that constitute? To what degree is there a consensus accepting that truth or is that 'consensus' a fallacy too? And so the epistemological questions continue. At the very least, curriculum developers should be aware of epistemology and be prepared to pose the fundamental questions involved in such a study.

Axiology

Axiology is that aspect of philosophy that is concerned with the nature of value. Axiological questions are a fundamental feature of our life in that the resulting decisions have a profound effect upon our behaviour. Questions such as: What is good? What is desirable to humans? are both fundamental to our very existence and constantly present in our daily lives. Thus axiological considerations are important in one's development of a curriculum for future generations.

Zais (1976:119) contends that axiological questions are usually divided into two main categories: ethics and aesthetics. *Ethics* is concerned with concepts of good and bad, right and wrong as they apply to human behaviour. When constructing curricula, developers need to be aware of both their *own* ethical positions and the ethical basis (hopefully not bias) that they are integrating into the curriculum. Thus developers will select objectives and contents that, in their mind, are more ethical both in terms of knowledge and process.

Students subsequently taught that curriculum will, hopefully to the developers, acquire certain ethical knowledge (what is right and wrong) as well as the skills required for making future ethical decisions. A school curriculum might, for example, include material about sanctity of human life. It may also include opportunities for students to acquire skills for future decision-making on human life issues such as abortion, death penalties, in-vitro fertilisation and so forth.

One thing is certain, however, and that is that a curriculum can never be value free in the sense that it can be constructed entirely objectively. We should be well aware that all curriculum developers naturally bring with them certain points of view, preferences, previous experiences and so forth which will influence the way they think about and construct curricula. Therefore in the curriculum development process we expect people to manifest some axiological positions, though hopefully these will not be blatant, excessive and imbalanced.

Rather, the issue of *vital* concern to curriculum decision-makers is how much *direct* inclusion of ethical concepts and processes should be included within a curriculum. Is an apparently low-value-oriented curriculum of a government school preferable to a medium-value orientation of an independent school to that of a very-high-value orientation of, say, an Islamic school in fundamentalist Iran? This very issue is also an ethical consideration itself!

Robert Zais summarised the situation succinctly: 'Education, after all, is a process of deliberately influencing children and youth in such a way that they become what they would not otherwise become. And the curriculum is the master plan by which this purpose is accomplished' (1976:119). At this point it is important to raise these issues and questions in the mind of curriculum developers—not to answer them. That will be achieved in a wider forum, and there is increasing evidence in recent years that elements of Australian society want a greater, more purposeful input into the ethical aspects of school curricula.

Aesthetics is concerned with such value issues as beauty and enjoyment of human experience. Aesthetics questions include: What is beautiful? What aspects of the senses produce enjoyment? And what aesthetic experiences yield 'higher-order' enjoyment?

The issues involving aesthetics produce particular difficulties for curriculum developers because individuals answer the above questions in very different ways. What is beautiful to one person may be ugly to another, particularly if they come from different cultures. And what produces aesthetic enjoyment to one individual, such as a fine spring morning, may produce hay fever in another! The sensory pleasures associated with a bottle of quality wine may be quite different for the wine connoisseur and the teetotaller who suffers from allergies.

While aesthetics remain essentially relative in their nature, the curriculum developer faces enormous problems over what to include and what to exclude from the curriculum. Some of the problems facing the curriculum developer may be expressed in the following questions. To what degree are aesthetics learnt naturally and therefore not required to be taught at school? What aesthetics should be taught? Should schools emphasise the process of aesthetic judgment-making or knowledge about what is aesthetically prized?

Strong consensus has emerged within schooling that a curriculum should include elements of aesthetical appreciation and skill acquisition. Thus art, music, theatre, dance, craft and so forth are commonly found in school curricula. But should the music be symphonic or rock? Should the art be acknowledged artists or street graffiti and should dance be ballet or 'break' dance? And how much of each should be included in a school curriculum?

In answer to these questions, curriculum developers in the past have opted for a more conservative, accepted view of what is beautiful and what is pleasurable. In more recent times this position has weakened and we have witnessed the emergence of more 'popular' aesthetics within the school curriculum. This has seen a re-examining of what is beautiful as well as the inclusion within the curriculum of modern dance, music, art, theatre, craft and so forth. Obviously the answers to aesthetics questions will always remain vexed and difficult to resolve.

These three sources represent the different aspects of philosophy that influence and are in need of consideration by curriculum developers. They raise fundamental questions that require thoughtful examination by curriculum developers both for their curricula directly and for themselves. We should also note that many curriculum developers employ the method of logic as a process in their decision-making. Clearly *logic*—the systematic treatment of ideas—is of immeasurable value to a curriculum developer and it is recommended that all curriculum developers employ it. Certainly it has a lasting value superior to intuition, 'ad hockery' and emotional consensus.

For the curriculum developer the value of philosophical considerations is abundantly clear. Ontology, epistemology and axiology provide a useful structure for examining one's own philosophical position as well as how philosophical stances affect the development of curricula. In these considerations, one might pose some typical philosophical questions that are useful to the curriculum developer:

1 On what grounds should content be selected or rejected?

2 How different is instruction from conditioning?
3 Are there distinct forms of knowledge?
4 How can specific curricula be justified?
5 Why are certain goals and objectives considered worthwhile?
6 How should content be structured within a curriculum?
7 Should a curriculum be differentiated for different students?
8 What is fact?
9 To what degree should 'new' reality be included within the curriculum?

These are but a sample of the philosophical questions that may be posed. What other questions are important? And to what degree are you as a curriculum developer prepared both to ask them and then act upon them?

Sociological sources

It is hardly surprising that society and culture exert enormous influences on the formation of the school curriculum or indeed any curriculum. After all as it was society that devised schooling to ensure the survival of the cultural heritage, we would expect to see an extensive influence of society and culture upon curriculum in schools.

Curriculum developers serve the function of translating traditional assumptions, ideas, values, knowledge and attitudes into curriculum objectives, content, learning activities and evaluation. Of these curriculum elements, sociological sources have their greatest impact on *content*. In acting this way, curriculum developers both transmit and reflect the culture of which they are part. Thus it is not possible to talk about a culture-free curriculum. Rather, one should consider a curriculum as a situation where judgments are made as to what aspects of culture are to be included and why.

Consequently, when developers devise curricula the cultural background of those developers will become evident in the content they select, the methods they include, the objectives they set and so forth. This phenomenon in part accounts for the differences existing between subject curricula amongst the Australian States and the differences between Australian curricula and those of other countries.

Indeed, an interesting phenomenon within Australian curriculum development has been the relative dearth of an ethnocentrically based curriculum. Traditionally Australian educators looked to Britain and Ireland for their curricula and this had a profound impact on nineteenth-century education. This influence was perpetuated until the middle of this century, although the last 30 years have witnessed a dramatically growing influence of education from the United States. The result of these combined external influences has been a curriculum general in nature, non-ethnocentrically oriented and largely lacking in national sentiment.

To a substantial measure, the behaviour of society today reflects the nature of curriculum taught to this adult generation when it was in school. A couple of brief examples will highlight this relationship. Australians have become well known as world travellers, more so than many other peoples. While this may be a factor of geographical isolation, a population originally from a wide diversity of countries or a high level of economic prosperity, it is also a factor of a school curriculum that has taught about other countries, their peoples, their history and their myths.

Examples are numerous throughout a child's schooling where students have studied topics ranging from a white Christmas, to ancient European civilisations, to medieval knights, to Swiss Alps and so forth. There is nothing necessarily wrong with this situation, depending upon how one answers the following curriculum question: What should be the *balance* between different learnings in the curriculum?

A corollary to the above example is the perceived lack of nationalistic sentiment evident amongst Australians. Any comparison between Australians and Americans, Germans, Japanese and many other countries reveals that Australians, at least in their own country, demonstrate little nationalistic behaviour. This phenomenon is probably a reflection of a diverse population base (although the same does not apply in America), a lack of major crises to draw people together, a long and close relationship with Britain as well as the nature of the school curricula.

Curricula in Australian schools, unlike those in other countries, have stored little value in nationalistically oriented content. The heroes and heroines in Australia's past are seldom lauded (unless they are sporting greats) and the major feats of the nation's people rarely acclaimed. In some considerable measure, then, the current lack of nationalistic fervour (other than in the sporting arena) can be attributed to the nature of past school curricula.

Influences of society and culture on curriculum

The societal and cultural influences that affect curriculum developers are evident in both conscious and unconscious ways and their impact is certainly profound. Australian education, manifest through the curriculum, reflects Australian society and culture, and that reflection is a result of curriculum developers being an integral part of that society and culture in both of the above ways. In this sense the curriculum more 'reflects' society than leads society to change.

Indirectly society and culture influence curriculum developers simply because they are members of a particular society. Cultural values, attitudes and beliefs are acquired by individuals unaware of that process, yet, once acquired, these cultural traits become consolidated and affect our social behaviour. And when the process of curriculum development takes place, the cultural traits within developers influence the very selection of objectives, content, methods and evaluation that constitute the curriculum they are devising.

Take, for example, a group of primary schoolteachers who decide to enhance the literacy component of an existing curriculum. On completion one could analyse the result to determine why they undertook the task, what objectives were formulated, what content was employed, how it was taught and how it was evaluated. In many instances, when probed deeply enough, the teachers would be unaware of the basis of their decisions. If story reading was a component of the revised curriculum, what proportion would be oral reading? Why? And how would that be assessed? What stories were selected for students? Why? These are typical of the questions that should be asked of curriculum developers when they construct curricula, and which reveal indirect influences of society and culture.

Alternatively, curriculum developers may be well aware of societal and cultural influences and have the deliberate intention in mind (or not) of reproducing aspects of that culture in the curriculum. The issue then becomes whether the curriculum should mirror society or whether it should become a tool for change. Those educators who envisage schooling in the vanguard of change would opt for a curriculum that leads future generations in particular directions. More conservative educators argue for a traditional perspective which sees schools as reflecting society and thus retaining the status quo. The reality, of course, is that elements of both positions exist in Australian curricula, although in most states the conservative educators and decision-makers remain dominant. Indeed, Peter Musgrave suggests that curriculum can even be defined in terms similar to the deliberative approach above. ' . . . the curriculum consists of that selection from the whole stock of knowledge available to a society which those in power in the educational system aim to pass on to succeeding generations' (Musgrave, 1979: 17).

In his useful book *Society and the Curriculum in Australia,* Musgrave (1979) poses several questions that are worthy of consideration by curriculum developers. In answering these questions, curriculum developers will have a more complete understanding of both Australian society and Australian schools as well as the curriculum manifest in the latter. These questions, arranged in related sets, are:

• *Control*: What groups controlled the educational system, or any one school or group of schools? By what methods did they exercise their control? What ideologies did they serve in the political conflicts involved in decisions about the curriculum, whether academic or moral?

- *Resource allocation*: What influence did decisions about how much could be afforded for education have upon the curriculum? Did decisions about the distribution of this amount between sectors within the educational system influence curricula? Who took such decisions?
- *Structural setting*: How have changes in the social structure influenced the institution of education? More specifically, how has the salience of various social institutions affected education? What was the source of such change—internal to or outside of Australia? Furthermore, through what groups were these changes mediated to decisions about curricula?
- *Ideological setting*: What part did intellectuals play in the process of curricular change? Were institutional or cultural intellectuals more important? Were the relevant intellectuals working in Australia or overseas?
- *Curricular dimensions*: Were there differences in the ways in which the academic and the moral curricula were decided? In addition, did social factors influence the curriculum differently along the differing dimensions of content, distribution, pacing and pedagogy? (Musgrave, 1979:38-9)

Culturally induced bias and the curriculum

One particular aspect of the social and cultural influences on the curriculum which deserves specific attention is that of culturally induced bias. As societies perpetuate themselves through implanting values in the young through institutions such as schools, it is distinctly probable that some of those values will be culturally biased. Indeed, these values may be so effectively integrated within schools and society that they are perceived not as biased but as accepted components, the very fabric of society.

It can be argued that until relatively recently the perception of the traditional occupational role for women was that of child rearing and domestic duties. A small range of stereotypical occupations such as nursing, teaching, secretarial duties and so forth were also condoned within society. But to imagine, even 30 years ago, women lawyers, engineers, politicians, pilots, judges and senior business executives would have been almost unthinkable.

Today the former view is perceived largely as ludicrous. But to have achieved this change in values and attitudes many barriers have had to be surmounted, not the least being pervasively held sex-stereotyped beliefs. These beliefs were so tightly woven into the fabric of society they were perceived as natural and essential. In changing these stereotypes, the school curriculum was seen as an important vehicle in promoting and consolidating the new values and attitudes. Traditionally the school curriculum had portrayed females as passive, accepting and supportive persons who would subsequently undertake occupations similar in nature such as nursing, secretarial work and teaching. Males, however, were portrayed as active, aggressive and leadership oriented and they would follow appropriate occupations. Ironically these stereotypes, inculcated and reinforced through the traditional curriculum, had an equally negative effect upon both girls and boys.

The 1970s and 1980s have witnessed many changes to school curricula in order to overcome such stereotypes. The content of literature has changed, course offerings in schools are more flexible (some secondary schools require boys to take home economics as part of a personal development component), career counselling has become more established, role models in schools have changed and more females have obtained senior positions within schools.

It can be seen, therefore, that social and cultural forces have a profound effect upon the curriculum in both indirect and direct ways. The exact degree that a society and its culture should influence the education system through the curriculum is a more debatable issue. Certainly curriculum developers, when considering the nature of their task, are well advised to reflect upon Musgrave's questions. But above all, curriculum developers—whether at systemic, local or school level within educational enterprise—should not forget that they are a product of their culture and that every decision that they make will be culturally related.

Psychological sources

The contribution of psychological sources to the foundations of curriculum is significant and growing. As this relatively young discipline matures, the scope for applying its concepts, principles, processes and values to curriculum development is becoming increasingly more apparent.

If the purpose of psychology is the study of human behaviour, then psychologists are concerned with describing, explaining, predicting and investigating the behaviour of humans. Curriculum, therefore, can draw upon psychology, particularly educational psychology, for at least five areas of information:

1 Educational objectives
2 Student characteristics
3 Learning processes
4 Teaching methods
5 Evaluation procedures

The study of psychology does not, at least for the moment, provide a source for content in a school curriculum (other than for a few subjects on psychological studies). Content is drawn from the domains of sociology and philosophy. However, psychology, through its understanding of learners and learning procedures, does indirectly influence the selection of specific content for students as well as the selection of learning activities for students to acquire content. Let us briefly examine the psychological sources that the curriculum developer can employ.

Educational objectives: A knowledge of the psychology of learning helps the curriculum developer devise and phrase appropriate goals and objectives. With this background the developer can determine if goals and objectives are suitable for various developmental levels and ages of learners and hence which are attainable and which are not. Subsequently, the formulation of curriculum goals and objectives has a profound influence upon the selection of content for the curriculum.

Student characteristics: An understanding of the nature of learners, particularly of individual differences and of personality, will assist the curriculum developer to make more appropriate choices in curriculum decision-making. The study of personality can tell us whether different personalities respond to learning experiences in different ways. Indeed, this is something the experienced teacher has long known and concerned teachers have endeavoured to accommodate these differences within their classrooms. Similarly, an understanding of individual differences is most useful to the curriculum developer. The more effective curricula in schools, for example, are able to accommodate differences in student skills and abilities.

Learning processes: Perhaps the greatest contribution that psychology makes to curriculum is an understanding of how people learn. The curriculum developer who has a sound grasp of learning and learning theory is in a commanding position to devise an appropriate curriculum for learners. In particular, an understanding of learning is essential to the effective selection of appropriate learning/teaching strategies.

Whether or not one supports a theory of operant conditioning (such as B.F. Skinner), some form of Gestalt theory (K. Lewin), Jean Piaget's approach to growth and development, or some other form of explaining how learning occurs, the final outcome will affect how the curriculum is shaped. Indeed, one of the difficulties encountered by curriculum developers is the vast array of theories, paradigms and algorithms that purport to explain the process of learning.

Teaching methods: Psychology makes a significant contribution to both the selection of learning experiences and the way that teaching is conducted in the classroom. In the school curriculum an understanding of psychology is essential to the curriculum developer in devising appropriate learning experiences and conditions for learning. In selecting learning experiences the curriculum developer should have taken account of learning theories, individual differences amongst students, motivation strategies, personality, cognitive and affective development, teaching styles, group dynamics, teaching methodology and learning styles. This extensive list of psychological factors suggests that the curriculum developer can make substantial use of psychological sources when selecting learning/teaching experiences.

Evaluation procedures: Psychology can also provide curriculum developers with directions for undertaking the evaluation of student and teacher performance. Educational psychologists have developed a vast array of techniques for measuring the degree of student learning, student attitudes towards learning/teaching and so forth, as well as the extent of teacher effectiveness.

Educational psychologists, as well as other educators, have been concerned with such evaluation issues as:

1 Norm-referenced assessment or criterion-referenced assessment.
2 The role of formative evaluation.
3 Appropriate instruments to measure student performance.
4 Determination of teacher effectiveness.

The five aspects of psychology outlined above indicate the range of influence that psychology has upon the development of curriculum. Detailed studies of each area may be found in the literature and should be consulted when appropriate. For our purposes we simply wish to alert curriculum developers to the areas of influence that psychology can have upon their curriculum decision-making.

To conclude this section, the contribution of philosophy, sociology and psychology to curriculum has been seen to be fundamental in nature. When curriculum developers undertake their task—whether they be a group working at systemic level, a group of classroom teachers, or those in educational but non-schooling situations—they will, knowingly or unknowingly, decide upon certain views of knowledge and values, interpret the nature of society to devise their content and employ psychological principles to make selections for their curriculum. The premise upon which this chapter has been based claims that a sound awareness of and familiarity with these foundation sources will facilitate more effective curriculum development.

Conceptions of curriculum

When curriculum developers get together to design and construct curricula, they bring with them very different ways of thinking about curriculum matters and the curriculum development process. They have different points of view as to what curriculum is concerned with, what it should try to achieve, let alone how one should be constructed.

To some extent the sources of our curriculum ideas discussed previously in this chapter help influence the way we think, write and act about curriculum. Our experiences in past curriculum development activities will similarly influence our decisions. Our perception of the curriculum task at hand, the organisations, if any, that we represent and our reading in the curriculum field will all have an impact upon how we perceive curriculum design and development.

The fundamental base from which we think and act about curriculum may be referred to as conceptions of curriculum. Eisner (1979) refers to these as 'orientations' and argues that there are five basic orientations to curriculum; while John McNeil (1985) devotes four chapters to a detailed analysis of his conceptions of curriculum. In this book it is contended that an additional conception emerges which reflects individual teacher and curriculum developer interactions with various conceptions such that an individualistic eclectic conception emerges. The five conceptions, based on the writings of McNeil (1985), Eisner (1979) and others, and their eclectic derivative, are:

1 Academic rationalist conception.
2 Cognitive processes conception.
3 Humanistic conception.
4 Social reconstructionist conception.
5 Technological conception.
6 Eclectic conception.

We study different conceptions of curriculum because this exercise helps us understand different perceptions of curriculum as well as clarify our own position. If we are able to understand where curriculum developers are coming from, we can better understand the curricula that have been devised and can thus be more consistent with the curriculum's intentions when it is implemented. Too often curricula are criticised without an understanding of the context in which they were developed and without particular reference to the developers involved. It would be quite acceptable, even preferable, for any curriculum document to include a statement of the developers' curriculum conception.

Furthermore, in the final model of curriculum development outlined in chapter 3, I've argued that the first phase of that algorithm is the organisational or presage stage. This involves examining curriculum developers in terms of what they bring to the developing task as well as the nature of the early stages of their interaction.

At the very beginning of curriculum development those involved spend some time discussing the proposed curriculum before the development phase actually begins. At this time the different conceptions or points of view about curriculum will come to the fore. In Walker's (1971) terms, participants have begun 'deliberations' using their 'platforms' as a basis for those deliberative discussions.

The different ways that developers conceptualise curricula will, it is suggested, result in different curricula. Some developers have very specific intentions in mind for their curricula and hence the impact that they will have upon students. Curriculum writers such as Eisner (1979), McNeil (1985) and Skilbeck (1984) have analysed the literature and classified these conceptions of curriculum into useful categories that are helpful when developing and analysing curricula in schools.

The following section will analyse five conceptions in a school context according to the criteria of purpose, content to be taught, approach or methods used, evaluation and examples of the conception in operation within schooling. It then concludes by suggesting that individual teachers will select from amongst these curriculum concepts and produce their individual eclectic conception.

Academic rationalist conception

Purpose: Academic rationalism, probably the oldest approach to conceptualising curriculum, argues that the major function of the school curriculum is to enhance the individual's intellectual abilities in those subject areas most worthy of study. Thus curricula in schools should both assist students to learn how to learn within the subject (examined further in the cognitive process conception) as well as to provide appropriate learning material (subject matter content).

This conception argues that schools, as special places for the development of our future society, should expose students to the accumulated wisdom acquired through a study of academic subjects. It is not the place of schools to address the curriculum towards perceived (and changing) social needs (such as drug education, self-concept enhancement, etc.) but rather the curriculum should provide students with the intellectual tools and understandings to face adult life. Such concepts and techniques may be found in a detailed study of the subjects from the academic disciplines.

The academic disciplines, such as history, chemistry, English, biology, geography, and so forth, are considered to be the depositories of our accumulated wisdom which we have systematically organised into fields of study and bodies of knowledge over the years. An academic discipline-based curriculum, with both appropriate processes and content acquired through studying such subjects, provides a sound basis for the student to become an effective member in adult society.

Content: A school curriculum that favours the academic rationalist conception would typically emphasise the knowledge, skills and values to be found in the various academic disciplines. It is argued that this conception includes more than just knowledge within content, but also the skills of that discipline, the values integral to it and, indeed, the very mode of thought associated with it. In a school setting, therefore, mathematics would be taught using the knowledge, skills and values associated with mathematicians, although simplified for the particular learning situation. These are updated constantly and hence the accumulated wisdom of the discipline grows in strength.

Approach: Within the school context a teacher-centred approach tends to be favoured by the academic rationalists. This emphasises didactic, expository methods for the transmission of knowledge and skills, and reveals values that are invariably acquired through role modelling. In the expository approach the discipline's main ideas have traditionally been ordered, illustrated and explored, and in so doing student minds filled to become individual reservoirs of valuable information.

To a considerably lesser degree, another approach employed within the academic tradition is the inquiry method although it sometimes appears at odds with the expository approach. Problem-solving, discovery learning, scientific methods or the inquiry approach all require the learner to resolve difficulties using logical, systematic reasoning. This develops the academic discipline skills of the learner which are later transferable to a variety of contexts. While this appears different from the expository approach, it is nevertheless an essential feature of working in the academic disciplines. This approach has been supported vigorously by academicians as being essential for young learners to understand the disciplines. Indeed, this was the fundamental rationale employed by many developers of curriculum projects, particularly in the 1960s and 1970s.

In recent times the range of teaching approaches has increased to provide a more diverse and useful range of teaching-learning strategies. This includes greater emphasis upon interactive strategies, small group teaching and individualisation. Furthermore, considerable use has been made within the academic subjects of developments in technology, particularly the use of personal computers, sophisticated computer programs and the technology of CD-ROM (compact disc—read only memory). Given the established strength of academic subjects in school curricula, and their ability to adapt to technological developments, it is highly likely that this conception will remain the pre-eminent approach to conceptualising school curricula (at the very least at the secondary school level).

Evaluation: Curricula based on academic rationalism emphasise examinations and the testing of knowledge and skills. Rigour and quality of learning are valued highly and assessment of student performance has become extensive. However, there is some concern that assessment is used more as an end in itself rather than as a means of providing feedback to learners and teachers. There is a very real danger that assessment will overpower the value of the learning situation itself as may be argued in the case of comprehensive external examinations of subjects at the end of secondary school such as the Higher School Certificate and the Tertiary Entrance Examination.

Examples: We don't have to look far to find examples of academic rationalism in practice. Upper-school subjects in Australian secondary schools have traditionally been oriented towards academic rationalism. Together with tertiary-level subjects, they have influenced the nature of both lower-secondary and even primary school subjects. Despite numerous attempts over the past two decades to unseat the academic disciplines from their control over secondary school curricula, this conception of curriculum is still dominant.

In addition, many of the major curriculum projects that influenced Australian education were academically oriented including Australian Science Education Project (ASEP), Social Education Materials Project (SEMP) and Individualised Science Instruction System (ISIS). Significant figures in the academic rationalist approach to curriculum development include Jerome Bruner, Joseph Schwab, Robert Hutchins, Alfred Kuhn and Paul Hirst.

Cognitive processes conception

Purpose: A significant criticism of the academic conception is that it is excessively content-bound and consequently underemphasises processes at the expense of content. Furthermore, much of this content is outdated before it even comes to be taught in schools. Therefore the principal purpose of the cognitive processes conception is to provide students with the necessary skills or processes to help them learn how to learn. A second, and closely related purpose, is to provide students with the opportunities to employ and enhance the variety of intellectual faculties that they possess.

This conception is premised on the argument that the mind consists of numerous cognitive faculties, such as the ability to solve problems, to visualise, to extrapolate, to synthesise, to conceptualise, to evaluate, to deal with ambiguity, to analyse, and so forth, which can, and should be, deliberately enhanced. But, muscle-like, these cognitive faculties require deliberate attention if they are to grow and assist the individual student.

Content: What is really important to learn, according to proponents of this curriculum conception, are the numerous skills that enable us to conceptually address the world and solve our problems. Thus it is more important to know how to use a dictionary to spell a word correctly rather than to learn vast lists of spelling. However, acquiring cognitive skills in isolation lacks meaning to learners. Hence the academic disciplines form the content base for the cognitive processes conception in that some framework or structure is required to make sense out of acquiring cognitive skills.

In a subject such as history, for example, the cognitive processes conception would still employ the framework of the subject as a basis for study. However, rather than emphasise the memorisation of vast numbers of facts, generalisations and so forth, students should acquire cognitive skills for processing information such as research skills, inquiry skills, information processing, reasoning skills and the like.

Approach: Advocates of the cognitive processes conception develop curricula that encourage teachers to use a combination of student-centred and teacher-centred teaching-learning strategies. The former emphasise inquiry strategies, group work and individualisation, while the latter emphasise interactive strategies.

Many proponents argue that students first need to learn the processes, from the teacher, before they can employ them satisfactorily by themselves. In particular, once students were competent with these skills they would be encouraged to solve significant problems. In very recent times it has been argued that group problem-solving using cognitive skills is vitally important for us to acquire and employ if we are to become economically competitive with other countries.

Evaluation: Emphasis in evaluation is placed upon concept acquisition and application which may be achieved through testing and use of problem-solving situations. Rigour and quality of learning are valued, particularly where they can be applied to specific contexts. Thus while testing of cognitive skills has some place, the application of those skills to resolving problems is valued highly.

Examples: While few curricula have been devised entirely on cognitive processes principles, there is evidence that this conception has influenced many curricula in schools. This is particularly so in terms of the many academic rationalist curricula found in our schools today. In primary schools much of the mathematics and science curricula have been dominated by a 'process approach' to teaching. Similarly, a social studies curriculum—MACOS (Man A Course Of Study), was developed on the lines of developing cognitive skills within students. The Australian-developed curricula, ASEP and SEMP, also had strong cognitive skills components within them.

Over the past decade, a wide acceptance has been evident of the need to incorporate a strong skills component in all subject-based curricula. It would be most unusual today to develop a subject curriculum that did not have strong components of skills and values as well as subject matter content. Significant individuals who support a cognitive processes approach to curriculum development include Jerome Bruner, J. P. Guilford, and Benjamin Bloom.

Humanistic conception

Purpose: The humanistic or personal relevance conception supports the view that the school curriculum should provide learners with intrinsically rewarding experiences to enhance personal development. This more recent view of a humanistic perspective relies much upon the work of the humanistic, experiential, phenomenological (third force) psychologists who argue for enhanced personal growth. They claim that the curriculum should provide opportunities to enhance the individual's self-concept in order to achieve self-actualisation. As John McNeil noted, 'The ideal of the self-actualising person is at the heart of the humanistic curriculum' (1985:4).

However, the concept of a humanistic curriculum is somewhat enlarged by writers who would include the notions of confluent education, mysticism and the radical critics of the late 1960s and 1970s under the humanistic umbrella. While this may be extending the concept too far, these groups have, as their ultimate intention, the enhancement of the individual through personal growth, integrity and autonomy.

Content: By adopting an holistic approach towards curriculum, humanistic educators effect an integration of the cognitive, affective and psychomotor domains. This approach gives the humanists a great strength in their approach to content selection as well as the possibility of producing a sense of unity within the learner. This is in marked contrast to the academic conception whose principal weakness is its lack of integration between subjects and the consequential demarcation between disciplines within educational institutions.

Content frequently consists of valuing situations, social emphasis and self-understanding experiences which produce a vital, enriching learning experience. Often the content in a humanistic curriculum cannot be predetermined as the final selection is determinant upon learner preferences. Nevertheless, content is important to this conception as it is perceived as a liberating force, one that enhances the learner's growth towards self-actualisation.

Approach: An essential feature of the humanistic perspective to curriculum is that the teacher must provide a supportive environment to enhance what is essentially self-learning. An holistic, integrated, 'real-life' approach to learning is emphasised where the teacher acts as a facilitator, resource person, supporter and understanding adult.

Experiential learning—learning by experiencing through one's senses—is a favoured approach in humanistic curricula. Other techniques, such as encounter groups, meditation and small group discussion, all attempt to enhance personal growth and all rely upon a bond of mutual trust between teacher and learner.

Evaluation: In the traditional sense of measuring student performance, the humanistic conception is opposed to evaluation. Humanistic educators emphasise personal growth rather than precise measures of student performance on some arbitrarily defined criteria. Qualitative measures that emphasise process rather than product are used frequently to monitor individual development. Thus techniques such as observation, interviews, personal diaries, participation, reflection and anecdotal records are employed. In all, assessment takes a low profile, with the experiencing of learning being far more important than the attainment of high marks.

Examples: Perhaps the best examples of the humanistic curriculum in practice can be found in the alternative school movement. Nearly two per cent of school students in Australia and the United States in the 1970s attended alternative schools that ranged from completely unstructured, 'free' schools to the Montessori schools. Summerhill, a school initiated by A. S. Neill (1960) was an influential example of an alternative school that emphasised personal growth and student participation in decision-making.

Early childhood education in Australia, particularly kindergarten and Year 1, displays a strong humanistic approach. A supportive learning environment, emphasising experiential learning procedures and the enhancement of personal growth, is fundamental to these classes.

Significant writers in the field include the third-force psychologists such as Abraham Maslow, Carl Rogers, C. H. Patterson and Arthur Combs. The radical critics include John Holt, Herbert Kohl, Jonathon Kozol and Charles Silverman. Together they provide a literature rich in ideas on how to educate our children and youth more humanistically.

Social reconstructionist conception

Purpose: Social reconstructionists would firmly oppose the previous conceptions of curriculum, arguing that they merely support the status quo. Rather, they claim, the school curriculum should effect social reform and help produce a better society for all. In this perspective the needs and betterment of society are placed above those of the individual.

Three strands of social reconstructionism may be determined from the literature, each representing a somewhat different purpose within the social reconstructionist conception:

1 Social adaptation—a relatively conservatively argued case for school curricula to be adapted to meet societal needs.
2 Social reconstructionism—a radical, critical perspective that demands rapid curriculum change to meet society's urgent, immediate needs.
3 Futurist perspective—a speculative view of what school curricula might be like in order to meet perceived needs of society.

All three perspectives seek to foster a sense of critical discontent within learners in schools , though they differ considerably as to how extensive that should be. Certainly all three favour students being more critically aware of their environment at large and hence being able to facilitate societal reform. However for the social adaptation perspective, reform should be small in scale, slow and minimally disruptive. The need for students to participate in career education, where student awareness of the world of work is enhanced, is an example.

By contrast, the social reconstructionist curriculum is also seen as a vehicle for fostering critical discontent, but of a different magnitude, pace and desired impact. By making students critically aware of their environment at large, it is argued, societal reform will be facilitated in the future through students who are both knowledgeable of societal problems and motivated to resolve them. The school curriculum, therefore, should serve as an agent for substantive social change rather than a bastion of the status quo.

A third perspective would use future planning as a basis for curriculum development. Futurologists argue for the power of persons to shape their own destiny and to plan the future (not plan for the future). The school curriculum is seen as an ideal vehicle for future planning.

Content: Supporters of a social reconstructionist curriculum would draw their content from an examination of societal needs, social issues, current ideals and future aspirations. Thus environmental issues, world peace, utilisation of limited resources, political corruption, racial prejudice, religious values, ethnic culture and so forth would be typical areas of study, particularly in subjects such as social studies, English, personal development, science and so forth. Indeed one way that social reconstructionists have made an impact on school curricula is through the introduction of controversial issues within the content of existing school subjects.

Nevertheless, processes and skills are perceived as vitally important for students to be able to assess problems effectively and make useful critical comments. Skills of analysis, deduction, information-processing, inquiry and so forth facilitate the organisation of critically oriented knowledge. In particular the development within students of critical thinking skills in a reflective manner is important (Apple, 1990; Smith & Lovat, 1991; Young, 1989).

The degree to which this content is covered varies with the perspective concerned. Thus the social adaptation perspective takes a minimal view of utilising this content, while social reconstructions take a strongly proactive view.

Approach: The methods used by students to acquire the content are less important than the nature of the content itself for the social reconstructionist. Of necessity most methods require group activity and include group discussions, group experiences to achieve social consensus, student involvement in community activities and group investigation of social problems. In this approach, cooperation with the community is stressed. Students may, for example, undertake a group investigation of a local environmental issue and, as part of that learning processs, would work closely with the community. Similarly students may become actively involved in current societal issues through both investigation and active participation in highlighting the problems concerned.

Evaluation: While social reconstructionists employ traditional assessment techniques such as examinations and tests, they recommend student involvement in their construction and administration. In this way, it is argued, the traditional, conservative, staus quo biases of these instruments can be overcome. Social reconstructionists also argue that the awarding of grades is less important than the experiential learning obtained from active participation of the learner.

Examples: Although there is little evidence of complete social reconstructionist school curricula in practice, an extensive literature in the field exists. More commonly we find examples of significant social issues integrated within existing school subjects. Thus in recent years we have witnessed many traditional school subjects changing to include an analysis of societal issues such as the environment, AIDS, racial prejudice and so forth.

Some specifically created courses on environmental studies, peace studies, women's studies and community cooperation can be found in secondary schools as well as tertiary institutions. In the 1970s greater evidence of social reconstructionist curricula was to be found and many of the newer universities, such as Murdoch University in Western Australia, had a decidedly social reconstructionist slant, not only to their curriculum, but also to their ethos and structure.

Perhaps a more obvious contribution of social reconstructionists can be found in the work of many writers, academics and left-of-centre politicians. The works of Michael Apple, Thomas Popkewitz, Henry Giroux, Ivan Illich, Paulo Freire, Jurgen Habermas, Robert Young, and the futurologist Harold Shane are well-known examples of social reconstructionist writing. A more obvious example of reconstructionist practice in education can be found with most of the Labor ministers for education at state and federal levels. Certainly John Dawkins took a social reconstructionist stance, at least in his early days as minister, towards the Commonwealth's involvement in education, even if tempered by some pragmatic, economically influenced political considerations.

Technological conception

Purpose: John McNeil notes that technology can be applied to curriculum in two important ways. 'First it comes as a plan for the systematic use of various devices and media, and as a contrived sequence of instruction based on principles from behavioural science . . . Second, technology is found in models and procedures for the construction or development and evaluation of curriculum materials and instructional systems' (1985:39–40). In both of these approaches, however, the technological methodology towards curriculum emphasises the effective and efficient resolution of predetermined ends. The task of the curriculum developer, then, is to determine the most efficient means, using technology, to achieve what was stated as being desired.

Content: The academic disciplines are invariably employed as a content base for the technological conception. Indeed, because there is so little intrinsic content involved in this conception (apart from learning how to use the technology itself), it is frequently considered as more of a means of facilitating other conceptions than as a conception in its own right.

Approach: a major strength of the technological conception is the nature of its relationship between the learner and the information source. Taking a behaviourist approach, learning is viewed as a process of reacting to stimuli and as such is considered to be predictable systematic behaviour. Thus learning can be made more effective by increasing the efficiency of the stimulus. The results of this line of thinking have led to various systems approaches to learning and instruction including Computer Assisted Learning (CAL), Individually Directed Instruction (IDI), programmed materials and even criterion referenced assessment procedures.

Evaluation: Traditional testing is a commonplace assessment procedure used in the technological conception where the emphasis is placed upon the effectiveness of the testing procedures. A unique assumption of this conception asserts that the responsibility for mastering the stated objectives lies with the program-maker, not the learner. If the learner fails to achieve the specified objectives, therefore, it is the technologist's responsibility to make the stimulus more effective.

One way to enable the learner to achieve the required objectives is to employ a mastery learning approach. In this approach pretested learners react to effectively presented stimuli and do not progress until they have mastered that learning to a predetermined level. Remediation procedures are devised to enable learners to reach that goal. Advanced learners proceed at a faster pace to achieve the specified goals. Students then acquire that learning, organised on a criterion referenced basis, at their own pace. In this manner all learners succeed at acquiring or mastering the required material.

Examples: Evidence of curricula devised entirely upon a technological conception is difficult to ascertain. However, there are numerous examples of aspects of curricula that have been technologically oriented. Programmed course and instructional books can be found as well as many examples of CAL. Some TAFE courses have been devised on a programmed learning basis and there is evidence of some secondary-school subjects moving in that direction. Significant individuals who advocate a more technological orientation towards curriculum development include James Popham, Michael Scriven, Robert Gagne, Robert Silverman and Eva Baker.

Eclectic conception

Curriculum developers often find themselves aligning their positions with two or more curriculum conceptions. Teachers, for example, may find themselves oriented towards both humanistic and academic conceptions when devising a primary school curriculum. A TAFE lecturer may be more technologically oriented as may a secondary maths teacher, while relying fundamentally upon an academic conception. In an alternative school, teachers may orient their curriculum towards a substantially humanistic interpretation of academic rationalism as this is perceived as best meeting student needs.

While it is quite feasible and even logical to relate to two or more conceptions, difficulties will occur if the conceptions are essentially opposite in nature. A social reconstructionist perspective will usually clash with an academic rationalist conception as will humanistic and technological conceptions. Curriculum developers must find their position for themselves and this requires some reflection about the differing conceptions. Ultimately, when pushed to make specific curriculum decisions, developers will find themselves emphasising one conception more than others.

In concluding this section on conceptions of curriculum it is important to reiterate that curriculum developers who understand these conceptions are better able to formulate their own ideas when devising curricula. Certainly those responsible for selecting curriculum development teams would do well to appreciate the difficulties that could emerge from people holding different conceptions firmly.

Similarly, curricula developed along the lines of a particular conception can be more readily understood if that development is consistent within that conception. Should the attributes of the conceptual approach adopted be disseminated along with the particular curriculum, its chances of being comprehended satisfactorily, and adopted successfully, are greatly enhanced. One aspect of curriculum development that requires participants to understand and reflect upon curriculum conceptions is known as curriculum design, which is addressed in chapter 4.

Curriculum planning

The model of curriculum development discussed in chapter 3 argues that the first phase of the curriculum process focuses on the organisation of the curriculum. That is the initial phase of curriculum development concentrates upon the various aspects of curriculum presage discussed in this chapter. However, we also have to consider the planning of the curriculum which precedes the second, or development, phase of the model.

When curriculum developers commence the task of constructing a curriculum, whether or not it includes a written document, they are participating in curriculum planning. That is, they conceptualise and organise the features of the curriculum they wish to construct.This usually involves them in thinking about the proposed curriculum, discussing it amongst themselves and with others and, particularly if it is a substantial curriculum, producing a written proposal for further discussion and reflection.

In this process of curriculum planning various curriculum presage factors become clearer and some become of vital significance in determining the structure of the final product. If, for example, a group of teachers in a particular primary school is devising a language arts curriculum to meet the needs of a special group of children, certain curriculum presage factors will influence the way they plan and prepare to construct such a curriculum. Perhaps their philosophical orientation will lead them to conceptualise a humanistically based curriculum. And when they come to design what their curriculum might look like, they may well opt for a learner-centred design which emphasises a humanistic perspective.

In a similar way, but with undoubtedly different effects, a centrally based syllabus committee composed of diverse members may plan and prepare to construct a curriculum for a statewide student population. Given different presage factors, the outcomes of this curriculum may be quite different. And if the syllabus committee was devising a curriculum for say Years 11 and 12, the design of the curriculum would undoubtedly appear quite different from the primary school example.

Summary

- Curriculum presage refers to those activities and forces that influence curriculum developers in their curriculum decision-making tasks.
- Curriculum developers play an important role in determining the final nature of a curriculum. Thus the selection or inclusion of particular developers is important.
- The determinants or foundations of curriculum are those basic forces that influence the content and organisation. They include:
— Studies of the nature and value of knowledge (philosophy)
— Studies of life and culture (sociology).
— Studies of learners and learning theory (psychology).
- Philosophical sources include ontology (what is real), epistemology (what is true) and axiology (what is good).
- Sociological sources provide the basis of content for curricula and thus the school curriculum reflects the nature of society. Culturally induced bias is a major concern of curriculum developers.
- Contributions to the curriculum from psychology include educational objectives, student characteristics, learning processes, teaching methods and evaluation procedures.
- There are many conceptions or orientations of curriculum and these explain how and why curriculum developers tackle their task in different ways. Five major groupings of conceptions are evident. These are:
— Academic rationalist conception.
— Cognitive processes conception.
— Humanistic conception.
— Social reconstructionist conception.
— Technological conception.
- The academic rationalist conception enhances the individual's intellectual abilities through the study of worthwhile subjects. It is commonplace in Australian schools, particularly secondary schools, and reinforces the status quo.
- The cognitive processes conception argues for the development of cognitive skills as the basis of a school curriculum. These skills enable students to learn how to learn and hence to resolve their needs and problems.
- The humanistic conception argues that schools should provide learners with intrinsically rewarding experiences to enhance personal growth. It is found in many alternative schools.
- The social reconstructionist conception claims that the school curriculum should effect social reform and help produce a better society for all. It has three directions:
1 social adaptation requiring minor redirection;

2 social reconstruction requiring radical change; and

3 future oriented social change.

- The technological conception seeks to produce a more effective and efficient resolution of objectives. It is seen mainly in small programs as facilitating the academic conception.
- An eclectic position, combining two or more reasonably compatible conceptions, is often taken by curriculum developers. Many teachers identify themselves with an eclectic position.

3 The curriculum process

Knowledge of some overall planning process provides some
structure, order, and direction amidst information overload and
the daily demands of teaching . . . It also provides a framework
and some common concepts, if not common language, for
cooperative curriculum planning . . . (Karen Zumwalt, 1989: 176)

The purpose of this chapter is to examine how curriculum developers can,
and do, devise curricula. It will focus on an analysis of how teachers may
develop curricula successfully as well as presenting a synthesis of the
literature explaining how teachers currently approach curriculum development. The former task will provide curriculum developers with both a
challenge and a useful guide as they tackle the process of curriculum
development.

An important reason for examining both of the above tasks is that
educators view the process of curriculum development in many diverse
ways. Clarity of understanding, let alone consensus, about the curriculum
process has been difficult to achieve. Yet a knowledge and understanding
of the curriculum process is of vital importance in the preparation of
effective curricula.

To understand the context of the model of curriculum development
presented at the end of this chapter, it is necessary to appreciate the range
of models employed by curriculum developers. Models may be classified
according to a continuum that ranges from rational through cyclical to
dynamic approaches of curriculum development. Curriculum writers tend
to advocate the use of cyclical or rational models when devising curricula
largely because of their explicit structure. Teachers, however, appear to
prefer a form of dynamic model, often adapted from a recognised model
such as Skilbeck's. What research is available (Walker, 1971; Brady, 1981;
Cohen & Harrison, 1982) suggests that there are numerous curriculum
models adopted by teachers, and that there is ample evidence of confusion
about curriculum and its development in schools.

For this reason, this chapter advocates the use of a model that
incorporates aspects of all three existing categories of models. The comprehensive model of curriculum development outlined at the end of this
chapter is at once logical and sequential in approach, cyclical in its
development of a curriculum product and yet concerned with applying
the model to realistic situations. It is a model that has the flexibility to

be used for developing systemic, regional, school or subschool curriculum documents as well as packages of curriculum materials and curriculum projects. The model is outlined later in this chapter and is fleshed out in subsequent chapters.

Curriculum practice

There is substantial evidence from the literature, research and by observation to inform us that classroom teachers are not actively engaged in using models in their curriculum development. This is particularly evident at the school level as mentioned in chapter 1 (Brady, 1981; Tom, 1973; Toomey, 1977; Cohen & Harrison, 1981; Deschamp, 1983; Print, 1990; Smith & Lovat, 1991). Some of the reasons forwarded for this situation are:

1　Lack of teacher understanding of curriculum models and the processes of curriculum development.
2　Insufficient experience, both practically and theoretically, with curriculum models.
3　Inadequate amount of time in which to enquire about and apply curriculum models.
4　Lack of support from colleagues for employing curriculum models.
5　Numerous and frequently conflicting conceptions of the nature of curriculum and curriculum development.
6　A misconception of the terms 'model' and 'algorithm'. Teachers avoid the former but use the latter, often unknowingly.

Regardless of the reasons, and whether educators refer to models, theories, paradigms or algorithms, it is essential that curriculum developers bring a conceptual consideration to their task. If they are to overcome the weaknesses inherent in intuitive approaches to curriculum development, some sound theoretical underpinning to the curriculum process is essential.

Models, algorithms and theories

A model is a simplified representation of reality which is often depicted in diagrammatic form. The purpose of a model is to provide a structure for examining the variables that constitute reality as well as their interrelationships. Zais (1976:91) considers models to be '. . . miniature representations that summarize data and/or phenomena and thus act as an aid to comprehension'. Similarly, van Dalen (1973:53) refers to models or paradigms as ' . . . simplified or familiar structures which are used to gain insights into phenomena that scientists want to explain'. In curriculum development we use models to examine the elements of a curriculum (the variables) and how those elements interrelate. At this point it might be worthwhile consulting the glossary for definitions of 'curriculum elements', 'curriculum development' and 'curriculum process'.

A general term gaining greater acceptance as a means of explaining the curriculum process is 'algorithm'. The *Oxford English Dictionary* defines an algorithm as a '. . . step-by-step procedure for solving a problem or accomplishing some end' and may well be a more appropriate term than 'model' (simplified representation) or 'paradigm' (outstandingly clear or typical example). Certainly there is evidence that teachers conceptualise curricula more in an algorithmic sense than as a model (Deschamp, 1983; Deschamp & Ryan, 1986; Toomey, 1977). Nevertheless, the literature in the area of curriculum development has accepted the use of the term 'model' to explain both the nature and process of curriculum development.

Models may be considered in many different ways, depending upon the purpose for which they are intended. For example, models may be physical representations of reality, such as a globe of the world, a cross-section of an orbital engine or a scaled version of a yacht such as *Australia 11* (and its 'winged' keel) to be used for water testing. In these cases the physical reality is represented in a simplified replication of the actual object. The variables that constitute that object may then be analysed and so comprehension of reality is facilitated.

More abstractly, models may be conceptual or verbal in nature. This type of model endeavours to clarify meanings and assist the comprehension of complicated theories and phenomena. Thus models may be seen as a portion of a theory and, indeed, one of the main functions of models is to aid in theory-building. Such models are used extensively in the study of curriculum.

This second type of model frequently employs metaphors in order to enhance comprehension. Thus conceptual models include explanations of the dissemination of innovations (for example the problem-solver model which likens the spread and acceptance of an innovation to the process of problem solving), and the factory-like nature of schools, where schools are seen as factories for the processing of raw materials (students).

Mathematical models reduce complex phenomena in the physical sciences to regular mathematical expressions. Typical of this type are mathematical equations, chemical equations and, probably the most well known equation in physics, Einstein's $E = MC^2$. Finally, models may be graphic representations which depict, by drawings or diagrams, the components of the item being examined. Such diagrams also show the relationships between the variables within the model. The models that follow in this chapter, and indeed much of curriculum theory, may be depicted in diagrammatical form. This facilitates easier understanding of quite complex processes.

Sometimes in the literature the terms 'model' and 'theory' are used synonymously. More accurately the former must be seen as a portion of a theory, something that aids in explaining complicated theory. Van Dalen makes this point quite emphatically.

> Both theories and models are conceptual schemes that explain the relationship of the variables under consideration. But models are analogies (this thing is like that thing) and therefore can tolerate some facts that are not in accord with the real phenomena. A theory, on the other hand, is supposed to describe the facts and relationships that exist, and any facts that are not compatible with the theory invalidate the theory. (van Dalen, 1973:54)

We have seen that models are useful when developing theories because they can summarise effectively and economically a mass of data and complex phenomena. They achieve this by explaining limited aspects of a total theoretical domain. In other words, they concentrate upon selective variables and how they interrelate within the theory under examination. In curriculum we frequently use graphical models as they enable curriculum developers to visualise curriculum elements, their relationships, and the processes of development and implementation.

A continuum of models

Consensus about the relationships between curriculum elements, their order and their exact nature has largely evaded those writing in the field of curriculum. Views of what the curriculum process is about or, more accurately, what it should be concerned with, abound in the literature. A representative sample of the more significant viewpoints has been included in the form of a continuum of curriculum models.

The continuum depicts two extremes of the curriculum process as seen in figure 3.1. The rational or objectives models are sequential, rather rigid approaches to viewing the curriculum process, while at the other extreme may be found dynamic or interaction models, which view curriculum processes as flexible, interactive and modifiable. In between, models gradually change from one type to the other.

Figure 3.1   Continuum of curriculum models

Rational/objectives models	Cyclical models	Dynamic/interaction models
Tyler	Wheeler	Walker
Taba	Nicholls	Skilbeck

It is possible to distinguish cyclical models as those that are rational in approach, but are becoming increasingly more flexible in application. Each of these models will be examined in some detail, with emphasis placed upon particular proponents of models. Figure 3.1 shows the relationship between these models and the names of their developers.

Rational models: Tyler, Taba

Sometimes referred to as objectives/classical/means-end models, these approaches to the curriculum process emphasise the fixed sequence of curriculum elements, beginning with objectives and following a sequential pattern from objectives to content, method and finally evaluation. In this pattern, objectives serve as a basis for devising subsequent elements, with evaluation indicating the degree of achievement of those objectives. Two principal proponents of rational models are Ralph Tyler and Hilda Taba.

Ralph Tyler

In his seminal work *Basic Principles of Curriculum and Instruction* (1949), Tyler argued that curriculum development needed to be treated logically and systematically. His book attempted to explain '. . . a rationale for viewing, analysing and interpreting the curriculum and instruction program of an educational institution.' Further, he argued that to develop any curriculum, one had to pose four fundamental questions:

1 What educational purposes should the school seek to attain? (*objectives*)
2 What educational experiences are likely to attain these objectives? (*instructional strategies and content*)
3 How can these educational experiences be organised effectively? (*organising learning experiences*)
4 How can we determine whether these purposes are being attained? (*assessment and evaluation*)

Sometimes referred to as the father of the curriculum movement, Tyler sought to instil in developers of curricula a more logical, systematic, meaningful approach to their task. His work is now underrated by many curriculum writers because of the rigid nature of his objectives model. However, over time much of his work has been misinterpreted, treated superficially and even ignored. Brady, for example, in referring to the four questions posed above, suggests that: 'The four steps are sometimes simplified to read "objectives", "content", "method" and "evaluation"' (1992:58). Yet Tyler quite emphatically referred to 'learning experiences' in question 2 as ' . . . the interaction between the learner and the external conditions in the environment to which he can react' (1949:63).

Figure 3.2   Tyler model of the curriculum process

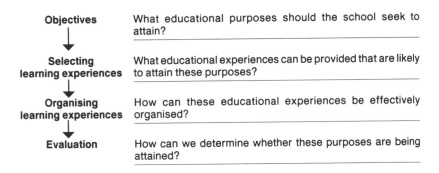

Objectives	What educational purposes should the school seek to attain?
Selecting learning experiences	What educational experiences can be provided that are likely to attain these purposes?
Organising learning experiences	How can these educational experiences be effectively organised?
Evaluation	How can we determine whether these purposes are being attained?

Source: After Tyler, 1949

Similarly, some writers have argued that Tyler doesn't adequately explain the source of objectives (Skilbeck, 1976; Kliebard, 1970). Yet Tyler devotes half of his book to just that task! He describes and analyses sources of objectives that come from learners, studies of contemporary life, academic subjects, philosophy and the psychology of learning.

Certainly Tyler has had a significant effect upon curriculum developers and writers for the past three decades. Briefly, his model for the curriculum process is outlined in figure 3.2. As the diagram suggests, Tyler saw the task of curriculum development as a logical, sequential resolution to the four questions posed. Once objectives had been determined, appropriate learning experiences could be selected which in turn would require effective organisation. The final step in Tyler's process was to determine whether the objectives had been achieved.

Hilda Taba

Of the several books that Hilda Taba wrote on curriculum, the most well known and influential was *Curriculum Development: Theory and Practice* (1962). In this substantial book Taba outlined her approach to the process of curriculum development. In so doing she modified Tyler's basic model to become more representative of curriculum development in schools.

While still linear in approach, Taba argued for more information input at each stage of the curriculum process. In particular, she suggested a dual consideration of content (logical organisation of the curriculum) and the individual learner (psychological organisation of the curriculum). To emphasise her point, Taba claimed that all curricula are composed of fundamental elements. 'A curriculum usually contains some selection and organization of content; it either implies or manifests certain patterns of

Figure 3.3   Taba model of the curriculum process

The order, as Taba perceives it, is:

Step 1: Diagnosis of needs
Step 2: Formulation of objectives
Step 3: Selection of content
Step 4: Organisation of content
Step 5: Selection of learning experiences
Step 6: Organisation of learning experiences
Step 7: Determination of what to evaluate and ways and means of doing it

Source: After Taba, 1962

learning and teaching . . . Finally, it includes a program of evaluation of the outcomes' (Taba, 1962:10).

Taba argued for a rational, sequential approach to curriculum development rather than a rule-of-thumb procedure. Furthermore, to be rational and scientific in one's approach, Taba claimed that decisions on the fundamental elements should be made according to valid criteria. These criteria may come from various sources—from tradition, from social pressures, from established habits. The differences between curriculum decision-making which follows a scientific method and develops a rational design and one which does not is that in the former the criteria for decisions are derived from a study of the factors constituting a reasonable basis for the curriculum. In our society at least, these factors are the learner, the learning process, the cultural demands and the content of the disciplines. Therefore, Taba contended scientific curriculum development needs to draw upon analyses of society and culture, studies of the learner and the learning process, and analysis of the nature of knowledge in order to determine the purposes of the school and the nature of its curriculum.

Finally, Taba claimed that if curriculum development was to be a logical, orderly task then one needed to examine closely the order in which curriculum decisions are made and how they were applied. 'This book is based on an assumption that there is such an order and that pursuing it will result in a more thoughtfully planned and a more dynamically conceived curriculum' (Taba, 1962:12). Taba perceived that the orderly way of developing curricula would follow seven sequential steps as outlined in figure 3.3.

For curricula to be a useful learning experience to students, Taba argued that it was important to diagnose the needs of learners. This was an important first step for Taba—what did the students want and need to learn? This information then became helpful with step 2—the formulation of clear and comprehensive objectives to form a base for the development of later curriculum elements. Certainly, Taba argued, the nature of the objectives would determine what sort of learning was to follow. To this degree Taba fervently supports the objectives or rational model, as can be seen in figure 3.3.

Steps 3 and 4 are integrated in reality, although for the purposes of studying curricula, Taba differentiated between them. To undertake these steps, teachers needed the previously formulated objectives as well as a deep understanding of the appropriate content.

Similarly steps 5 and 6 relate to the objectives and to the content that has been devised. To undertake these steps effectively, Taba suggested developers obtain an understanding of certain principles of learning, strategies of concept attainment and sequencing of learning.

In the final step, Taba sought to direct curriculum developers to conceptualise and plan evaluation strategies. As with Tyler, she wanted to know if the ends (objectives) of the curriculum were in fact being achieved.

These steps, presented sequentially in figure 2.3, represent a brief outline of Taba's systematic, logical approach to curriculum development. She is firmly located at the rational/objectives end of the curriculum models continuum, although she is far more expansive than Tyler. Her approach, with its emphasis upon the learner, comes in part from her extensive interaction with schools in California. Working with teachers she realised that they would become the major curriculum developers of the future and a systematic logical model would be valuable to them. As such, Taba's model is decidedly algorithmic in nature.

Strengths of rational models

The very nature of the rational model—its logical, sequential structure—provides it with a useful base for planning and devising curricula. By providing a recipe-type approach, these models have simplified what is a confusing, daunting task to many prospective curriculum developers. Given the pressures that teachers and curriculum developers work under, a rational model provides a straightforward, time-efficient approach to meeting the curriculum task. The practical approach to devising curricula is the essense of the rational model.

By emphasising the role and value of objectives, this model forces curriculum developers to think seriously about their task. Too much curriculum development, it could be argued, is carried out with little thought to the intended outcomes. By forcing people to conceptualise and then state objectives, rational thinking is encouraged and a clear guide to later planning is provided. Proponents of this approach also argue that *all* curriculum developers, regardless of their approach to curriculum, have objectives in mind, although some do not think about them systematically or state them logically.

In examining the curriculum process, one could argue that Tyler and Taba have found the inherent logic that underpins the construction of curricula, at least from a rationalist perspective. Using the sequence of developing objectives, formulating content and learning activities, and finally evaluating the extent to which objectives have been achieved, does have an obvious logical, rational appeal to it.

Should one begin with other elements, such as content or evaluation, one would have little direction or purpose in curriculum planning and confusion could well result. Besides, one could argue that those developers who commence planning with other curriculum elements have in reality thought about what they want to achieve, but have not formalised that thinking or not stated their objectives overtly. Furthermore, this thinking may well be related to teacher needs (I want to teach this material because I like it and am familiar with it), rather than student needs.

Weaknesses of rational models

Over time it has become increasingly apparent that the objectives model has flaws in terms of the reality of curriculum development. To a large measure one might claim that these apparent weaknesses are due to different ways of thinking and approaching curricula as well as the background experiences, or lack of them, of teachers. In other words, those not trained in the rational model and those who prefer not to think and develop logically and systematically will undoubtedly experience difficulties with this approach to curriculum development. As will be seen later, such developers tend to feel more comfortable with dynamic, interactive models.

A significant weakness of the objectives model arises from the unpredictable nature of teaching and learning. The model prescribes specified objectives to be achieved, but often learning occurs beyond these objectives due to factors that could not have been foreseen.

For example, in a science class certain objectives form the basis of the ensuing curriculum that is being taught. However, new information becomes available (a new theory, more information from space experiments, new approaches to research) that would be both pertinent and useful to the science curriculum. Should it be included if it is not consistent with the established objectives? What impact will this have on other elements of the curriculum, particularly evaluation? If we include this content, does its inclusion invalidate the curriculum? These are reasonable questions to pose of the objectives model.

Observation of curriculum development in practice has revealed that teachers frequently prefer not to follow a logical, sequential approach (see earlier in this chapter and chapter 1). Rather they prefer to begin with what they know—content—and work from there. This phenomenon may not be as much a weakness of the model as it is of those who might apply it. Certainly if developers are trained and experienced in the objectives approach, they find its logical, sequential approach simple and straightforward to follow.

Overemphasis on formulating measurable outcomes (such as behavioural objectives) has caused significant problems for the rational model. With limited time available, teachers have found themselves spending inordinate amounts of that scarce commodity on writing precisely phrased behavioural objectives. Consequently, where possible, classroom teachers have avoided objective models. However, this is more a case of misplaced emphasis and of the means overpowering the end. Objectives are designed to provide a guide to learning and curriculum planning, not an end unto themselves. Excessive time spent on phrasing and writing particular objectives reduces time for developing other elements within the curriculum. Furthermore, it encourages developers to avoid objectives in the first place.

Finally, the rational model is frequently criticised because its proponents, especially Tyler, do not *adequately* explain the sources of their objectives (Kliebard, 1970; Skilbeck, 1976; Brady, 1981; Marsh, 1986). In part the answer to this criticism lies in a sound reading of Tyler's and Taba's original works where, suprisingly, considerable space is devoted to explaining where objectives should come from. And in part the answer lies with the use of a non-specific, indeterminate term such as 'adequate'. What is adequate for some is obviously inadequate for critics.

Cyclical models: Wheeler, Nicholls & Nicholls

As can be seen from figure 3.1, cyclical models lie along the continuum between the extremes of rational and dynamic models, incorporating elements of both to provide a different approach to devising curricula. Basically, these models are an extension of rational models in that they are essentially logical and sequential in approach. However, differences do exist. Most importantly, cyclical models see the curriculum process as a continuing activity, constantly in a state of change as new information or practices become available.

Community pressure such as the need for improved physical health, for example, may require re-orientation of aims, and thus content, methods and evaluation. In this way the cyclical model is responsive to needs and indeed it is argued that these needs are ongoing, necessitating constant updating of the curriculum process.

Cyclical models view elements of the curriculum as interrelated and interdependent, so that the distinctions between the elements, as in the rational model, are less clear. An example of this might be when a developer is considering content, he or she may also suggest ideas for teaching methodology, although the consolidation of these teaching strategies would come later. Instead of regarding them as rigidly separate categories, cyclical models more realistically accept a degree of interaction between the various curriculum elements.

In the 1970s a new element was introduced into the curriculum process of cyclical models. Called situational analysis, it requires an analysis of those factors into which a curriculum is to be introduced (see chapter 5). In this way the subsequent curriculum more accurately reflects the needs of the students for whom it was intended. This element is integral to the dynamic models discussed later, but it is employed effectively in cyclical models as well.

Of the many cyclical models available, two will be discussed briefly. Another, my adaption, will be explained in more depth later in this chapter. The two selected here have both been influential over the past two decades, the former more with writers in the field, the latter more with classroom teachers, especially in Britain.

D. K. Wheeler

In his influential book *Curriculum Process,* Wheeler (1967) argued for curriculum developers to employ a cyclical process in which each element is related and interdependent and follows a cyclical pattern as evidenced in figure 3.4. Yet his approach to devising curricula is still essentially rational in nature.'Each phase is a logical development of the preceding one, for, most commonly, work in one phase cannot be attempted until some work has been done in a preceding phase'(1967:30).

A former member of the University of Western Australia, Wheeler developed and extended the ideas forwarded by Tyler and particularly Taba. He suggested five interrelated phases in the curriculum process which, when developed logically and temporally, would produce an effective curriculum. As can be seen in the five phases listed below, they incorporate the essential elements outlined by Tyler and Taba, although they are presented in a somewhat different manner.

Wheeler's phases

1 Selection of aims, goals and objectives.
2 Selection of learning experiences to help achieve these aims, goals and objectives.
3 Selection of content through which certain types of experience may be offered.
4 Organisation and integration of learning experiences and content with respect to the teaching–learning process.
5 Evaluation of each phase and the attainment of goals.

Figure 3.4   Wheeler model of the curriculum process

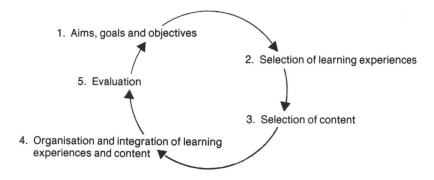

1. Aims, goals and objectives

2. Selection of learning experiences

5. Evaluation

3. Selection of content

4. Organisation and integration of learning
   experiences and content

Source: After D.K. Wheeler, 1967.

Wheeler's significant contribution to curriculum development was to emphasise the cyclical nature of the curriculum process and the interdependent nature of the curriculum elements. His model is outlined in figure 3.4, although he admits that this is a simplified view of the curriculum process. The diagram shows how the rational approach is still evident by requiring curriculum developers to follow steps 1 through 5 in a sequential pattern. However, figure 3.4 also indicates that these steps are in a continuous cycle that responds to changes within education.

At a time when the writing of objectives was gaining momentum, it is unfortunate that Wheeler overcomplicated the idea of determining curriculum outcomes with an undue emphasis on goals. His requirement for the writing of ultimate, mediate and proximate goals, from which specific objectives are to be devised, received little support from classroom teachers or indeed from other curriculum writers. Nevertheless, his notion of a cyclical curriculum process, emphasising the interdependent nature of curriculum elements, has stood the test of time well.

Audrey and Howard Nicholls

By contrast, the team of Audrey and Howard Nicholls, in their book *Developing a Curriculum: A Practical Guide* (1978), devised a straightforward cyclical approach that covered the elements of curriculum briefly but succinctly. First published in 1972, the book was enormously popular with teachers, particularly in Britain, where curriculum development at the school level has long been established.

The Nicholls model emphasised the logical approach to curriculum development, particularly where the need for new curricula emerged from changed situations. They argued that '. . . change should be planned and

Figure 3.5   Nicholls model of the curriculum process

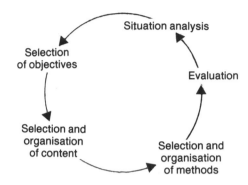

Source: After A. and H. Nicholls, 1978.

introduced on a rational and valid basis according to a logical process, and this has not been the case in the vast majority of changes that have already taken place' (Nicholls & Nicholls, 1978:17).

They refined the work of Tyler, Taba and Wheeler by emphasising the cyclical nature of the curriculum process and the need for a preliminary step—a situational analysis. The authors contend that before the more obvious elements in the curriculum process are undertaken, the context or situation in which curriculum decisions are made requires detailed and serious consideration. Situation analysis, then, is a preliminary stage which makes curriculum developers cognisant of the factors impinging upon the curriculum they are devising (see chapter 5).

Five interdependent stages are needed in this continuous curriculum process as seen below and in figure 3.5.

1 Situation analysis.
2 Selection of objectives.
3 Selection and organisation of content.
4 Selection and organisation of methods.
5 Evaluation.

The inclusion of the situation analysis phase was a deliberate move to force curriculum developers in schools to be more responsive to their environment and particularly to the needs of learners. The authors argued for a 'much wider and more comprehensive approach to diagnosis, an analysis of all the factors which make up the total situation followed by the use of knowledge and insights derived from this analysis in curriculum planning' (Nicholls & Nicholls, 1978:21).

As each of these stages will be discussed later in this chapter it is unnecessary to repeat them here. It is possible, however, to examine the work of earlier curriculum writers and see how the concepts posited by the Nicholls model have been refined over time. The diagrammatic representation of the model (figure 3.5) shows how the authors were indebted to their curriculum predecessors.

Strengths of cyclical models

While cyclical models incorporate the advantages inherent in objective models, they also overcome many of the latter's disadvantages as well. Thus cyclical models exhibit the strengths derived from a logical sequential structure upon which curricula may be devised. For example, such models, by emphasising the role of aims, goals and objectives, require the curriculum developer to have conceptualised the task before proceeding. This enhances rational thinking with the probability that a more effective curriculum will result.

By employing situational analysis as a starting point, cyclical models provide baseline data upon which effective objectives may be devised. Although Wheeler did not refer to situational analyses specifically, he did examine the sources of aims and goals. Certainly objectives cannot be phrased in a vacuum and it is the data, both quantitative and qualitative (including intuitive), that are obtained by undertaking a situational analysis that helps curriculum developers make effective decisions. This approach is essential if teachers are to become actively engaged in school-based curriculum in an effective manner.

The nature of cyclical models is such that the various elements of curriculum are seen to be in continuous motion, able to cope with new situations and consequently reacting to changing circumstances. The model is flexible in that as the situation changes so corresponding changes are made to subsequent elements of the model. For example, if a school is changed suddenly by an influx of a large group of students who are different from what existed previously, then the situation upon which the existing curriculum was based has to be altered. The model allows for, and indeed demands, a revision of the new situation and subsequent changes to the other curriculum elements (objectives, content, methods and evaluation). A school curriculum based on a cyclical model could cope, for example, if there was a sudden influx of migrant adolescents, if a change in societal demands became evident (such as literacy or career education) or if student needs changed (such as non-academic upper secondary subjects).

Cyclical models, being less rigid in their application, are more relevant to school situations and hence are more appropriate to curriculum development by teachers. Experience has also indicated a reduced dependence on using specifically stated objectives in cyclical models, particularly those phrased in behavioural terms. Together with its greater flexibility in terms of development, the cyclical model offers greater scope for effective curriculum development in schools.

Weaknesses of cyclical models

Inherent weaknesses within cyclical models are more difficult to locate largely because this approach to the curriculum process is so successfully employed by curriculum developers. It is possible, however, for the cyclical model to be ignored by developers because of its initial logical approach. As a model must begin somewhere, the cyclical model commences with a situational analysis and then proceeds through the successive elements of curriculum.

However, once the cycle has been established it is possible that the stimulus for change may be originated from any curriculum element. For example, where a school curriculum is in operation the need to revise the cycle may originate with new content, a different approach to teaching/learning being adopted from the results of an evaluative study or a changed situation due to the arrival of additional students. Nevertheless, once the stimulus for revision has been initiated within the cycle, it needs to run its course as it impacts on subsequent elements.

A second weakness of this model arises for many people from its apparently logical and sequential nature. For many, cyclical models are little different from rational models and hence maintain the weaknesses described above. Third, the manner in which the model is implemented may be construed as a weakness. A fundamental problem in utilising such models is the amount of time required to undertake an effective situational analysis. In order to be well appraised of the situation, developers must employ numerous techniques to elicit data about the learning situation. This can become extremely time consuming and classroom teachers often prefer to rely upon their experienced intuition rather than the more systematic collection of situationally based data.

Dynamic models: Walker, Skilbeck

Interactive or dynamic models of curriculum offer an alternative view of the process of curriculum development, as seen in figure 3.1. Proponents of these models (Walker, 1971; Skilbeck, 1976; Macdonald & Purpel, 1988) argue that the rational and cyclical models do not reflect the reality of curriculum development in educational organisations. The curriculum process, they contend, does not follow a lineal, sequential pattern. Rather, curriculum development can commence with any curriculum element and proceed in any order. Indeed, curriculum developers may move through the various elements of curriculum several times before they are satisfied with the final curriculum product. As well, the needs of learners are seen as more important in determining curriculum planning than some pre-determined set of information to be acquired.

It should be noted that the dynamic models have emerged from a more *descriptive* approach to curriculum where researchers have observed the behaviour of teachers and developers as they devise curricula. This, they argue, represents the essential base for formulating theory. Consequently the analytical and prescriptive approach, the very basis of the objectives and cyclical models, is not prominent in dynamic models. Several writers have produced interpretations of dynamic models of the curriculum process. Two significant contributions outlined below have been developed by Decker Walker (1971) and Malcolm Skilbeck (1976).

Decker Walker

In the early 1970s Decker Walker argued that the objectives or rational models of the curriculum process were, contrary to accepted opinion in the literature, neither popular nor successful. Walker (1971) contended that curriculum developers do not follow the prescriptive approach of the rational sequence of curriculum elements when they devise curricula. Rather, they proceed through three phases in their 'natural' preparation of curricula as seen in figure 3.6.

These conclusions were derived by Walker's analysis of reports on

Figure 3.6   Walker model of the curriculum process

(beliefs   theories   conceptions   points of view   aims,objectives)

Platform

Deliberations

(applying them to practical situations, arguing about, accepting, refusing, changing, adapting)

Curriculum Design

(Making decisions about the various process components)

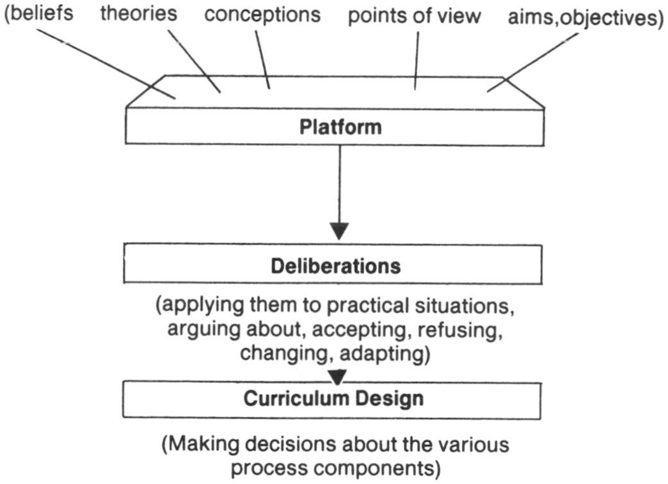

Source: After D. Walker, 1972

curriculum projects such as CHEM Study, BSCS and SMSG and his personal participation in a curriculum project in art (1971:63). This analysis led him to describe what he saw as a 'natural' model of the curriculum process. 'It is a naturalistic model in the sense that it was constructed to represent phenomena and relations observed in actual curriculum projects as faithfully as possible with a few terms and principles' (Walker, 1971:51).

In the first stage, Walker argues, 'platform' statements are recognised by curriculum developers. These statements consist of a hotchpotch of ideas, preferences, points of view, beliefs and values that are held about the curriculum. They may not be defined clearly or even logically, but they form the basis or platform upon which future curriculum decisions are made by curriculum developers. Figure 3.6 shows the relationship between the first and subsequent stages.

After all, Walker contends, curriculum developers do not commence their task with a 'blank slate'. The ideas, values, conceptions and so forth that developers bring with them to the curriculum-development process indicate their predilections and also serve as a base, or platform, from which curricula may be devised. Walker suggests that 'The platform includes an idea of what is and a vision of what ought to be and these guide the curriculum developer in determining what he should do to realize his vision' (1971:52).

Once the interaction between individuals begins, they are then said to enter the deliberation phase. Walker contends that during this phase individuals defend their own platform statements and push 'spur of the moment' ideas. Together these events provide a situation where developers seek to clarify their ideas and reach a consensus. From this apparently chaotic period, the deliberative phase produces considerable illumination (and not a little heat!).

The deliberation phase is not precisely laid out in a series of steps or procedures as would occur in an objectives model. It is a complex, randomised set of interactions that eventually achieves an enormous amount of background work before the actual curriculum is designed. Walker chose to characterise this phase by quoting from Joseph Schwab.

> [Deliberation] . . . treats both ends and means and must treat them as mutually determining one another. It must try to identify, with respect to both, what facts may be relevant. It must try to ascertain the relevant facts in the concrete case. It must try to identify the desiderata in the case. It must generate alternative solutions. It must take every effort to trace the branching pathways of consequences which may flow from each alternative and affect desiderata. It must then weigh alternatives and their costs and consequences against one another, and choose, not the right alternative, for there is no such thing but the best one. (Walker, 1971: 52–3)

The final phase of Walker's model (figure 3.6) is what he terms 'design'. In this phase developers make decisions about the various process components (the curriculum elements). Decisions have been reached after extended discussion and compromise by individuals. The decisions are then recorded and these become the basis for a curriculum document or specific curriculum materials.

To conclude, it is useful to view Walker's model in comparison with the classical, objectives model that he condemned.

This model is primarily descriptive, whereas the classical model is prescriptive. This model is basically a temporal one: it postulates a beginning (the platform), an end (the design), and process (deliberation) by means of which the beginning progresses to the end.

In contrast, the classical model is a means-end model: it postulates a desired end (the objective), a means for attaining this end (the learning experience), and a process (evaluation) for determining whether the means does indeed bring about the end. The two models differ radically in the roles they assign to objectives and to evaluation in the process of curriculum development. (Walker, 1971:58–9)

Malcolm Skilbeck

An alternative interactive or dynamic model of the curriculum process has been posited by Malcolm Skilbeck, former director of Australia's Curriculum Development Centre. In a well-publicised article, Skilbeck (1976) suggested an approach for devising curriculum at the school level. As part of the argument for pursuing school-based curriculum development (SBCD), Skilbeck provided a model by which teachers could realistically develop appropriate curricula. Such a model may be considered dynamic in nature and that was certainly Skilbeck's intention.

Dynamic or interactive models suggest that the curriculum developer may commence with any curriculum element and proceed in any sequence rather than the fixed sequence advocated by the rational model. Skilbeck supports this notion, although he adds that it is important that developers be aware of the source of their objectives. To understand these sources, he contends, a situational analysis must be undertaken. This phenomenon is examined further in chapter 5.

The model (figure 3.7) claims that for SBCD to work effectively, five steps are required in the curriculum process. Although Skilbeck (1976:95) suggested that the model could be applicable equally to curriculum development, observing and assessing curriculum systems and for theoretical analysis of curriculum, its applied value lies with the first alternative.

While it is tempting to argue that the apparent logical order of the model is rational by nature, Skilbeck warns us not to fall into that trap. He suggests that curriculum developers may commence their planning at

Figure 3.7   Skilbeck model of the curriculum process

```
        ┌──────────────────────► ┌─────────────────────────┐
        │                        │   Situation analysis    │
        │                        └─────────────────────────┘
        │                                      ↓
        │                    ┌─────────────────────────┐
        │                    │   Goal formulation      │
        │                    └─────────────────────────┘
        │                                      ↓
        │              ┌─────────────────────────┐
        │              │   Program building      │
        │              └─────────────────────────┘
        │                                      ↓
        │         ┌─────────────────────────┐
        │         │  Interpretation and     │
        │         │  implementation         │
        │         └─────────────────────────┘
        │                                  ↓
        │    ┌─────────────────────────────┐
        │    │  Monitoring, feedback,      │
        └────┤  assessment,                │
             │  reconstruction             │
             └─────────────────────────────┘
```

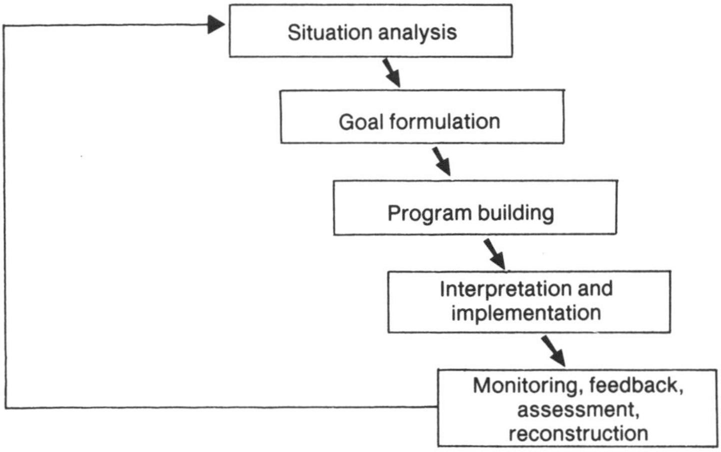

Source: After M. Skilbeck, 1976

any of the five stages and proceed in any order, perhaps even handling different stages concurrently. In one sense the model above is confusing as it indeed appears to support a rational approach to curriculum development. However, Skilbeck states: 'The model outlined does not presuppose a means-end analysis at all; it simply encourages teams or groups of curriculum developers to take into account different elements and aspects of the curriculum development process, to see the process as an organic whole and to work in a moderately systematic way' (1976:97).

It is difficult to summarise the model succinctly and the best way is to employ table 3.1 as devised by Skilbeck.

Strengths of interaction models

Proponents of dynamic models of the curriculum process claim that these are far more realistic ways of handling curriculum development. By avoiding the obsession with writing objectives, and indeed behavioural objectives at that, developers are free to be more creative. Certainly there is substantial teacher resentment to the writing of excessive numbers of objectives, particularly when they are required to be expressed in behavioural terms. Thus interactive models are more realistic, feasible procedures for curriculum development, especially from the viewpoint of the overworked classroom teacher.

Such models also offer developers considerable flexibility when approaching the development task. This flexibility emerges from the

Table 3.1   Features of the curriculum process

1 Situational analysis	
Review of the change situation	Analysis of factors which constitute the situation
a external	i cultural and social changes and expectations including parental expectations, employer requirements, community assumption and values, changing relationships (e.g. between adults and children), and ideology; ii educational-system requirements and challenges, e.g. policy statements, examinations, local authority expectations or demands or pressures, curriculum projects, educational research; iii the changing nature of the subject matter to be taught; iv the potential contribution of teacher-support systems, e.g. teacher training colleges, research institutes v flow of resources into the school.
b internal	i pupils: aptitudes, abilities and defined educational needs; ii teachers: values, attitudes, skills knowledge, experience, special strengths and weaknesses, roles; iii school ethos and political structure: common assumptions and expectations including power distribution, authority relationships, methods of achieving conformity to norms and dealing with deviance; iv material resources including plant, equipment, and potential for enhancing these; v perceived and felt problems and shortcomings in existing curriculum.

2 Goal formulation

The statement of goals embraces teacher and pupil actions (not necessarily manifest 'behaviour') including a statement of the kinds of learning outcomes which are anticipated. Goals 'derive' from the situation analysed in 1 only in the sense that they represent decisions to modify that situation in certain respects and judgments about the principal ways in which these modifications will occur. That is, goals imply and state preferences, values and judgments about the directions in which educational activities might go.

3 Program building

a   design of teaching-learning activities: content, structure and method, scope, sequence;
b   means-materials, e.g. specification of kits, resource units, text materials etc.;

c design of appropriate institutional settings, e.g. laboratories, field work, work-shop;
d personnel deployment and role definition, e.g. curriculum change as social change;
e timetables and provisioning.

---

4 Interpretation and implementation

Problems of installing the curriculum change, e.g. in an on-going institutional setting where there may be a clash between old and new, resistance, confusion, etc. In a design model, these must be anticipated, pass through a review of experience, analysis of relevant research and theory on innovation, and imaginative forecasting.

---

5 Monitoring, feedback, assessment, reconstruction

---

a design of monitoring and communication systems;
b preparation of assessment schedules;
c problems of 'continuous' assessment;
d reconstruction/ensuring continuity of the process.

Source: M. Skilbeck, 1976:96

suggestion that developers may commence at any point in the curriculum process that is appropriate to their needs. Certainly the objectives model, and to a lesser extent the cyclical model, require developers to proceed in a rigid, sequential order. Furthermore, dynamic models allow for flexible movement *within* the curriculum process so that developers may move about in any order of events, retrace their steps and proceed in whatever way they find preferable. This lack of constraint is prized highly by many developers of curriculum.

Finally, it can be argued that interaction models reflect the reality of curriculum development, albeit complex and confusing. By reflecting the situation, particularly in schools, it can be claimed that a more suitable, less dysfunctional approach is advocated to those learning the task of curriculum development.

Weaknesses of interaction models

Presenting the relative strengths and weaknesses of the various models depends largely upon the perception and preference of the person involved. It has been stated earlier that my preferred approach to the curriculum process is that offered by the cyclical model and thus one might expect a greater emphasis upon the weaknesses of interaction models than would come from supportive writers.

It is not difficult to suggest that dynamic models appear confusing and lacking in direction. With a non-systematic approach recommended, such models will undoubtedly be confusing in operation and there is the very real danger that pooled ignorance will result. Although these models supposedly reflect reality, one might question if reality is necessarily good or useful.

In a similar vein, some dynamic models offer so little direction that developers are left perplexed as to what to do. Such models assume that developers understand curriculum theory and curriculum elements but I contend that this is a dubious stance to take. One of the problems emerging from curriculum development in schools today is that too few teachers understand what they are doing in terms of curriculum development. Thus interactive models, except perhaps Skilbeck's, provide little guidance to curriculum developers and this facilitates confusion rather than clarity.

A question that is often asked by opponents of interaction models is—How do you know where you are going if you pose few or no objectives? If objectives provide guidance and direction, the argument goes, then they must be stated in order to be effective. Although Skilbeck refers to goals, he plays down their impact, particularly in terms of their planning capabilities. Walker also refers to aims and objectives but sees them as only one of several factors that comprise platform statements. Thus one important weakness of interaction models, some would claim, is the lack of emphasis placed on the construction and use of objectives and the direction they can provide.

It could also be claimed that by not following a logical sequence in developing curricula, developers waste significant amounts of time meandering around the curriculum maze. Spending time in the deliberative stage is time lost from effective development and, in turn, this may partly account for the curriculum confusion evident in schools!

In all, one can argue that there are numerous weaknesses with the interaction model of the curriculum process. However, this must be tempered with the knowledge that other approaches to devising curricula have weaknesses as well. At this stage those interested in the relationship between the various models of the curriculum process should reflect upon Figure 3.9. One may then be in a better position to determine which is the most appropriate model for a curriculum developer's needs.

Model of curriculum development

The model of curriculum development advocated here has been devised in an attempt to provide a useful and easily understandable approach to developing curricula. The approach adopted is essentially algorithmic in that it is sequential and logical, and hence appropriate to the needs of curriculum developers, particularly teachers performing that role. As such, the model is a relatively prescriptive approach which suggests how curriculum development should be undertaken, essentially in a step-by-step procedure.

There seems little to be gained by continuing to elaborate dynamic models which describe what is happening when teachers and developers devise curricula. That situation is characterised by confusion and chaos and thus requires clarity not exemplification. Considerable research (Cohen & Harrison, 1982; Brady, 1981; Toomey, 1977; Tom, 1973; Print, 1986) substantiates the claim that teachers have little clear understanding of curriculum terms, concepts and models. From their major research study, Cohen & Harrison (1982) concluded that there was no common definition of curriculum shared by teachers in Australian schools, and that there is justifiable concern about the effectiveness of curriculum development.

> As well as the diversity of perceptions (of curriculum) across Australia generally, there was differing perceptions between states and between principals, department heads and teachers. Of more crucial importance, however, is that, even within individual schools, there were differing and often conflicting views. (Cohen & Harrison, 1982:205)

Therefore what is needed is a clear, logical, prescriptive approach to curriculum development that will provide positive guidance for developers of curricula. Such a model should have a wide range of applicability, be straightforward in approach and yet be sufficiently complex to provide an algorithmic base to curriculum development.

The structure of the model (figure 3.8) lends itself to application in different curriculum contexts. Some of the appropriate situations that could employ the model include the development of:

1 System curricula, for example, the curriculum for all schools in New South Wales; the curriculum for Catholic schools in Queensland.
2 Subject curricula, for example, the curriculum for K10 English; the curriculum for secondary home economics.
3 School curricula, for example, the curriculum for Kapinara Primary School; the curriculum for Sydney Girls High School; the curriculum for Bruce Technical College.
4 Subschool curricula, for example, the junior primary school curriculum; the upper secondary school curriculum.
5 Project curricula, for example, a curriculum project on environmental studies; a curriculum for science in Australian schools (such as Australian Science Education Project—ASEP).

Three sequential phases—organisation, development and application—are considered to form the basis of this model of curriculum development. To understand what happens, or more accurately what *should* happen, in curriculum development, the model argues that we need to understand what happened as a prelude to development (presage); how we are to devise a curriculum document, project or materials (development) and finally how the document/materials may be applied and modified in practice (application). Figure 3.8 depicts the three phases by emphasising the activities that should occur within them.

Phase 1: organisation

Curriculum presage considers the nature of those participants involved in the curriculum development task and the curriculum planning they undertake before the development phase commences. The model suggests that an important commencement point in any curriculum development lies with a formalised procedure of curriculum presage. In other words, to begin developing a curriculum we must first look at those who will be responsible for developing it, what backgrounds they bring to the task and what forces have shaped their thinking. This group may be part of a school staff, a subject department or even people appointed at a systemic level, depending upon the nature of the curriculum task at hand. In a school context the group will often consist of a group of teachers given the charter to develop a curriculum in a particular subject.

What is important in this phase is that probing questions are posed of the intended curriculum developers. The answers to these questions will provide a valuable guide to understanding the final curriculum produced and, indeed will affect its very nature. Of these people, then, we should pose the following questions:

1 Who is involved in this curriculum development, and what, if anything, do they represent?
2 What conceptions of curriculum do they bring with them?
3 What underlying forces or foundations have influenced the developers' thinking?

The answers to these questions will reveal a most interesting insight into the product most of us would recognise as a curriculum. Would a curriculum devised by a group of independent schoolteachers be different from one devised by government schoolteachers? How similar would be a curriculum developed by tertiary academics to one devised by teachers? And would a state department-devised curriculum reflect the requirements of an independent school or indeed would it be similar to the curriculum developed by government teachers? These questions were considered in chapter 2 in substantially more depth.

In chapter 1 the notion of curriculum as a manipulative strategy and as a cultural construct was raised. If one agreed with this notion, then it could be argued that a curriculum, and hence the 'products' of that curriculum, the students, would consequently follow the direction decision-makers

Figure 3.8   Model of curriculum development

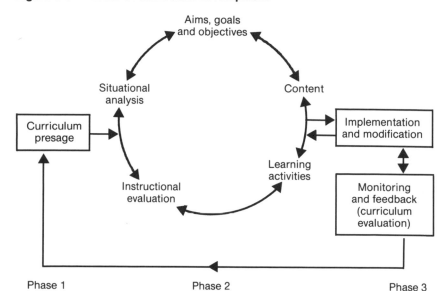

prescribed. But what conceptions do they have of curriculum and what specific directions do they have in mind for this curriculum and for learners? For example, should the curriculum be academically oriented, or devoted towards basic skill development or even directed towards enhancing positive self-concepts within students? To answer these, and the questions raised above, we need to know about the curriculum developers, what they represent and their understandings of curriculum.

As part of this process curriculum developers need to be aware of how they perceive the curriculum when they undertake the development task. It will be argued later that those involved in curriculum development tend to view that process in one of five ways. The viewpoint adopted then affects the curriculum decisions that are made and hence the ultimate nature of the written curriculum.

Writers in the field (Eisner, 1979; Skilbeck, 1986; McNeil, 1985; Tanner & Tanner, 1980; Eisner & Vallance, 1974; Schubert, 1986; Print, 1988) argue that there are numerous conceptions of, or ways of thinking about, curriculum evident that will affect the way curriculum developers conceptualise, plan and construct curricula. One of the more comprehensive examinations of this question (Eisner & Vallance, 1974) suggests that there are five orientations of curriculum, although it has also been argued that there are really four (McNeil, 1981). I contend that there are essentially five conceptions, to which I add a sixth composed of two or more elements of the original five conceptions.

1 Academic disciplines conception.
2 Cognitive processes conception.
3 Humanistic conception.
4 Social reconstructionist conception.
5 Technological conception.
6 Eclectic conception.

Chapter 2 examined these conceptions in some depth and showed how they influence the process of curriculum development. At this point we need to acknowledge that curriculum developers will bring different approaches to conceptualising about curriculum into the development task and this will affect the way they think about and act on curriculum design and curriculum development.

The final question to be posed of curriculum developers in curriculum presage concerns the foundations or forces that influence developers' ways of thinking about curriculum. These curriculum foundations, provided from philosophical, sociological and psychological sources, will have different effects upon individuals and hence we can expect different forms of curricula. These and other factors are discussed in greater depth in chapter 2.

Together, all of these factors influence the ways curriculum developers conceptualise and plan curriculum design and how they will construct curricula. Consequently the selection of persons to participate in the curriculum development process will be significant, particularly upon the final outcome of the curriculum document.

Phase 2: development

The second phase in this model requires the group assembled for the curriculum-development stage to devise the curriculum document, materials or project. Whatever the nature of the curriculum task, it is the responsibility of the development group to devise a workable product in this phase. Invariably, but not always, the presage and development groups will be the same. Where they are not, perhaps at systemic levels, it is important for close ties to be maintained between the groups if the written curriculum is to be effective.

To achieve the second phase developers follow the cyclical procedure in the model (figure 3.8). In other words, they follow the sequence of curriculum elements that begin with situational analysis and continues with aims, goals and objectives; content; learning activities; evaluation and then continuing on to situational analysis again. The following chapters will elaborate this sequence in more detail.

Should a group of teachers, for example, be interested in developing a particular science curriculum for lower secondary students, they would follow this cyclical procedure. Having been made aware of their approach to and conceptions of curriculum through the presage phase, the group of teachers (developers) is now in a position to undertake the next phase in the construction of this curriculum document as evident in figure 3.8.

By undertaking a situational analysis, the teachers become aware in a systematic manner of the needs of their students and the resources they have available to meet those needs. From this data they can make meaningful statements about the educational intent of their curriculum, that is, they can state useful and appropriate aims, goals and objectives. With these statements as a base, developers can then devise appropriate content. Similarly appropriate learning activities can be organised so that the content is learnt effectively and thus the objectives achieved.

Finally, evaluation requires the developers to devise effective assessment procedures to determine the degree to which students have achieved the objectives. This can be termed instructional evaluation for it concentrates upon a form of product evaluation, namely determining how well students have achieved the intentions of the curriculum. As shall be seen in later chapters this is a different emphasis and direction from other forms of evaluation, particularly curriculum evaluation.

By the time the curriculum document has been employed, the initial situation may well have changed. This will require a revised situational analysis to take place and so demand changes in other curriculum elements. The continuous, cyclical nature of the curriculum development process is therefore evident. But a detailed explanation of this phase appears later in the unfolding of events. For the moment, we are concerned that the curriculum developers, in devising a curriculum document, curriculum materials, a curriculum project or whatever, have a systematic, logical procedure to follow. Phase 2 of this model provides such a systematic procedure and each step is outlined more substantially in chapters 5 to 9.

Phase 3: application

If we are to seriously consider what happens after the development of some curriculum object (a written curriculum document, a curriculum project package or a set of curriculum materials), and we reflect upon the definition of curriculum stated in chapter 1, then we must take cognisance of what happens when that object is used by students in classrooms. This involves the third phase of the model—application—which in turn incorporates three sets of activities as seen in figure 3.8:

1 Implementation of the curriculum.

2 Monitoring of and feedback from the curriculum.

3 The provision of feedback data to the presage group.

For any curriculum document, materials or project to be implemented in a school or school system, change must occur. To make this change occur effectively and with minimal disruption and confusion, a plan for implementing the curriculum innovation must be devised. If not, one can expect extensive resistance to the degree that the innovation may fail to be accepted. Similarly, it is insufficient merely to devise a curriculum and hope that schools will adopt it, as that is a recipe for disaster.

In the early stage of implementation it is likely that modifications will be made to the curriculum. This is to be expected, indeed anticipated for a curriculum cannot possibly be devised to anticipate the myriad of variables operating in schools. The degree of successful implementation will reflect to a large measure the ability and willingness of developers to accommodate modifications to their curriculum.

The monitoring stage (figure 3.8) of the curriculum implementation is similarly an important step in gauging the success of the curriculum activity. Feedback from the curriculum over a longer period of time will invariably involve the application of a comprehensive curriculum evaluation, that is, an analysis of the effectiveness of the curriculum activity as a whole. Further feedback will be obtained from a study of product evaluation, that is, how well students have achieved the educational intentions. While the implementation of the curriculum is a short-term activity, the monitoring and feedback aspects of the third phase are likely to span several years.

The final set of activities in the third phase of the model relate to the forwarding of feedback data to the curriculum presage group. The model assumes that the presage group or a similar group will remain intact to accommodate the monitoring and feedback received. Most educational institutions have some form of group responsible for curriculum accountability (for example, curriculum committee; studies committee). If the presage group and/or development group is disbanded, matters relating to curriculum feedback should be forwarded to the curriculum accountability group.

During the period in which the curriculum has been developed, then implemented, modified and monitored, changed circumstances in education have undoubtedly occurred. Changes may well have occurred to the nature of students taking the curriculum, new educational directions may have emerged from government policy, additional resources may have become available and so forth.

To account for, and where necessary accommodate, those changes, the curriculum model must be reconsidered. This may involve major changes to the structure of the curriculum, simple cosmetic alterations or something in between. What is important, however, is that the continuation of the model is seen as standard procedure. As the variables that affect education are in continual change, so curriculum must take account of positive variations and reflect those changes. In this way we can be assured that we have the basis for an effective, responsible curriculum document, material package or project. This final phase in the curriculum model is detailed in chapter 10.

Appropriate curriculum model

This book does not suggest that only one model of curriculum development is appropriate in all contexts and to all curriculum developers. Rather, one has been advocated but others explained as well, so that prospective curriculum developers may select the most appropriate for their context.

To assist developers to make a more informed selection, figure 3.9 suggests that models of curriculum development may be related to each other in terms of two dimensions—the degree of prescription/description involved and the rational/dynamic emphasis given to the respective models. If we examine curriculum models in terms of these dimensions we will be in a better position to determine which is the most appropriate to meet our specific needs.

The prescription/description dimension contends that models may be analysed in terms of the degree to which they demand a sequenced order of events. Models that are high in prescription require curriculum developers to follow a rigid set of activities. Models low in prescription (high

Figure 3.9   Curriculum models

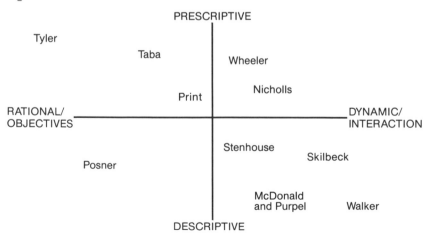

in description) are more flexible in approach and emphasise what does happen rather than what should happen in the process of curriculum development.

The rational/dynamic dimension states that some models are more logical, sequential and objectives-based in their approach to curriculum development. Alternatively, models may be low in rationality and high in interaction thereby approaching curriculum development in a non-sequential randomised approach. Figure 3.9 simply provides curriculum developers with a different perspective for selecting an appropriate model for curriculum development. Which model of curriculum development do you prefer? Can you justify your decision according to the two dimensions described above?

The curriculum development process in practice

To show the relationship between theory and practice we can examine the way in which curricula are developed by major educational organisations. Each state has a curriculum and assessment agency charged with the legal responsibility for developing and assessing tertiary entrance subjects. In most states these bodies also influence the development of the lower secondary curriculum as well. And in New South Wales the

Figure 3.10 Curriculum development process (New South Wales)

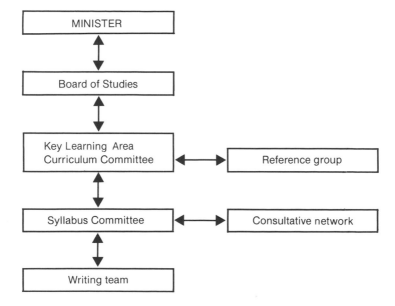

Board of Studies, a statutory authority, has curriculum responsibility for all subjects from Years K to 12.

The process by which these bodies develop curricula (what they call syllabuses) is reasonably similar across the country. The diagram below indicates the type of groups involved in constructing and influencing the development of subject-based curriculum documents. The principal group is the syllabus committee, that group charged with developing the curriculum document for later use in schools. Often a sub-group of the syllabus team (usually called a writing team) will actually prepare the draft curriculum which is then debated and refined within the larger group, though it is still the responsibilty of the syllabus committee for supervising the complete curriculum development task.

In the case of a specific subject, say history Years 7–10 in New South Wales, the curriculum development process required by the Board of Studies would be as outlined in Table 3.2.

It can be seen that the tasks outlined follow approximately the model of curriculum development discussed earlier. While the organisational phase (curriculum presage—phase 1) is not specifically stated, it is nevertheless present in the conceptualisation and preliminary planning of the task. For example, the creation of a reference group and the use of a consultative network indicate the awareness of the Board in involving a broad-based decision-making process. But who is selected to participate

Table 3.2   New South Wales Year 7–10 syllabus development process

Task	Responsibility
1 Research and development—needs assessment	BOS project officers and curriculum officers
2 Issue Identification e.g. content, gender issues	Curriculum reference group BOS officers
3 Syllabus committee created—identify writing brief, team and consultative network	BOS curriculum and project officers
4 Forward writing brief upwards for approval	BOS officers
5 Forward writing to reference group and consultative network	Syllabus committee and BOS officers
6 Consultation with school systems	BOS officers
7 Devise draft syllabus and support documents	Syllabus committee and writing team
8 Draft syllabus upwards for approval	Syllabus committee and writing team
9 Draft syllabus to reference group, consultative network and schools	BOS project officers
10 Revision of syllabus based on feedback from groups	Syllabus committee and writing team
11 Syllabus through levels to minister	BOS project officer
12 Distribution to schools	BOS project officer

in this task? And on what basis? And what perceptions of curriculum and the subject matter do they bring with them? A different mix of people will clearly produce a different curriculum product and this needs to be kept in mind when selecting participants in the various groups.

Phase 2 activities may be seen in the tasks of needs analysis, issue identification, development of writing briefs and the preparation of documents.

Phase 3 activities include consultation with school systems, testing documents with consultative network and schools, syllabus revision and final distribution. In the New South Wales example it is interesting to note that the Minister for Education is integrated into curriculum development loops, allowing for direct involvement in the evolution of the curriculum document. This is usually the case in other states as well but only with tertiary entrance subjects. This direct involvement, though usually used minimally, offers the politicians a final say in any curriculum which may become politically sensitive. In this time of the politicisation of education we must expect these things to occur and, indeed, to witness political parties and pressure groups 'driving' curriculum policy-making.

Summary

- In this chapter we have seen that there are many ways to view the curriculum development process. While these approaches are not radically different from each other, they do represent different areas of emphasis.
- Models are simplifications of reality that are designed for purposes of analysis. A model of curriculum development is a convenient way of demonstrating the working of essential curriculum elements and their interrelationships.
- Essential curriculum elements include situational analysis, intentions, content, learning activities and evaluation.
- Rational models, such as those of Tyler and Taba, follow a logical, sequential approach to curriculum development. In these models the statement of objectives is very important and the other curriculum elements follow in fixed order.
- Cyclical models are an elaboration of rational models in that they are essentially logical and sequential in approach. However, cyclical models view the curriculum process as a continuous activity that is constantly updating itself. The Nicholls and Wheeler models are examples.
- Dynamic models lie at the other end of the continuum from rational models. Here developers begin with any curriculum element, progress in any sequence of elements, interrelate between elements constantly and tend to relate more directly to perceived learner needs. The Walker

and Skilbeck models are essentially descriptive of what happens in school-level curriculum development.

- The final model of curriculum development takes an eclectic position amongst the models. It emphasises:

  1 Curriculum presage procedures in the organisational phase.
  2 A cyclical approach in the development phase.
  3 Implementation and monitoring of the curriculum in the application phase.

- No single curriculum model is favoured by teachers when they develop curricula at the school level. The final model is recommended as a means of providing effective direction in curriculum development and is the basis for chapters 5 to 10.
- In practice curriculum developers adopt variations on any curriculum model they may employ. The NSW Board of Studies follows a 'syllabus development process' which resembles the model of curriculum development discussed at the end of this chapter.

4 Curriculum design

The design element is central in many applied fields. 'Utmost simplicity' is sometimes seen as a desirable characteristic of good design. Our concern in curriculum planning is more than just simplicity. We seek a larger context in order to cope with necessary diversity and complexity. (Paul Klohr, Ohio State University)

Curriculum planning and design are essential preliminary ingredients in the curriculum development process. This chapter examines the concepts of curriculum planning and design, how they function as an integral part of the curriculum development process and what this means for curriculum developers. The chapter also examines the nature of the design process and considers the principal forms or types of commonplace curriculum designs found in schools and educational systems. It then suggests some ways by which curriculum designs may be created and lastly addresses the important issue of teacher curriculum planning.

Before the detailed construction of a curriculum document occurs, curriculum developers are involved in planning and designing their proposed curriculum. Indeed it is not possible to develop a curriculum without some form of curriculum design, though some curriculum developers address this issue more systematically and substantively than others. And while curriculum planning and design may be essentially conceptual in nature, they may also be quite overt acts of groups of curriculum developers who, together, resolve issues relating to the design and planning of the proposed curriculum.

This book argues that a well-conceptualised approach to the process of curriculum development is an effective use of resources and hence suggests that time will be profitably spent on substantive curriculum planning and design. As Karen Zumwalt suggests, 'Given the view that professional teachers should have the knowledge to enable them to create sound educational programs . . . it is essential that teachers have knowledge of some planning process that enables them to think about curriculum beyond the individual lesson.' (1989:176)

Terminology

By *curriculum planning* I mean that process whereby curriculum developers conceptualise and organise the features of the curriculum they wish to construct. This involves a broad analysis of the curriculum intent and context (what you wish to achieve), conceptualising the curriculum's design (what it will look like), organising the sequencing of developmental tasks (how to construct the curriculum) and arranging for the process of implementation and evaluation. Thus curriculum planning is an integral part of the curriculum development process.

In some cases, perhaps where the curriculum task is small in scale, curriculum planning may be largely a mental activity. More commonly, the task of curriculum planning is extensively conceptualised, discussed and written. From the basis of this planning, the curriculum development process continues with the construction of the curriculum, usually in the form of a document. Indeed, many models of the curriculum development process have been created over the past fifty years as a means to assist those involved with planning curricula. Some of these were discussed in chapter 3 and one was elaborated in greater detail.

Curriculum design refers to the arrangement of the elements of a curriculum. An essential feature of any curriculum is the conceptualisation and organisation of its various parts. These parts are known as curriculum elements and they are the essential building blocks of any curriculum. By organising curriculum elements in particular ways, different designs emerge. Curriculum design has been defined in slightly different ways by curriculum writers, though there is general agreement with the view that defines curriculum design as:

> . . . the arrangement of the components or elements of a curriculum . . . Ordinarily, the components or elements included in a curriculum are (1) aims, goals and objectives; (2) subject matter or content; (3) learning activities; and (4) evaluation . . . Thus the nature of these elements and the pattern of organization in which they are brought together as a unified curriculum constitute the curriculum design. (Zais, 1976:16)

Curriculum design usually takes place as part of the curriculum planning process. That is, early in the conceptualisation of the curriculum, decisions are made about the nature and arrangement of the various curriculum elements. Usually this is a deliberative activity, though inexperienced curriculum developers may be unaware of the decisions they are making. In the development of substantial curricula, by experienced curriculum developers, the task of curriculum design is often demanding and time consuming as developers work their way through the curriculum planning phase.

Considerable agreement exists amongst curriculum writers that while curriculum design refers to the arrangement of the elements of a curriculum, many forms of design may be found. And as Gress & Purpel note, 'One may be distinguished from another on the basis of the nature and organisation of its elements—objectives, subject matter content, learning experiences, evaluation scheme.' (1988: 199)

For many teachers curriculum design means only the pattern of *content* organisation. Most curricula have documents depicting the arrangement of content and hence the association is to be expected. Some of the more commonly accepted curricula have organised their content according to principles inherent in the major curriculum patterns of the subject design, the discipline's design, and the broad field's design.

However, as seen in the above definition, curriculum design refers to the interrelationship between *all* curriculum elements. Designs based on problem-solving, activities and learner-centred approaches emphasise less the content and more of the other curriculum elements. Regardless of the approach employed, curriculum design is concerned with planning and organising the ultimate nature of the entire curriculum. As such, it is an extremely important task.

Curriculum design process

Where does the curriculum design process begin? In the curriculum presage phase of the model of curriculum development discussed in chapter 3, we find curriculum developers brought together to prepare for the development phase, or construction of the curriculum. In that model we saw that an examination of curriculum conceptions and curriculum foundations that have influenced the curriculum developers was an important consideration to be made. One specific and useful application of curriculum foundations and curriculum conceptions may be seen in the design of curricula.

When developers set out to develop curricula they usually have some notion of curriculum design in mind (part of Walker's (1971) platforms as seen in chapter 3). For some individuals this notion is held firmly before development commences, while for others it emerges more clearly as curriculum development proceeds. As early as possible it is important for curriculum developers both to be aware of the different groupings of curriculum design and also to strive for internal consistency within the design selected. The result will be a more consistent, effective curriculum.

Design forces

The two principal forces employed in the organisation of curricula are the dimensions of horizontal and vertical integration. These are discussed in some depth, specifically in terms of organising content, as the architectonics of content (see chapter 7). At a broader level these forces may be extrapolated to facilitate the organisation of the curriculum in general.

Horizontal organisation, often referred to as scope or horizontal integration, is concerned with the arrangement of curriculum components at any one point in time. It asks, for example, what is the relationship between chemistry, biology, physics and geology in a lower-secondary school science curriculum? How much of each is required and how are they interrelated? Alternatively, it may ask what is the balance between subjects in the primary school and how much of each should be studied at any one time given that basic skills of reading and writing are to be mastered?

The second dimension is known as *vertical organisation* or sometimes as sequence or vertical integration. Its concern lies with the relationship between curriculum components over the entire duration of the curriculum's application. In a primary school curriculum, for example, emphasis may be placed upon literacy, numeracy, personal development and social growth in the first three years, while the later years may see the emergence and increasing emphasis of mathematics, English, science, social studies and similar subjects. Vertical organisation asks what learnings should be included, how much is required over time and what should be the balance between different learnings over the duration of a course.

In Australian schools today there is evidence that insufficient thought has been devoted to curriculum design. Many school curricula have grown like Topsy and it can be argued that they are in serious need of review (see chapter 7 on the overcrowded and finite curriculum). At both primary and secondary levels new subjects have been added in order to make the school curriculum appear more relevant and more accountable. But what has happened to the existing areas of study and how do the new areas relate to them?

This situation, in part, has necessitated a considerable number of inquiries into school curricula, particularly at the secondary level. The result has been a proliferation of reports that will hopefully lead to curricula with purposeful designs that feature a high degree of internal consistency. The results of these inquiries have been presented in reports such as: *Core Curriculum* (1980), Curriculum Development Centre all schooling levels; the Beazley Report (1984), Western Australia lower secondary; the McGowan Report (1981), New South Wales lower secondary; the Blackburn Report (1985), Victoria post-compulsory schooling; Directions in Curriculum (1987), Victoria; the Carrick Report (1989), K-12 schooling in New South Wales; and the Print Report (1990) on social studies curricula in Western Australia.

Curriculum designs

Over the years it has been possible to distil a number of different approaches to curriculum design. Broadly, they may be classified into four groups, though different curriculum writers suggest differing patterns of designs (Smith, Stanley & Shores, 1950; Taba, 1962; Saylor, Alexander & Lewis, 1981; McNeil, 1985; Gress & Purpel, 1988; Print, 1988; Wiles & Bondi, 1989). The four recognised groups of designs are subject-centred designs, learner-centred designs, problem-centred designs and core designs. Different curriculum designs largely reflect differences in the organisation and consequential focus of subject matter.

School curricula designs have been distinguished on the basis of how the subject matter is delivered (instructional emphasis) while most emphasise what subject matter is delivered (curriculum emphasis). In this book I have emphasised a curriculum approach. Indeed this is arguably the most common and fruitful way of conceptualising curriculum design (Smith, Stanley & Shores, 1950; Taba, 1962; Saylor, Alexander & Lewis, 1981; Print, 1988).

Thus curriculum developers, drawing upon personal experiences, their preferred conception of curriculum and their understanding of curriculum drawn from the curriculum foundations, have constructed curricula according to designs which may be categorised as:

1 subject-centred designs
2 learner-centred designs
3 problem-centred designs
4 core designs

Subject-centred designs

This group of designs revolve around the teaching of an established body of *content* that has been derived from the accumulated wisdom of the academic disciplines. Content considerations are the basis for decisions about the horizontal and vertical dimensions of the curriculum while other curriculum elements have considerably less impact. Three related, though distinct, designs have emerged.

Subject designs

This is probably the oldest and most widely used form of curriculum organisation found in schools and educational systems, enjoying a long tradition at least in the Western world. In essence, this design is based on the classification and organisation of subject matter into discrete groups which we have called subjects. These groupings, which have become known as school subjects, were initially based on evolving divisions of labour in research that produced physics, history, literature, geography, mathematics and so forth. In more recent times practical areas such as typing, home economics and industrial arts have become accepted as subjects.

Emphasis in subject designs is placed on the acquisition of subject matter knowledge, and content is structured sequentially, such as in mathematics or history. The subject approach is commonly employed in Australian schools, particularly at secondary levels, though not without some concern. Because these subjects have been studied in isolation from each other, a factor reflecting the development of the subject design, it has been extensively criticised over the years.

Academic disciplines design

This approach to organising curriculum is essentially a post-Second World War phenomenon, gaining greatest support in the 1960s. Predicated on the inherent organisation of content, as is the subject design, the academic disciplines design emphasises the role played by those distinct entities called academic disciplines. These can, it is claimed, be clearly delineated in terms of knowledge, skills and values.

Thus, in a school setting, the content of this design would focus on what an academic does, that is, how a biologist, historian, mathematician actually works at that discipline. That is, how the disciplinarian thinks, what research is done, how that research is carried out, how data are analysed, how research is reported, and so forth. The result, it is hoped, is that the schools would produce mini versions of academic disciplinarians.

To assist students to acquire the knowledge, skills and values of the academic disciplines, numerous curriculum projects were developed in the 1960s and 1970s. Among the more well known are:

BSCS: Biological Sciences Curriculum Study
HSGP: High School Geography Project
ASEP: Australian Science Education Project
SMSG: School Mathematics Study Group
ISIS: Individualised Science Instruction System
MACOS: Man A Course of Study

In these curriculum projects the principal thrust was for students to understand the structure of the disciplines, that is, the relationship between its key ideas, concepts and principles as well as the integration of the skills and values associated with that discipline. It is interesting to note that despite the initial level of support for many of these projects, especially ASEP and SEMP, virtually none of these discipline-based projects is used extensively in schools today.

Broad fields design. This third design was developed to overcome a perceived weakness in the subject design that was evident in the nineteenth and early twentieth centuries. Essentially the broad fields design attempts to rectify the fragmentation and compartmentalisation evident in the subject design by combining two or more related subjects into a single, broader and integrated field of study.

Furthermore, the broad fields design was deemed more suited to younger learners and to those less able to cope with the rigours of subjects and academic disciplines. Through the process of subject amalgamation, not only were subjects to be made more integrated, but also pedagogically modified to suit the needs of learners. Examples found commonly in Australian schools include:

1 Social studies: history, geography, economics, sociology, politics, anthropology and current events.
2 Language arts: reading, writing, spelling, speaking and composition.
3 General science: physics, chemistry, biology, geology and astronomy.
4 Mathematics: arithmetic, algebra, trigonometry and geometry.

In Australia the broad fields design is commonly found in primary and lower-secondary schools. Attempts to introduce broad field subjects into upper-secondary school have been resisted largely on the grounds that they are inadequate preparation for tertiary education. With the changing nature of upper-secondary school enrolments in recent years, we are witnessing some change to this resistance. The proposed Vocational Certificate Training System (Carmichael, 1992) may well produce a modified version of broad field subjects based around the concept of 'key competencies', though strictly speaking these competencies are an instance of a core curriculum design. What we don't know at this stage is what form the competencies will take when implemented into the school curriculum.

Features common to the three subject-centred designs include:

1 Classification and organisation of all content into subjects or subject-like groupings.
2 Subjects are clearly defined and distinguished.
3 A hierarchy of subjects is commonly found according to their perceived value.
4 Methodology implied, and practised, is largely teacher-centred and expository in nature.

Learner-centred designs

Supporters of these curriculum designs generally view society in democratic terms and perceive individuals as being 'naturally good'. Hence learner-centred designs emphasise individual development and their approach to organising the curriculum emerges from the needs, interests and purposes of students. As a result, there are two essential differences between this and the subject-centred designs.

1 Learner-centred designs take their organisational cues from individual student needs rather than a body of subject matter.

2 Consequently learner-centred designs are usually not as preplanned as other designs, for they evolve from teacher–student interaction in relation to learning tasks. In some cases the curriculum may have no preplanning at all and may emerge as a group of students reveal their concerns, interests and needs. More commonly, however, curriculum developers have purposeful intentions which are learner oriented and these may be modified later upon interaction with students.

Two forms of learner-centred designs can be distinguished in the curriculum field:

Activity/experience design

This approach is based on determining the genuine needs and interests of learners which in turn form the basis of the curriculum (Smith, Stanley & Shores, 1950). An important claim of this approach is that 'People only learn what they experience . . . Learning in its true sense is an active transaction' (Taba, 1962:401). Consequently it is very difficult to preplan, although with experience certain trends emerge. An important role for the teacher, therefore, is to develop the ability to ascertain genuine student interests and then create an appropriate curriculum around them. To do so implies competence with the curriculum development process.

Other features of this design include a lack of formal subjects, joint planning of learning experiences between curriculum developers and students and, finally, skills and knowledge taught as the individual requires or needs them. It should be noted that this approach to organising curricula is found mostly in the literature, with few examples in reality. In some alternative schools, such as Summerhill, examples of activity/experience curriculum may be found and most preschools/kindergartens use the activity design as a basis for their curriculum.

Humanistic design

Similar in approach to the experience design, the humanistic design emphasises the meeting of individual needs in a conducive, supportive learning environment. The humanistic approach to curriculum design may well incorporate all the features of the experience design with the additional factor of providing a supportive environment for the individual learner. Alternatively, it may offer some subject structure as a guide to learners.

This design has emerged from the humanistic conception of curriculum which seeks to provide learners with intrinsically rewarding experiences for self-development, that is, to enhance an individual's self-concept through a supportive learning experience. As a further guide, the writings of Carl Rogers, Arthur Combs, John Holt, Mario Fantini, Jonathon Kozol and C. H. Patterson should be consulted.

Alternative schools, particularly of the open variety, provide examples of the humanistic curriculum design in operation. You may be able to identify specific examples of schools that have a humanistic design as the basis of their curriculum, or have components of a humanistic curriculum within a broader curriculum design.

The essential difference between the two designs is that the curriculum developer in the humanistic design has some preconceived views, based on the intents of humanistic psychology, on what is of value to learners and that these ideas are integrated into a curriculum based upon the learner's needs. The intent of this design then is to deliberately provide a curriculum which purposively reflects those supportive features from humanistic psychology such as caring, support, enhanced self-concept and the like.

Problem-centred designs

These curriculum designs direct learners to focus their attention on, and attempt to resolve, problems of living that are both individual and social in nature. As this is such an enormous task, considerable variations in the nature of problems to be studied may be found. Themes might include persistent life situations, contemporary social problems, personal concerns of youth, major social functions and worldwide problems such as peace and environment.

Generally a preplanned approach, the problem-centred curriculum design seeks to provide learners with opportunities to resolve problems they are likely to encounter, or already are, in their life. Unlike the learner-centred designs, emphasis is placed on group welfare, group activities and the group resolution of problems. At least two variations of problem-centred designs may be found in the literature on curriculum design.

Thematic design

The argument for thematic designs is based on the artificiality of other curriculum designs in providing appropriate learning experiences which reflect what we experience in real life. A curriculum design should, it is suggested, reflect the types of experiences we encounter in our lives in order to be useful and meaningful. Designs based around non-realistic bases, such as subjects, academic disciplines, broad fields and so forth, are remote from reality and from students' perceptions of what they need to learn. A useful thematic approach, by contrast, can meet those needs. Significant themes may be based on studies (interdisciplinary in nature) which provide an insight into the real world. For example, a study of the theme of environment would involve students in biology, geography, history, politics and English. Themes for study might include urbanisation, war, pollution, peace, transportation, healthy lifestyles, family life and other aspects of 'real' adult life.

Thematic approaches to curriculum design are employed commonly in Australian preschools and primary schools. In many primary schools teachers have deliberately programmed their curriculum across subjects in order to produce a more useful thematic approach.

Problem design

This curriculum approach argues that learners should encounter substantial real life problems in order to understand the world. Like the thematic approach, the problem-centred design argues for a more meaningful basis to curriculum design in order to involve learners in what they perceive as relevant. However, distinct emphasis is placed upon the concepts of identifying, addressing and resolving multifarious problems. Through this process, it is argued, students will obtain meaningful learning and be able to play a more purposeful role in society.

Here the curriculum would be designed so that students might study problems experienced by people that are of both an individual and group nature. The emphasis in this curriculum design is upon resolving the problem to the satisfaction of the learners. Examples of typical problems would be:

1 What can we do about air pollution in our cities?
2 How can adolescents live harmoniously at home?
3 Should a new freeway be constructed to solve the traffic problem in our area?
4 Can conflict in Northern Ireland be resolved?
5 How far should genetic research be allowed to proceed?
6 How can nuclear waste be stored effectively?
7 What should one aspire to in life?
8 Where should a new airport be located in our city/town?

This curriculum design appears to be most appropriate to the various life-skills curricula that are now emerging. Certainly those students for whom the traditional academic curriculum designs are inappropriate would benefit from a problem-oriented curriculum. This situation is particularly applicable to the increasing numbers of non-tertiary-bound students remaining in upper-secondary schools.

Core learning designs

Many forms of core learning design may be distinguished and there is evidence of this design having been used for some time (Smith, Stanley & Shores, 1950; Zais, 1976, CDC, 1980; Kirk, 1986: Marsh & Stafford, 1988). More recently in Australia and Britain, a new wave of curriculum policy initiatives in the area of national curriculum (Dawkins, 1988; Kennedy, 1989; Hughes, 1990; Print, 1991; Ruby, 1992) suggests the re-emergence of a core learning design of a new variation and at a national level.

Core design

The notion behind a core design, usually called a core curriculum, is that there exists a set of common learnings (knowledge, skills and values) that should be provided to all learners in order for them to function effectively in society. The core concept, however, does vary considerably in interpretation and one writer has suggested that it is possible to distinguish no less than six forms of the core design (Zais, 1976:42–3). For our purposes, it is sufficient to understand that a curriculum may be organised around the idea of a core as a set of learnings essential for all students.

The key issues in any core design for a curriculum are:

1 What should be included in the core?
2 How large should the core be, i.e. what percentage of the total content within the written curriculum?
3 What should be excluded from the core?
4 Is a core required of all learners?

In Australia the notion of a core design has usually referred to a small, separate group of subjects that are compulsory to study, while the curriculum is topped with options or elective subjects. Typically the 'core' consisted of English, mathematics, science, social studies (or equivalent subjects such as history and geography) and physical education, for these

Table 4.1   Core learning areas for Australian schools

1 Communication
2 Scientific and technological ways of knowing and their social applications
3 Mathematical skills and reasoning and their applications
4 Moral reasoning and action
5 Social, cultural and civic studies
6 Environmental studies
7 Arts and crafts
8 Health education
9 Work, leisure and lifestyle

Source: Curriculum Development Centre, 1980

were the subjects studied by all students. To these were then added a number of optional subjects such as art, home economics, music, languages, drama and so forth.

However, the CDC publication *Core Curriculum for Australian Schools* (1980) devised an eclectic approach to the concept of a core curriculum, emphasising the thematic and social problem types of cores. The emphasis of this approach to core curriculum was that all students would experience a set of common and essential learnings that were necessary for learners to function effectively in society. Nine areas of learning were described in this way.

The document created considerable initial interest amongst educators, though it had little direct influence upon curriculum design at the time. Subject curriculum designs dominated the thinking of those responsible for curriculum development within state education departments at that time, and it must be remembered that interstate rivalries were still strong at that time. However, the CDC document appears to have influenced the thinking of numerous subsequent investigations into curriculum and education such as the Beazley Report (1984), Blackburn Report (1985) and the Carrick Report (1989). One can also draw parallels between the CDC document and the eight learning areas designated by the AEC in its recent approval of a 'national curriculum initiative' (Kennedy, 1989; Print, 1991; Ruby, 1992).

The existence of a core curriculum can be readily seen in New South Wales since the creation of Key Learning Areas in *Excellence and Equity* (1989). The newly elected Liberal government argued that prescription in the overall pattern of study by students was not only necessary, but also without opposition (1989:13). Indeed the document further stated:

> As a fundamental point, the Government accepts responsibility for ensuring that all students in our schools have access to a balanced and relevant core curriculum (1989:13).

Table 4.2   KLAs in New South Wales

Primary schools	Secondary schools
English	English
Mathematics	Mathematics
Science and Technology	Science
Human society and its environment	Human society and its environment
Creative and practical arts	Creative arts
Personal development, health and physical education	Personal development, health and physical education
	Technology and applied studies
	Modern and classical languages

Source: Excellence and Equity, 1989

The result was the formation of Key Learning Areas (KLAs) in which all students are required to study core learnings. In primary schools six KLAs were created, while secondary schools have eight KLAs.

National core curriculum designs

In recent years the concept of a core curriculum has taken on new meaning as pressures have intensified for some form of national curriculum (Kennedy, 1989; Ruby, 1992). In 1989, stimulated by Dawkins' earlier statement (Dawkins, 1988) and subsequent action through the AEC (Ruby, 1992), this became a realistic manifestation with the proclamation of the 'Hobart Declaration'—*The Common and Agreed National Goals for Schooling in Australia* by the Australian Education Council (see Appendix). The very existence of the statement meant that a high degree of consensus had already been reached, at least at the political level, that a core of essential learnings should exist for Australian schools.

Following the AEC statement, several significant decisions about national curriculum activity as well as cooperation between the states have been made and implemented (Kennedy, 1989; Ruby, 1992). In summary, these decisions include:

- Agreement upon the need for, and analysis of, eight learning areas through national mapping exercises (until mid 1991), literature reviews and audits (after mid 1991) of those areas.
- Development of eight national 'core' learning areas with a statement to describe the essential features of each learning area. These are in various stages of construction with the last due for completion late in 1993. The eight areas are: English, mathematics, science, study of society and the environment, technology, the arts, languages other than English, and health (including physical education and personal development).
- Explicit inclusion in these statements of reference to the principles and objectives of the 1990 *National Policy for the Education of Girls in Australian Schools* (Ruby, 1992).
- Creation of national profiles (descriptive statements of learning outcomes) in each of the eight learning areas which will form the basis of a common assessment system.
- Creation of the AEC's Curriculum and Assessment Committee (CURASS) to supervise the development of the national statements as well as assessment profiles for those learning areas.
- Removal of barriers to different handwriting styles so that children may move from one state to another and not have to change style.
- Working towards creating a common age of school entry across the different state school systems.

- Establish equivalence of Year 12 certificates and statements of achievement through the work of the Australasian Conference of Assessment and Certification Authorities (ACACA).
- Creation of a national report on schooling in Australia.
- Appointment of Review Committee on Young People's Participation in Post-Compulsory Education and Training (Finn Committee, 1991) to recommend pathways and opportunities for post-compulsory schooling.
- Appointment of the Mayer Committee (1992) to produce a discussion paper on Employment Related Key Competencies for Post-Compulsory Education and Training. These were subsequently taken up, in the Australian Vocational Certificate Training System (1992), or, as it has become known, the Carmichael Report (1992).
- Creation of the Curriculum Corporation to act as a national body to assist, where appropriate, the curriculum development undertaken by the states.
- Enhancing the effectiveness of teachers in schools through the National Project on the Quality of Teaching and Learning (NPQTL). This project has numerous elements, all of which have been designed to result in improvements in the effectiveness of classroom teaching (Ruby, 1992).

Thus one form of national core design could be considered to be the national curriculum statements made, or in the process of development, in the eight areas. Those learnings associated with the proposed key competencies that have evolved from the Finn (1991), Mayer (1992) and Carmichael (1992) reports, as well as from federal government and business pressures, may well form another example of a national core curriculum design. Table 4.3 outlines those key competencies.

Table 4.3   Key competencies: Australian vocational certificate

1 Language and communication
   - speaking
   - listening
   - reading
   - writing
   - accessing and using information
2 Mathematics
   - computation
   - measurement
   - understanding mathematical symbols
3 Scientific and technological understanding
   - understanding scientific and technological understandings
   - understanding the impact of science and technology on society
   - scientific and technological skills including computing skills
4 Cultural understanding

- understanding and knowledge of Australia's historical, geographical and political context
- understanding of major global issues
- understanding the world of work, its importance and requirements
5 Problem solving
  - analysis
  - critical thinking
  - decision making
  - creative thinking
  - skill transfer to new contexts

In this chapter we have seen how curricula may be designed and the many forms of curriculum design that have evolved over the years. Teachers involved in the curriculum development process need to be aware of these concepts and processes as well as the types of curriculum design they are teaching within or the curricula they are developing.

Summary

- Curriculum design may be defined as the arrangement of the elements of a curriculum. The different parts (intention, content, learning experiences, evaluation) of any curriculum are known as curriculum elements and they are the essential building blocks of any curriculum which may be arranged in different ways to produce different designs.
- By curriculum planning we mean that process whereby curriculum developers conceptualise and organise the features of the curriculum they wish to construct. This involves a broad analysis of the curriculum intent and context (what you wish to achieve), conceptualising the curriculum's design (what it will look like), organising the sequencing of developmental tasks (how to construct the curriculum) and arranging for the process of implementation and evaluation.
- Curriculum design is an example of the application of curriculum presage in practice. In the curriculum presage phase, developers are influenced by various forces and conceptions which helps account for the different curriculum designs that emerge.
- Design forces in curriculum are referred to as horizontal and vertical organisation.
- Horizontal organisation, often referred to as scope or horizontal integration, is concerned with the arrangement of curriculum components at any one point in time.
- Vertical organisation, sometimes known as sequence or vertical integration, addresses the relationship between curriculum components over the entire duration of the curriculum's application.
- The main categories of curriculum designs are:

1 Subject-centred designs
  — subject designs

— academic discipline designs
— broad field designs
2 Learner-centred designs.
— activity/experience designs
— humanistic designs
3 Problem-centred designs.
— thematic designs
— problem designs
4 Core designs
— core designs
— national core designs

5   Situational analysis

No single source of information is adequate to provide a basis for wise and comprehensive decisions about the objectives of the school. (Ralph Tyler, 1949:4)

In this chapter we examine the concept of situational analysis, why it is needed, how to conduct one and what are the principal factors involved. As well we examine a needs-assessment technique which may be used as an important part of the situational analysis procedure or additonally it may be employed as an independent diagnostic tool at one or more later points in the curriculum development process.

Situational analysis is a term that has gained greater credence in the field of curriculum in recent years. However, the underlying concept has been around for many years and was outlined by Hilda Taba (1962) in what she described as a 'diagnosis of needs'. Simply put, situational analysis is a detailed examination of the context into which a curriculum is to be placed and the application of that analysis to the curriculum being developed. This argument claims that a systematic analysis of the situation must be conducted in order for a curriculum to be developed effectively. Just what the situation is exactly, and at what depth and breadth the analysis will be conducted, vary significantly and will be discussed later in this chapter.

A situational analysis may be conducted at broad educational levels, such as groups of schools, regions within an educational system or even at entire systemic levels. The principles involved are the same as a situational analysis at the school (site-specific) level, although the level of analysis and extrapolation are naturally more general and broadly based. As seen in chapter 3, the NSW Board of Studies undertakes a needs assessment task at the very beginning of developing systemic curricula in that state, as do most curriculum and assessment agencies and state departments of education in other states.

However, a situational analysis is frequently conducted at the individual school level where it is invariably a precursor to some form of school-based curriculum development (SBCD). Here teachers analyse the situation of their school in order to develop appropriate curricula to meet student needs. Teachers developing appropriate curricula for non-tertiary-bound upper-school students, for example, typically undertake such a task. If they want their curricula to be useful in schools they must first be cognisant of the context in which that curriculum will be developed.

Definition

Situational analysis may be defined as the process of examining the context for which a curriculum is to be developed and the application of that analysis to curriculum planning. It involves a detailed analysis of several factors that relate to that context, albeit a school, group of schools, region or system. This analysis is then incorporated within the subsequent planning for and development of curriculum intent, curriculum content, learning activities and evaluation. Nicholls & Nicholls refer to the proces of situational analysis as:

> . . . a situation which is made up of a number of factors such as pupils, pupils' homes and background, school, its climate, it staff, facilities and equipment. Analysis of these factors, together with a self-analysis, followed by study of their implications for curriculum planning constitutes one step towards the rational approach . . . [of curriculum]. (1978:22)

The need for conducting a situational analysis is a fundamental precept of effective curriculum development. Developers commencing their task should ask important questions such as: 'What do we know about the context—the students, teachers, school environment—of this curriculum and why is it needed?' This provides them with an information base to pose an even more fundamental question: 'What do our learners need?'

Many developers believe they intuitively know the answers to these questions and hence a formalised situational analysis to them is unnecessary. They rely on their past experience and their intuitive understanding of the curriculum context. But how do they know that they are accurate? They don't—they believe they are but only an effectively conducted situational analysis can determine if, indeed, their intuition is accurate. Thus the real need for conducting a situational analysis is to collect useful data that can become a basis or springboard from which other curriculum elements can be devised. With such a base, for example, developers are better able to devise appropriate curriculum aims, goals and objectives; better able to develop appropriate content and so forth.

A situational analysis is an obvious commencement point for the construction of a curriculum. It is an ideal opportunity for curriculum developers, aware of the curriculum presage factors affecting them, to bring a reasoned, rational approach to the development of curricula. Above all, it is an opportunity for curriculum developers to take account of *local* factors when developing curriculum to meet student needs.

With a new school, region or system, curriculum developers would have the luxury of beginning their deliberations with something of a blank slate. By undertaking a situational analysis they could create an appropriate curriculum for all concerned (students, parents and teachers). But such an event is uncommon. A more realistic scenario for conducting a situational analysis is an existing school, region or system in which curriculum changes must be implemented. In this context a problem or need has undoubtedly been expressed and a curriculum resolution is required.

Concern may be voiced, for example, at the level of student literacy skills within a school. This may have arisen from a needs-assessment technique such as the one described later in this chapter. Or it may reflect the apprehension voiced by teachers and parents. At the point where the school decides to initiate curriculum change to rectify the perceived problem, a situational analysis may be applied. In this example it would involve teachers (and perhaps parents and external consultants) analysing the context of the school and the specific problem.

On completion of the situational analysis, the resulting recommendations would be incorporated within the subsequent curriculum development. This may produce a revised English course, a special reading program (such as USSR—Uninterrupted Sustained Silent Reading), an integrated approach to literacy across the curriculum and so forth.

Although such tasks may be difficult, time consuming and demanding, their value to effective curriculum development is obvious nevertheless. The argument for undertaking a situational analysis may therefore be summarised as:

1 Identifying local needs of students, parents, teachers and the community.
2 Understanding the local curriculum context.
3 Facilitating planning and subsequent curriculum development.
4 Providing a systematic database for devising curriculum goals and objectives.

Needs assessment

A useful technique for determining the starting point of a situational analysis, for collecting data within a situational analysis, or for undertaking reviews of aspects of curricula at other times, is the technique known as needs assessment. John McNeil defines needs assessment as:

> the process by which one defines educational needs and decides what their priorities are. In the context of curriculum, a need is defined as a condition in which there is a discrepancy between an *acceptable* state of learner behaviour or attitude and an observed learner state. (McNeil, 1985:74)

The needs-assessment procedure has been included for our purposes in this chapter on situational analysis. Essentially a needs assessment is a means of reaching consensus over future directions for a curriculum by determining the discrepancy between current and preferred situations. In turn this requires a procedure to ascertain the nature of the discrepancy and this is outlined below.

A needs assessment may be used by curriculum developers to determine and prioritise educational needs. This is extremely useful in facilitating a situational analysis and for laying the foundations for an effective set of curriculum aims, goals and objectives.

Conducting a needs assessment

While there are numerous ways available for curriculum developers to undertake a needs assessment, the following procedure is straightforward and useful. The algorithm suggests using a five-phase approach employing a discrepancy concept to determine needs. It assumes the needs assessment activity is being conducted at a school level though it may be conducted at other levels such as regions and systems.

Phase 1: formulate goal statements

Those involved in conducting the needs assessment (teachers, perhaps parents and students) make statements of acceptable, but preferred, student behaviour. These goal statements may relate to literacy levels, numeracy competencies, personal skills, content knowledge, subject skills, self-concept, physical development and so forth. Stated briefly, the goal statements represent positions that the curriculum decision-makers believe is of value to students. For example:

1 Students should be literate in English to an acceptable level.
2 Students should develop a positive self-concept.
3 Students should understand the nature of Australian government.

Phase 2: rate goal statements

The goal statements developed in phase 1 have priorities assigned to them by a group such as those from phase 1 or a broader group of teachers, parents and students. Goals are rated on a scale (say 1 to 5) by individuals and then averaged amongst the group. For example:

Goal statement 1 = 4.51
Goal statement 2 = 3.27
Goal statement 3 = 3.77
Goal statement 4 = 4.21

Phase 3: rank goal statements

The averaged ratings are then ranked in order to determine a priority of importance for the preferred goals. A ranked list now exists of preferred learning goals. Ranking the above goals, the result is:

Goal statement 1
Goal statement 4
Goal statement 3
Goal statement 2

Phase 4: determine goal statements

By examining each goal statement, either subjectively or objectively, in terms of what is happening within the institution, a discrepancy factor may be determined which represents the difference between reality and the preferred learner state.

Subjectively this may be achieved by using teachers to act as judges and to then rate the goals in terms of what is happening in reality. Objectively data may be collected (through tests, exams and so forth) to determine levels of learner proficiency and a rating given.

Where a discrepancy exists between what is preferred (ranked goals) and what exists (observed learner state), a need is indicated. It is possible that the goals ranked highest may not produce the greatest need, although this obviously depends upon the level of discrepancy evident between the observed and preferred learner states. However, those goals ranked highest usually tend to have high discrepancy factors simply because they are judged to be important. Extending the example above we find different levels of discrepancy have resulted:

Goal 1 = moderate discrepancy
Goal 2 = high discrepancy
Goal 3 = negligible discrepancy
Goal 4 = high discrepancy

Phase 5: developing plans of action

Goal statements with high discrepancy factors and to which high priority is attributed demand immediate attention. Using the discrepancy as a basis for change, curriculum developers then set about to create or adjust curricula that will resolve the perceived problems. New curriculum objectives will be required, and from these subsequent curriculum elements will be developed or altered.

An example of this technique may be a school that decides to examine the relevancy of its curriculum on a regular basis. Before it can develop a new curriculum, staff need to reflect upon the existing situation. Rather than react intuitively, a needs assessment is recommended and a small group of staff, together with a small group of parents, create a list of goal statements of preferred behaviour for the students of the school. These statements are rated and ranked by a larger group of staff and parents in order to determine priorities. With data collected on student performance, discrepancies between actual and preferred learner states can be determined. Once the areas of greatest discrepancy have been ascertained (perhaps student literacy skills and student self-confidence), curriculum action may be taken. Curriculum developers may develop an integrated approach to enhancing literacy as well as a specific program of student self-concept. In this way curriculum developers react systematically to areas of perceived need.

In a somewhat different way, Wiles & Bondi (1989) advocate a needs assessment of a far more substantive nature. They contend that a needs assessment is basic to all curriculum development and should represent a comprehensive inquiry into educational operations of a school system. As such they appear to argue for a situational analysis of a most thorough nature.

Conducting situational analysis

While the need for undertaking a situational analysis is considered beyond dispute in most of the curriculum literature, it may nevertheless be resisted by uninitiated curriculum developers who perceive it as a difficult, time-consuming task. Some curriculum developers may argue that they don't need a situational analysis to understand the context of their curriculum. After all, they have an intuitive understanding of student needs and necessary curricula to meet those needs! However, we should question curriculum developers as to where this intuitive response comes from and to what degree is it valid.

Amongst other things, a situational analysis provides a clearer vision of the curriculum context as well as a systematically devised database, both of which provide a more reliable and valid source for later curriculum decisions. This is not only a more systematic way of conceptualising and conducting curriculum development than an intuitive understanding approach, but one likely to gain substantially greater support from other participants in the curriculum development process. The approach of curriculum developers being remote and isolated from the curriculum context and then imposing the devised curriculum upon users is long gone, as seen in the discussion on composition of syllabus committees in chapters 2 and 3.

Table 5.1   Situational analysis factors

External factors to the school

---

1 **Cultural and social changes and expectations** This includes major changes to society such as unemployment patterns, societal values, economic growth and family relationships. Parental, employer and community expectations of schools are included (e.g. the need for improved literacy and numeracy).

2 **Educational system requirements and challenges** Includes systemic influences such as policy requirements, inquiry reports, external examinations, major curriculum projects and significant educational research. Major inquiries such as McGowan (NSW, 1981), Beazley (WA, 1984), McGaw (WA, 1984) and Blackburn (Vic., 1985) have all been very influential at the systemic level.

3 **Changing nature of content** The subject matter taught in schools requires constant revision to update it with developments in the outside world. Examples include new knowledge acquired, technological developments and new literature.

4 **Teacher support systems** A variety of external systems can contribute to enhancing teaching/learning strategies, content updates, evaluation techniques, audio-visual material and other resources. Support may come from tertiary institutions, educational institutes (ACER, CDC), local teacher centres, curriculum consultants, advisory teachers, in-service courses and subject associations (e.g. Science Teachers Association).

5 **Resources** Curriculum developers need to be aware of the availability and flow of resources into the school. These may come from Commonwealth sources (Priority Schools Project, projects of national significance), state education departments, the community and business organisations.

Internal factors to the school

---

1 **Pupils** Significant data that may be gathered on students include abilities, physical and psychological development, aptitudes, emotional and social development and educational needs. An accurate understanding of the nature of students allows for effective curriculum planning.

2 **Teachers** What are the skills, experience, teaching style, values and special strengths and weaknesses of a school teaching staff? Special strengths may broaden curriculum offerings (e.g. aeronautics, horticulture, meditation) and allow for curriculum enrichment and extension.

3 **School ethos** The school climate/environment is a significant factor influencing curriculum and includes principal involvement, power distribution, social cohesiveness, operational procedures and professional cohesiveness.

4 **Material resources** What exactly does the school possess in terms of buildings, equipment, resources (books, curriculum materials), land and vehicles as well as financial resources for future purchases? Knowledge of resources facilitates curriculum planning (e.g. can we offer horticulture, rowing and photography?).

5 **Perceived problems** Major stimulus for curriculum change emanates from a perception of needs or problems. Curriculum planners ascertain these from parents, teachers, students and the community. Needs-assessment techniques may be used.

Source: After M. Skilbeck, 1975

How, then, does one conduct a situational analysis? Several sets of procedures are available and they may appear somewhat daunting and formidable. Nevertheless, time and effort spent on undertaking an effective situational analysis will be well rewarded in the later stages of curriculum development and in terms of the overall effectiveness of the curriculum development task.

Malcolm Skilbeck (1976) was instrumental in devising and disseminating an approach to situational analysis through his widely acclaimed model of SBCD (see chapter 3). He considered that a 'critical appraisal' of the learning situation was an important beginning, as from this situation the curriculum for a school would emerge. To undertake this critical appraisal Skilbeck suggested a review of factors that were both internal and external to the school which constituted the situation (see table 5.1).

A somewhat different approach to undertaking a situational analysis has been devised by I. Soliman and others (1981) in their model of SBCD. They developed an elaborate Situational Analysis Checklist (SAC), incorporating factors such as societal expectations, resources, educational system requirements, content, forms of knowledge, internal factors and learning processes. The SAC might then be applied to a perceived problem and data collected by using one of the Situational Analysis Techniques (SAT). Despite their somewhat elaborate procedures, they fundamentally agree with Skilbeck on the procedure for undertaking a situational analysis.

Situational analysis procedure

A recommended approach to conducting a situational analysis involves four steps: (i) identify problems in context; (ii) select appropriate factors; (iii) data collection and analysis; (iv) make recommendations.

Curriculum developers beginning the development phase of the curriculum model outlined in chapter 3 should devote considerable time and effort to a situational analysis as it will pay handsome returns with the development of other curriculum elements. Figure 5.1 illustrates how the situational analysis procedure can be sequenced.

Figure 5.1   Situational analysis procedure

Identify problems in context
↓
Select appropriate factors
↓
Data collection and analysis
↓
Make recommendations

The problems

The problems that initiate a situational analysis may be specific (prepare a course for non-tertiary-bound upper-school students), general (improve student literacy abilities at primary school) or fundamental (create a curriculum for a new school). The need to address these problems could well be so obvious that the school would encounter significant difficulties if they were ignored. The increasing numbers of non-tertiary-bound students in Years 11 and 12 are a case in point. Should schools serve up the traditional curriculum diet to these students continually, enormous problems will ensue. A thorough analysis of student needs and expectations is required as a preliminary to later curriculum development. Indeed, this has been the brief of the Finn Report (1991), the Mayer (1992) discussion paper and the Carmichael (1992) recommendations for a Vocational Training Certificate.

It may be that teachers are not well aware of problems and felt needs of students and/or parents. Regular investigation of these attitudes is a useful activity by teachers for keeping the curriculum relevant and valued. A needs-assessment technique may be helpful here as seen earlier in this chapter. In many instances feedback to students and parents will also provide a beneficial public relations function. Skilbeck and Soliman have suggested various factors to use in a situational analysis, as have Nicholls and Nicholls. In most cases of conducting situational analysis at the individual school level, the Nicholls' factors are appropriate for collecting data relating to the nature of the curriculum problem. This approach requires an analysis of the following: pupil abilities and backgrounds; teacher strengths and weaknesses; school environment; school resources; school climate (after Nicholls & Nicholls, 1978).

Appropriate factors

Upon determining which needs and problems are to be addressed in the situational analysis, the curriculum developer can then relate to the appropriate factors suggested by Skilbeck (table 5.1). It may be that the problems are so obvious that progress direct to data collection is warranted, but often that is not the case. A careful consideration of Skilbeck's factors will illuminate the nature of the problems concerned. It should be noted, however, that the curriculum developer is not expected to collect and analyse data from all of the factors outlined by Skilbeck, rather those that are relevant to the problem/need. Should the need be extremely general, it would then be appropriate to collect data on all factors, but in most cases some selection of factors is sensible.

Data collection and analysis

How are data to be collected which will throw light on the selected factors being analysed? Many teachers will adopt an intuitive approach, relying upon their experience and intuition to explain the situation. Others, to their peril, may simply ignore this stage. However, a more systematic approach to data collection provides useful information that often conflicts with intuitive understanding.

Table 5.2 suggests some techniques useful in data collection and the types of data that may be obtained. Curriculum developers then analyse these data to determine their significance in the context of the specific situation. It is not possible to provide an analysis of the data-collection techniques mentioned in table 5.2. Nevertheless, it is important for curriculum developers to be knowledgeable about these forms of data collection.

The use of the above techniques will vary with the nature of the situational analysis being undertaken. A small-scale review of a physical education program might only require informal interviews with students and a brief survey of parental attitudes. A more substantial example might involve an entire school staff in an analysis of student numeracy skills. Such an analysis may require special student ability tests; students self-reporting scales; questionnaires to parents; inventory of school mathemat-

Table 5.2   Data collection techniques

Factor	Techniques	Data collected
Pupils[a]	Interviews	Student information and attitudes
	School records	Background and achievement data
	Systematic observation	Student behaviour patterns
	Questionnaires	Student attitudes (large scale)
	External exam	Comparative student performance
	Psychosocial environment	Student perceptions of room climate
	Self-reporting scales	Student attitudes
Teachers	Anecdotal records	Information on teacher behaviour and attitudes
	Staff profiles	Records of staff skills and abilities
	Questionnaires	Teacher attitudes
School ethos	Systematic observation	Impression of school climate
	Psychosocial environment	Aggregated classroom climate
	Interviews	Student/teacher/parent attitudes
Resources	Inventory Checklist	Listing of school resources
	Systematic observation	Impression of school resources

Notes: [a] These represent a sample of factors from Skilbeck's model (see table 5.1)
Source: M. Print, 1988

ical resources; analysis of school records and external exam results, as well as interviews with staff to elicit teaching strengths and interests. The latter is obviously a time-consuming task, although clearly the data collected would provide a sound foundation for developing appropriate curricula.

Another example may revolve around a problem of student attitudes towards the school and perhaps schooling in general. An examination of the school ethos is recommended and several forms of data can be collected. Employing instruments to measure the psychosocial environment of classrooms (Fraser & Fisher, 1983), curriculum developers can ascertain student perceptions of that situation. These instruments basically determine, according to a number of dimensions, student differences between actual and preferred classroom environment. Armed with this information, curriculum developers are then in a position to take positive action.

Once data have been collected they must be analysed to determine trends and areas of consistency. This does not usually require sophisticated statistical treatment but rather a systematic analysis and synthesis of the collected data to determine what patterns are revealed. From these patterns developers are able to recommend directions for action.

Recommendations from a situational analysis

The final step in the situational analysis model (figure 5.1) requires curriculum developers to make recommendations based on the analysed data. This would typically consist of a list of recommended actions based on the previous goal statements. Examples of recommendations may be:

1 Students require substantial literacy development to establish secure English communication skills.
2 An advanced course in Japanese culture is needed to support Japanese language courses for upper school students.
3 Staff have expertise to offer introductory units in aeronautics, marine biology and yachting.
4 The school and staff have appropriate resources to address the needs of locally based gifted and talented students.

The value of undertaking a situational analysis is diminished considerably without the translation of results into recommendations or plans of action. The resulting recommendations will serve to guide the curriculum team with the development of goals and objectives, content, learning activities and strategies for evaluation.

Situational analysis links

Developers, now armed with valuable data from a situational analysis, are able to continue with the effective preparation of the curriculum. Utilising situational analysis data, for example, developers are better able to address the problematic task of devising a purposeful curriculum. When considering the curriculum intent for learners, developers will know about contextual factors, teaching resources, the nature of learners, school facilities, school ethos and so forth. This information will provide a substantively sound basis for their future deliberations as seen in the next chapter.

Similarly, a soundly conducted situational analysis will facilitate curriculum developers with their deliberations on suitable curriculum content, appropriate learning activities, useful forms of student assessment and even how to facilitate effective implementation of the curriculum document.

Summary

* Situational analysis is defined as the detailed examination of the context (situation) into which a curriculum is to be placed and the application of that analysis to curriculum planning.
* A needs assessment is a useful technique for defining needs and determining their priorities. It is particularly helpful in schools when conducting a situational analysis as a base for curriculum planning.
* Conducting a needs assessment involves:
  — Formulating goal statements.
  — Rating goal statements.
  — Ranking goal statements.
  — Determining discrepancies.
  — Developing plans of action.
* In a school setting a situational analysis covers many factors which are both external and internal to that setting, but which nevertheless have a profound effect upon the school.
* To undertake a situational analysis, a curriculum developer is required to:
  1 Identify problems in context.
  2 Select appropriate factors.
  3 Collect and analyse data.
  4 Make recommendations.
* After undertaking data collection and analysis in a situational analysis, curriculum developers make recommendations for the proposed direction and structure of the curriculum.

6   Curriculum intent

By definition, teaching is a purposeful activity and reponsible
teachers should be able to explain their purposes and defend
them . . . Objectives are seen as a way of helping new teachers
focus their teaching and help set priorities. (Karen Zumwalt,
1989:178)

'Curriculum intent' is a term which is not widely used in the literature yet as a concept it is commonly and constantly applied in practice. It may be defined as the direction that curriculum developers wish learners to go as a result of participating in the curriculum. Curriculum intent incorporates the various forms of aims, goals and objectives found in curriculum documents which together provide directions that will hopefully be achieved by learners as they interact with the curriculum. As such, aims, goals and objectives provide guidance to teachers and developers (as well as to learners) to plan appropriate content, learning opportunities and evaluation strategies for students. This chapter examines the numerous concepts related to curriculum intent, examines their sources and considers some recent developments.

In many curriculum models and algorithms it is suggested that the sequencing of curriculum elements is unimportant and that developers may commence with any element and progress in any order (Skilbeck, 1975; Brady, 1992; Walker, 1972). Nevertheless, there is a logic in dealing with situational analysis and curriculum intent before developing content, learning activities and evaluation procedures (though this may not be the only occasion when situational analysis data might be used).

If the formulation of aims, goals and objectives is undertaken at this point in the development process, a clear direction is provided for subsequent development. Instead of relying upon intuition and experience for the subsequent selection of content, learning activities and evaluation strategies, the curriculum developer has a sound foundation for later decision-making by using the stated goals and objectives to provide direction. Thus from objectives comes content, from objectives and content together comes learning activities, and the three elements together then help to direct evaluation strategies.

This has far more value than constructing goals and objectives after content, as would appear to be the case in some practice. The latter approach requires objectives to fit the content, rather than the other way around, and questions the very purpose of writing objectives at all. It is both logical and useful, therefore, to use a situational analysis as a starting point for formulating curriculum intent, and for facilitating the formulation of other curriculum elements. The subsequent aims, goals and objectives would then be used to develop appropriate content, learning activities and evaluation procedures. While this may appear an arduous task, it proves to be rewarding when the process of developing curriculum unfolds.

Aims, goals and objectives

What are aims, goals and objectives, and what are the relationships between them? The literature abounds with various terms that describe curriculum intent and it is fair to say that substantial confusion occurs over the use of the respective terms, though not the concepts underpinning these terms. In recent years this confusion has spread to the public arena with the publication of numerous documents which amply demonstrate this confusion.

A study of the literature reveals minor levels of confusion over the *terminology* associated with these concepts. A few writers in the field (Brady, 1992; Pratt, 1980) refer to the component parts of curriculum intent in the order—goals, aims and objectives, rather than aims, goals and objectives. This is regrettably confusing to students when the great majority use the hierarchical relationship indicated previously.

However, an examination of the *concepts* involved reveals that the differences occur only in the *labels* (terminology) associated with these concepts. Thus when Brady and Pratt talk about 'goals', they refer to the concept that we term aims. Thus the definitions of the terms are essentially the same, only the labels differ. Similar confusion of the terms has been exacerbated in numerous Commonwealth and state education documents which refer to 'goals' when what is meant is 'aims'. A distillation of the academic literature reveals the following terms and relationships.

Aims: A useful way to think about educational aims is to consider them as statements of societal expectations and desires. More particularly, aims are broadly phrased statements of educational intent. Aims state what is to be hopefully achieved by the curriculum. They are purposely stated generally because they are developed for a general level of education and by society (whatever form that may take). Mostly aims are considered to be developed at a system level such as an education department or system (for example, the Tasmanian state education system or the Catholic education system). Aims are long term in nature and may cover a time span of many years, even the entire school life of a child (see table 6.2). Examples of aims may be found in most government curriculum-related documents and two recent documents are good instances of the concept (though not the label). Both examples refer to 'goals' when they mean 'aims', though the concept behind the label is the same. Table 6.1 lists the aims as they are presented in the respective documents.

In *Excellence and Equity* (1989), the New South Wales Department

Table 6.1   Educational aims

Common and agreed national goals for schooling in Australia

1 To provide an excellent education for all young people, being one which develops their talents and capacities to full potential, and is relevant to the social, cultural and economic needs of the nation.
2 To enable all students to achieve high standards of learning and to develop self-confidence, optimism, high self-esteem, respect for others, and achievement of personal excellence.
3 To promote equality of educational opportunities, and to provide for groups with special-learning needs.
4 To respond to the current and emerging economic and social needs of the nation, and to provide those skills which will allow students maximum flexibility and adaptability in their future employment and other aspects of life.
5 To provide a foundation for further education and training, in terms of knowledge and skills, respect for learning and positive attitudes for life-long education.

New South Wales aims

To develop in students:
* the skills of English literacy, including skills in listening, speaking, reading and writing;
* skills of numeracy, and other mathematical skills;
* skills of analysis and problem solving;
* skills of information processing and computing;
* an understanding of the role of science and technology in society, together with scientific and technological skills;
* a knowledge and appreciation of Australia's historical and geographical contexts;
* a knowledge of languages other than English;
* an appreciation and understanding of, and confidence to participate in, the creative arts;
* an understanding of, and concern for, balanced development and the global environment; and
* a capacity to exercise judgment in matters of morality, ethics and social justice.
* To develop knowledge, skills, attitudes and values which will enable students to participate as active and informed citizens in our democratic Australian society within an international context.
* To provide students with an understanding and respect for our cultural heritage including the particular cultural background of Aboriginal and ethnic groups.
* To provide for the physical development and personal health and fitness of students, and for the creative use of leisure time.
* To provide appropriate career education and knowledge of the world of work, including an understanding of the nature and place of work in our society.

Source: Australian Education Council, 1989 (see appendix); NSW Ministry of Education, 1989

of School Education document which has set the direction for schooling in New South Wales for the 1990s, the ten statements of educational intent are identical to those of the national aims stated in the Hobart Declaration. It is an interesting comment upon the role of educational aims that two very significant documents can have identical aims, yet the translation of those aims into curriculum documents appears to be somewhat different. The degree of that difference we shall witness as the 1990s unfold.

Goals: Goals are more specific, precisely worded statements of curriculum intent and are derived from aims. Usually phrased in non-technical language, goals are directed towards student achievement by emphasising content and skills. Another way to conceptualise goals is to consider them as the ways institutions and organisations within society facilitate the achievement of educational aims. That is, if an aim of an education system is to make students literate and numerate, then goals are the ways by which educational institutions generally address those aims.

Curriculum developers often devise goals, as do others working at higher levels of curriculum development such as subject syllabus committees. Goals are medium to long term depending upon how they have been translated from aims (see tables 6.1; 6.2). The examples below provide a range of goals.

1 Students will examine the main issues in Australian society 1850–1900.
2 To understand the rules and exhibit appropriate skills and values in playing the sports of hockey, netball, football, tennis and cricket.
3 To prepare and cook a variety of foods to meet the requirements of three nutritionally balanced meals.

Objectives: These are specific statements of curriculum intent, that is, what students should learn through interaction with this curriculum. They are expressed in terms of changed learner behaviour. Derived from an analysis of aims and goals, objectives are phrased precisely, using technical language and frequently in behavioural terms. Objectives may also be seen as the working statements whereby educational institutions translate goals into specific statements of educational intent.

Objectives are invariably devised by teachers, or groups of teachers, for use within the school, or groups of educators within an institution. They are short term in nature and, as such, may cover a lesson, a day, a week, a term or a semester (see table 6.2). Some examples of objectives are:

1 Children will understand reasons for the first settlement in Australia.
2 Given appropriate apparatus, students will conduct an experiment to prove Archimedes' principle, to the teacher's satisfaction.

3 Students will write a letter to a potential employer seeking an advertised position.

4 Given the necessary information, students will construct a right-angled triangle with 100 per cent accuracy.

A useful distinction is drawn between *general* or *unit* objectives and *specific* (including behavioural) objectives. The former are used in developing curriculum documents on a more general scale, while the latter are appropriate for daily classroom teaching. This distinction will be examined later in this chapter.

A temporal, hierarchical relationship exists between aims, goals and objectives where the first two are regarded as abstract, vaguely worded statements of program intent, while objectives are specific, teacher-prepared statements of what learners will experience.

As figure 6.1 suggests, there exists a direct relationship between the three levels of curriculum intent. The aims of any curriculum may be translated into many goals. Each goal in turn may be translated into numerous unit objectives. At this point a prepared curriculum document may well evidence adequate specificity for the later curriculum elements—content, learning activities and evaluation—to be determined. Finally, at the practitioner level, such as the classroom teacher, specific objectives may be devised based upon the curriculum's unit objectives. Specific objectives then guide the teacher as the curriculum is put into practice in a school. Table 6.2 summarises the relationship between aims, goals and objectives as well as detailing the nature of each.

Figure 6.1   Curriculum intent

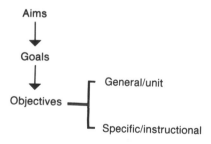

Source: Print, 1988

Table 6.2   Relationship between aims, goals and objectives

Criteria	Aims	Goals	Objectives
1 Definition	Generally phrased statements of what should be achieved by a curriculum.	More precisely phrased statements of curricula intent derived from aims.	Specific statements of program intent; derived from goals.
2 Expression	Broadly phrased, non-technical language.	Generally phrased in non-technical language, although more precise than aims.	Phrased in technical language, using precise key words; may use behavioural terms.
3 Time	Long term, usually covering many years.	Medium to long term, depending upon how they are translated from aims.	Short term, may cover a lesson, a day, a week, a term or a semester.
4 Stated by	'Society' through forms such as politicians, education systems, major inquiries, pressure groups.	Education authorities at system, region and subject level; subject syllabus committees; school policy documents.	Classroom teachers individually; groups of teachers. Some curriculum documents (unit objectives).
5 Examples	Develop positive self-concepts in students.	Students will examine19th C Australian novelists	Given a tennis racquet and ball, students will serve over the net correctly each time.
	Students will develop mathematical and computer skills.	Students will construct three pieces of furniture employing woodworking skills.	Students will draw the physical features of Australia on a prepared outline.
	Demonstrate an understanding of the role of the skilled tradesperson in society (TAFE).	Students will understand reading readiness procedures.	Students will know the correct use of capital letters.

Sources of aims, goals and objectives

Where do our ideas that form the basis of our aims, goals and objectives come from? Certainly our conceptions of curriculum, as discussed in earlier chapters, will be an influential factor in determining how we perceive appropriate curriculum intent. Similarly, our past experience in teaching and curriculum development will influence how we perceive aims, goals and objectives. However, there are other influences of import-ance that must be considered when developing aims, goals and objectives.

The following are the major depositories from which curriculum developers draw their inspiration for creating statements of aims, goals and objectives.

Empirical sources

Two sources of data have emerged that provide guidance to the curriculum developer in formulating statements of curriculum intent. These are the curriculum foundations discussed earlier though classified in a somewhat different manner.

1 Studies of society. By looking at existing society, educators can pose the question: What do we wish to pass on to the next generation? To ask this question a preceding question must be posed, namely, What knowledge is of most worth? How you answer these questions will affect your view of curricula and what you perceive should be included therein. In recent years, for example, growing acceptance of multiculturalism and ethnic diversity as important components of the school curriculum and the pressures from what has been called 'economic determinism' have influenced the nature of curriculum intent.

2 Studies of learners. By examining the needs of learners, educators can determine what should be included in a curriculum. The important question to pose is: What does a person need to function as an adult? A specific example of such a source may be seen in recent reviews and policy statements relating to post-compulsory schooling (Finn, 1991; Mayer, 1992; Carmichael, 1992). These studies of non-tertiary bound learners have demanded a more relevant curriculum and in turn these studies have become the basis for developing appropriate curriculum intent.

In both studies of learners and of society, *empirical* data can be collected to provide a base for stating objectives, that is, data empirically collected provides information about the current situation upon which to base statements of curriculum intent.

Philosophical sources

These sources provide suggestions as to what *ought* to happen to children and adolescents in our schools. Curriculum developers need to pose the philosophical questions—What is a good life? What is of value? What is true? What is real? when considering curriculum intent. By examining these questions from a philosophical perspective, educators can make meaningful contributions to a curriculum's aims, goals and objectives. In so doing, educators manifest notions of a philosophy of education as well as a personal philosophy on life.

Subject-matter sources

Zais (1976) suggests that the most common source of aims is probably subject matter, that is, the established body of knowledge from which school subjects are derived. In the Australian context, subject-matter sources have been particularly influential at the level of formulating goals. The aims of education are general, but when applied at the level of goals they are translated through the medium of subject matter. This is particularly the case when subject syllabus committees in the various states develop curricula in their respective subject areas.

Thus one of the Beazley Report's stated aims, 'Educate towards social responsibility' (1984: 25), is translated at the level of goals through the activities of the various subject syllabus committees and the K10 Social Studies Syllabus. The result is a number of goals that are expressed in terms of subject matter, for example, to study the interrelationship of humans and the environment and to appreciate the needs of others in society. Similarly the broad curriculum intention found in *Excellence and Equity* (1989), 'To develop in students skills of numeracy, and other mathematical skills', may be translated through the Mathematics Syllabus Committee into a K–6 Mathematics Syllabus and a 7–10 mathematics syllabus.

Curriculum conceptions

In chapter 2 various conceptions of curriculum were described and analysed. They represent the culmination of many factors and in turn synthesise those influences into an approach when dealing with curriculum matters. These conceptions also provide a source of and influence over the selection of aims, goals and objectives. Those who favour a humanistic conception, for example, will tend to support the inclusion of humanistically oriented aims, goals and objectives. These may emphasise the enhancement of individual self-concept, personal interaction skills, an understanding approach towards others and so forth.

In similar ways, proponents of the social reconstructionist, technological and academic conceptions would select aspects of aims, goals and objectives influenced by their curriculum conception. This is particularly evident in the formulation of aims and goals where the formative selection of content and learning experiences is undertaken. For example, advocates of technological conceptions have impacted substantively upon some curricula in recent years. A specific example may be found in *Excellence and Equity* (1989) where a major curriculum intention is stated as '. . . skills of information processing and computing', while another states in part: '. . . an understanding of . . . technology in society, together with . . . technological skills.'

Situational analysis

An obvious source of objectives for a curriculum may be found in the deliberations undertaken in a situational analysis. As seen in chapters 2 and 5, when teachers and curriculum developers participate in a situational analysis an enormous amount of data can be generated. This data reflects student interest and abilities as well as teacher strengths, parental wishes, school resources and so forth. A distillation of this information will produce a set of recommendations suitable for inclusion in a statement of goals and objectives.

As a result of a situational analysis, for example, a school-based curriculum-development team may recommend that the school emphasise basic literacy and numeracy skill acquisition while providing opportunities for more able students to extend themselves. Furthermore, the enhancement of positive self-concept within students would be facilitated at all stages of teaching. Such recommendations would be an effective base for a school-level curriculum, and the development of a school's goals (within a system's aims) would reflect these suggestions.

Educational forces

The increased politicisation of education in general, and of curriculum specifically, in the past decade has witnessed the creation of numerous curriculum policy documents which have impacted upon curriculum development. These documents have consequently exerted a significant influence over the formulation of curriculum intent by curriculum developers, both at systemic and school levels.

In New South Wales, for example, a plethora of policy documents which reflect the impact of various forces upon curriculum development have been thrust on to the educational stage in recent years. Beginning with the Carrick Report (1989) into schooling in New South Wales, we find such policies as *Excellence and Equity* (1989), *The Values We Teach* (1989, 1991); *Flexible Progression* (1991), *Curriculum Requirements for NSW Schools* (1991) and *Curriculum Outcomes* (1992).

At a broader level, numerous policy documents and policy initiatives have emerged at the national level with the deliberate intention of affecting curriculum practice. Beginning with Federal Minister Dawkins' initiative, *Strengthening Australia's Schools* (1988), we find deliberate statements on the direction of curriculum.

> We need a curriculum that is relevant to our time and place in the world. A curriculum that is sound in content and which instils positive habits of learning, and attitudes and values such as initiative and responsibility, the pursuit of excellence, teamwork and competitiveness.
>
> What is required is the development of a common framework that sets out the major areas of knowledge and the most appropriate mix of skills

and experience for students in all the years of schooling, but accommodates the different or specific curriculum needs of different parts of Australia (1988:4).

Similarly we find the *Common and Agreed National Goals for Schooling in Australia* (AEC, 1989) serving as another educational force in influencing the creation of curriculum intent within recent curriculum development. Even more specifically, the development of national statements in English and mathematics as well as the development of statements in the other six areas have been further influences upon the construction of curricula at state level.

Thus when curriculum developers undertake the task of considering curriculum intent they are increasingly being forced to take cognisance of such policy documents. This is all the more apparent in the past decade with the increasing politicisation of both education in general and curriculum in particular.

As a general statement then, we can say that curriculum developers do not create statements of curriculum intent in a vacuum. Rather, they are influenced by a myriad of factors and forces which impinge upon the way they construct aims, goals and objectives.

Functions of objectives

Classroom teachers are unlikely to be involved in formulating aims and goals for systemic curricula, though they certainly may be involved with school-level goals. One exception is the teacher who becomes part of a subject syllabus committee and in that curriculum development process aims may and goals will be created, in a sense, by a teacher. As can be seen in table 6.2, a teacher is principally concerned with interpreting and translating goals into operational objectives, that is, specific statements of learner intent that can be applied to the classroom context. When writing objectives, therefore, the teacher should be cognisant of both aims and goals in order to place each level of curriculum intent in harmony and perspective.

It is important when writing objectives to reflect upon the functions that they serve. First, objectives provide a sense of direction to anyone interested in the educational process such as students, teachers, administrators, parents, superintendents and so forth. If learners and teachers know what is expected of them, it is more likely that they will get there.

Second, a function of objectives is to provide a basis for rational and logical curriculum planning. If teachers are aware of what is expected of learners, they are able to plan appropriate experiences to achieve these objectives. This would involve selecting and employing appropriate content, learning activities and evaluation strategies. Such an approach is clearly superior to a haphazard, intuitively based approach to the selection of experiences for learners.

Third, an important function of objectives is to provide a basis for student assessment. While assessment is frequently perceived as an odious but necessary activity, its true value is frequently overlooked. Assessment may be seen simply as the measurement of student performance on the stated objectives. The results of this assessment then provide feedback to learners which allow them to make appropriate adjustments to their learning. This function of objectives should be kept in mind when they are written. The important role of feedback (Hattie, 1992) should also be kept in mind when undertaking assessment of student work.

Types of objectives

There are different types of objectives that serve different purposes within a curriculum. Curriculum developers and teachers need to be familiar with all objectives when developing curricula.

General or unit objectives

These are written as a guide for preparing a unit or section of a curriculum. A typical unit of study would cover a term, a semester or a year. General objectives represent a translation of goals into more specific directions for action although they are expressed more generally than instructional objectives. A semester unit, for example, might have six to eight unit objectives which give us a guide as to the nature of that section of work and from which specific instructional objectives can be devised.

Typically, a curriculum document, such as a syllabus, will have a list of general objectives, flowing from previously stated goals, that teachers can later translate into specific classroom action. Examples of general objectives include:

1 Students will use and understand fractions.
2 Students will analyse Rolf Boldrewood's Robbery Under Arms and Tom Collins' *For the Term of His Natural Life.*
3 Students will construct a four-legged wooden table using dowling joints and glue.
4 Students will prepare a nutritionally balanced two-course evening meal using the microwave oven.

Specific or instructional objectives

When teachers prepare objectives for a lesson or a day's teaching, they are writing instructional or specific objectives. These are precise statements of educational intent and relate to a small amount of manageable time. They are gleaned from general or unit objectives, or sometimes directly from goals, and represent the teacher's attempt to place those objectives into specific classroom learning. In classrooms, some examples might be:

1 Students will understand and draw triangles, squares and rectangles using a protractor and compass.
2 Students will demonstrate the skills of trapping and passing the ball in soccer.
3 To distinguish between silver soldering and arc welding.
4 Students will understand the five principal causes of the Russian Revolution.
5 To bake scones, with sultanas, given the correct ingredients.

Behavioural objectives

Another way of expressing specific curriculum intent is to use behavioural objectives. These are specific statements of intended learner outcome describing the change in terms of observable learner behaviour, that is, the outcomes of instruction should be seen in terms of demonstrated student behaviour. To write a behavioural objective, three criteria are required as outlined by Mager (1962):

1 A description of student observable, terminal behaviour (observable behaviour).
2 A statement of the important conditions under which the behaviour is to occur (conditions).
3 A definition of the standard of acceptable performance (standard).

Some people prefer to name these three criteria in more colloquial terms, such as:

1 Given what, the student (conditions) . . .
2 Does what (observable behavioural),
3 How well? (standard).

Conditions state specifically the material the student is given to work with and/or the problem to be solved and/or prescribe the boundaries for the learning situation, that is, the learner knows exactly what is expected in terms of the learning situation. A common way of expressing the conditions component of a behavioural objective is to use the word 'given' and to begin the objective with the condition statement. For example:

1 Given a 20 ounce (565 gram) hockey stick and ball . . .
2 Given the formula for the area of the triangle . . .

3 Given a blank map of Australia . . .
4 Given a still-life object . . .

Observable behaviour refers to exactly what the student has to achieve in order to demonstrate completion of the objective. Stated in terms of demonstrated student behaviour, a set of specific verbs assists in this expression.

Recommended verbs	*Verbs to avoid*
List	Know
Explain	Understand
Describe	Appreciate
Design	Believe
Evaluate	Enjoy
State	Familiarise
Select	Realise
Identify	Acquaint
Distinguish	and similar vague verbs
Construct	
Calculate	

For example:

1 Given a 20 ounce (565 gram) hockey stick and ball, the student will dribble the ball a distance of 20 metres . . .
2 Given the formula for the area of a triangle, the student will construct three different examples . . .
3 Given a blank map of Australia, the learner will locate the principal iron-ore deposits . . .
4 Given a still-life object, the artist will draw a charcoal sketch . . .

Standards refer to the precisely worded level of achievement required of the learner. In some subjects this is a relatively straightforward task, while in areas such as art, English, home economics and so forth, this task is far more difficult. In these cases the expert judgment of teachers is usually required. Behavioural objectives may then be written in terms of standards from three alternative positions, depending upon which is most appropriate: (1) state a specific standard, (2) state an acceptable standard by a judge or (3) imply a level of standard. For example:

1 . . . with 90 per cent accuracy.
2 . . . to the teacher's satisfaction.
3 . . . write the list *correctly*. (Correctly implies with 100 per cent accuracy unless stated otherwise.)

The previous examples all require the standards component to be added to them. Can you complete that task? You can perhaps devise your own behavioural objectives. Here are some different examples to provide a guide:

1 Given a list of words, students will spell them with complete accuracy.
2 Given a smoothing plane, students will name the component parts (standard implied).
3 Students will label each noun and adjective correctly from a mixed list of twenty nouns and adjectives (implied 100 per cent accuracy through the use of 'correctly').
4 Given a set piece, students will type it within five minutes, with a maximum of ten per cent errors.
5 Students will bake a sponge, given the correct ingredients, to the teacher's satisfaction.

The arguments for and against the use of behavioural objectives have waxed and waned over the past twenty years. The total picture is still somewhat unclear although it appears that in certain places (some states in the United States) and some subjects (maths and science) the use of behavioural objectives is extremely pervasive. In recent years in Australia, however, there has been a move away from the rigid application of behavioural objectives.

Indeed, the opposition to the comprehensive or exclusive use of behavioural objectives has been so intense that Elliot Eisner (1979) developed the concept of 'expressive outcome' or expressive objectives. Eisner, and indeed many others, objected to the excessive rigidity of behavioural objectives and argued against their preformulated approach to curriculum intent. Rather, he claimed, one should use 'outcomes' which are statements of what one ends up with when the curriculum interacts with learners.

> Expressive outcomes are the consequences of curriculum activities that are intentionally planned to provide a fertile field for personal purposing and experience . . . Curriculum planning and schooling in general need not always be singleminded in their pursuits, forever focusing on objectives that are by definition always out of reach. Purposes need not precede activities; they can be formulated in the process of the action itself.
> (Eisner, 1979:103–4)

While Eisner's concept of an expressive outcome has not received extensive acceptance, it is nevertheless a provocative idea that some learning at least need not be planned in specific detail beforehand. Where this applies to the more aesthetic and creative aspects of the school curriculum (art, craft, drama, dance and so forth), the argument is even more compelling. In the latter part of the 1980s and into the 1990s however, the concept of 'outcomes' has gained significant importance within many state educational systems, though in a slightly different sense.

Features of effective objectives

As a measure to determine the effectiveness of objectives, one can employ the following criteria in a screening manner. Effective objectives will thus require these features to be present to a substantial degree. It is incumbent upon curriculum developers in general, and teachers in particular, to refer to these criteria when constructing objectives.

Comprehensiveness

To be effective, objectives must cover everything established by the previously designed aims and goals. If aims and goals give a curriculum its broad purpose, objectives provide its specific intent. And in that specificity, objectiveness must be comprehensive.

But what does one use as a source and a guide for the construction of objectives? From the sources mentioned earlier in this chapter, curriculum developers should employ the major reports that guide their profession. These reports supposedly represent the distilled wisdom of leading figures in that profession and hence may be used as a guideline.

For classroom teachers there are numerous recent reports that provide directions for education. Many of these have explicit statements of aims and goals while others are implied. Some of the more recent significant reports include: Carrick (New South Wales), Keeves (South Australia), Beazley (Western Australia), Blackburn (Victoria), Swan/McKinnon (New South Wales). From these reports and other more general reports such as Karmel (1973), curriculum developers can generate a comprehensive set of aims and goals from which they may derive their objectives. In the Karmel Report (1973), entitled *Schools in Australia,* the functions of schools were outlined. As such they reflect an effective, if succinct, statement of the *aims* of schooling. Further elaboration, as shown earlier, can produce goals and objectives and hence a comprehensive base for curriculum intent. The functions, as outlined in the Karmel Report, are listed below.

This perspective of the school reflected its context in time and political development. In recent years, what may be termed the 'Dawkins years'

Table 6.3   Functions of the school (Karmel)

1 Acquisition of knowledge and skills.
2 Initiation into the cultural heritage.
3 Valuing of rationality.
4 Broadening opportunities to participate in artistic endeavours.
5 Confident self-initiated learning.
6 Creative response.
7 Development of a sense of identity.

Source: Karmel, 1973

of Commonwealth involvement saw numerous government reports on future directions for Australia's schools. The most significant of these, *Strengthening Australia's Schools* (1989), reflects Dawkins' approach to education in a time of greater economic accountability.

Other major guides useful in the construction of objectives are the various taxonomies developed in the past three decades. The best known and comprehensive of these are those developed under the leadership of Bloom (1971), Krathwohl et al. (1964) and Harrow (1972). Bloom and his associates classified objectives according to a *cognitive domain,* while Krathwohl and his group extended the taxonomy of educational objectives to include the *affective domain.* Later Anita Harrow (1972) developed a taxonomy for the psychomotor domain.

Consistency

Not only should objectives be comprehensive but they must also be consistent with each other and with the goals from which they come. When constructing objectives it is important to see that objectives relate effectively to each other. If one objective for enhancing student self-concept, for example, emphasised a supportive, nurturing environment, and another required all learning experiences to be assessed through rigorous, multiple-choice testing procedures, then inconsistency and a clash would occur.

To maintain a logical development and extension of the fundamental curriculum intent, objectives must be consistent with the statements of aims and goals. One source of confusion within schools, for example, would occur where objectives have been written without consideration of school goals or wider-level aims. In this case the objectives would be clearly inconsistent with the initially stated curriculum intent. This phenomenon has occurred in some Australian schools, leading parents to become extremely dissatisfied with the schooling offered to their children.

Attainability

For objectives to be viable they must be attainable by students. Levels of student competency and experience, the availability of resources and the availability of time must be taken into account when devising objectives in order to ensure they are attainable.

It may well be sensible for students to understand and appreciate, for example, the scale of the Murray–Darling River system. However, it would be extremely difficult, in terms of time and cost, for students to acquire that learning experientially. If the objective is important, it would need to be constructed in a way that was attainable (by using audio-visual material perhaps). Similarly, an objective on jet propulsion in primary school science may be unattainable for many students. Such an objective may well be beyond their level of cognitive understanding and experience.

Suitability

The issue of suitability of objectives is a somewhat vexed one as educators hold different opinions as to what those needs are and who will decide them. Curriculum developers agree that objectives must be suitable to learners' needs, but what are these needs and who decides if they are suitable? Furthermore, are the objectives suitable for learners given their level of maturation and the social context within which they function?

Curriculum developers may decide, for example, that all students in primary schools should learn about human reproduction. This appears to be a logical need of students, particularly in the context of modern society where the acquisition of such knowledge may be, at best, haphazard. But do all curriculum developers agree that this learning should be acquired by students? And at what age? And do the students want this information or do certain adults suggest they do? Are objectives based on this knowledge suitable for students? These are some of the fundamental questions that must be posed in order to determine the issue of suitability of objectives. And underlying this is the fundamental issue—*who* decides *what is* suitable for students to learn?

Validity

In order to be valid, objectives must reflect the reality they purport to represent. In other words the objectives must state what we wanted them to state. If, for example, a set of aims and goals refer to standards of student literacy and the ensuing objectives refer only to literature, then these objectives are likely to be invalid. Similarly if a set of objectives was created to cover the period 1901–45 in Australian history, but the objectives did not include Australia's role in the Second World War, they would be, in part, invalid. This criterion is particularly important when applied to the assessment of student learning where it is essential that what is measured is indeed part of the curriculum.

Specificity

To avoid ambiguity and to be readily understandable to all concerned, objectives should be phrased precisely. Objectives that lack specificity and thus perhaps clarity are likely to be misunderstood by both learners and instructors. To some curriculum developers this means writing objectives in behavioural terms. However, as mentioned earlier, behavioural objectives are waning in popularity. Furthermore, an objective may be written precisely, although not in strict behavioural terms, and still meet the criteria of specificity.

Together these criteria serve the useful function of enhancing the effectiveness of objectives. As so much of curriculum is concerned with the statement of objectives, and as they are so important in subsequent curriculum planning, it is a worthwhile investment of time and effort to make them effective. Using the above criteria as a screening device, curriculum developers will enhance their objectives and hence their subsequent curriculum.

Curriculum outcomes

In recent times the terms 'curriculum outcomes', 'educational outcomes', or 'outcome statements' have been used with increasing frequency in the literature, particularly in publications emanating from departments of education, curriculum and assessment agencies, and the like. Late in 1991, for example, the NSW Board of Studies published the document *Curriculum Outcomes,* a statement of the role of outcomes in the curriculum development process.

The document represents what appears to be the direction of the 1990s—an emphasis upon predetermining the learnings undertaken by students and representing them by statements to be achieved before the curriculum is completed. As such the concept is nothing new, reflecting the competency-based movement and the mastery-education movement of the 1970s, neither of which had significant impact in Australia.

Curriculum outcome statements may be defined as the intended results of the teaching learning process as identified in a curriculum document (usually called a syllabus) and expressed as a set of broad, comprehensive, assessable and observable indicators of student achievement. Taken together, a set of curriculum outcome statements should cover not only the knowledge and skills domains of a subject syllabus but also the attitudes and values domain as well.

Curriculum outcome statements are expressed in general terms because they are not meant to provide a list of specific behavioural outcomes. The relationship between outcome statements and curriculum intent may be seen in the following example. A general or unit objective, say in a unit of work in a history/social studies curriculum may be expressed as:

To develop practical skills in researching primary sources.

Subsequently this general objective could be expressed in terms of such curriculum outcome statements as:

• Locates primary sources in libraries.

- Makes precise and accurate analysis of documents.
- Constructs accurate relationships between events.
- Uses equipment purposively and effectively.
- Presents findings in clearly understandable ways.

The 'need' for outcome statements has been said to be to assist in defining curriculum intent more precisely, clarifying student progress through more precise means, assisting schools to communicate student progress effectively and providing a focus for teacher assessment of student performance (NSW Board of Studies, 1992). This development reflects not only societal demands for greater educational accountability but also the greater politicisation of the curriculum.

Summary

- Curriculum intent provides direction for subsequent development by specifying the ends for learners to achieve. A statement of curriculum intent includes the aims, goals and objectives to be achieved by learners.
- Aims are broadly phrased statements indicating what is hoped to be achieved by the curriculum in terms of general student behaviour.
- Goals are more specific, precisely worded statements of curriculum intent and are derived from aims.
- Objectives are specific statements of curriculum intent, are derived from goals and are expressed in precise terms, including specific student behaviour.
- The sources for aims, goals and objectives include curriculum foundations (philosophy, society, learners), subject matter, curriculum conceptions, situational analysis and educational 'forces' such as government reports.
- Objectives may be written as:
    general or unit objectives;
    specific or instructional objectives;
    behavioural objectives.
- Effective objectives are characterised by the presence of features such as comprehensiveness, consistency, attainability, suitability, validity and specificity.
- Curriculum outcomes are related to curriculum intent and, as the intended results of teaching and learning, are expressed as general statements of expected student achievement.

7 Curriculum content

> *The school curriculum is not neutral knowledge. Rather, what counts as legitimate knowledge is the result of complex power relations, struggles, and compromises among identifiable class, race, gender, and religious groups.* (Michael Apple, 1992:4)

> *Only in education, never in the life of farmer, sailor, merchant, physician, or laboratory experimenter, does knowledge mean primarily a store of information aloof from doing.* (John Dewey, 1916:186)

Many people involved with curriculum development, including many teachers in schools, believe that the starting point for constructing a curriculum lies with the formulation of content. This appears to be a natural phenomenon as the teaching of content is the daily fare of teachers in schools. Consequently many teachers tend to think in terms of what content students should learn and what content is of value to learners when they begin to plan for curriculum development. However, this is a tendency that must be resisted. Like driving a car before one has integrated the constituent skills of driving effectively, curriculum developers can end up in a crash if they begin with content without taking cognisance of other curriculum elements.

To those who may wish to commence curriculum development by first formulating content one should ask: How does one know *what* content to select if some form of objectives have not been formulated? 'I just know,' says the experienced teacher. But is intuition a sufficient source for content selection, even if based upon years of experience? And what of the neophyte teacher? How do inexperienced teachers select content appropriately without the guide of objectives or some form of curriculum intent?

The reality is that *all* curriculum developers employ objectives in some way when constructing curricula. Most follow the path suggested here and write objectives based on predetermined aims and goals. We can see these in the many syllabus documents which are created by educational authorities and distributed to schools as a basis for schools' curricula. For these developers there is a sense of systematic logic and direction to their curricula as they grow out of statements of curriculum intent and take the form of statements of curriculum content.

For others, objectives are developed more intuitively and may not be expressed overtly. Nevertheless these curriculum developers still have intentions for their curricula in mind, although they may not write them into a curriculum document. Consequently the content of their curricula appears to materialise miraculously, although that is not the case. Such an approach may appear to work for an experienced curriculum developer, but there are still difficulties to be faced. A teacher who has taught for many years, for example, may argue that content of a subject can be written without recourse to objectives. The reality is that those very years of experience have honed the teacher's mental objectives to a point where they appear to be an effective base for curriculum development. But in this situation how does one really know if they are effective? What can the developer say when asked to defend the selection of content? Does such an approach also encourage people not to change their perspective and become more relevant to changed circumstances? And how can it be ascertained which content is being taught without reference to objectives? With these questions in mind the forewarned curriculum developer, guided by statements of curriculum intent, is able to plan and develop appropriate curriculum content effectively.

The nature of content

All too readily 'content' is equated directly with 'knowledge'. Many educators believe that content consists only of the facts, concepts and generalisations, or the knowledge, related to a particular subject or theme. And of course content docs consist of knowledge—but it also includes more.

For our purposes content is defined as the subject matter of the teaching–learning process and it includes the knowledge (facts, concepts, generalisations, principles and so forth), processes or skills associated with that knowledge base and the values associated with subjects or whatever is being learnt. R. Hyman, for example, has defined content as consisting of: *'Knowledge* (i.e. facts, explanations, principles, definitions), *skills and processes* (i.e. reading, writing, calculating, dancing, critical thinking, decision-making, communicating) and *values* (i.e. the beliefs about matters concerned with good and bad right and wrong, beautiful and ugly)' (Hyman, 1973:4).

A social studies curriculum, for example, would include not only the facts, concepts and generalisations associated with this particular body of content, but also the related skills and values (including attitudes) from the social sciences. One of the best curriculum documents to illustrate this is the Western Australian Education Department's *Social Studies K10 Syllabus* (1981). This well-prepared curriculum document was devised around three strands of knowledge, skills and values distilled from the social sciences. The content of the subject, in terms of knowledge, skills and values, has been clearly laid out over Years Kindergarten to Year 10 and has stood the test of time very well (Print, 1990).

A hypothetical social studies curriculum for lower secondary students, as depicted in table 7.1, would include the three components of content—knowledge, skills and values. This example does not take into account the balance between the three components, though it illustrates broad relationships between the components and it only provides a brief selection of what the content might be.

In the past few years a new domain of educational research has addressed the issue of the content knowledge of effective teachers. The seminal conceptual work and research of Lee Shulman (1986; 1987) has been followed by numerous studies examining a wide diversity of aspects related to teacher content knowledge (Ball, 1990; Grossman, Wilson & Shulman, 1989; Kennedy, 1990; Print, 1990; Shulman, 1986, 1987; Wilson & Wineburg, 1988). The result of this research indicates that prospective teachers need to be knowledgeable about the subjects that they teach i.e. the subject matter knowledge, the skills and the values associated with that content area. This content knowledge has three components (Shulman, 1986, 1987; Kennedy, 1990) which teachers require in order to be effective practitioners:

1 Subject matter knowledge—facts, principles, generalisations and so forth found in the subject concerned.
2 Pedagogical content knowledge—the methods used by the teacher to translate subject matter knowledge into meaningful understanding for learners, i.e. metaphors, ryhmes, sayings, similes and so forth.
3 Curricular knowledge—understanding of the curriculum requirements of the context to teach the subject matter knowledge.

Table 7.1   Course content

Social studies curriculum (content)[a]

1 Knowledge
   Australian society
   Solar system
   Australian history
   Asian societies
   Environmental studies
   Local history

2 Skills
   Mapping
   Researching information
   Report writing

3 Values
   Equality but difference
   Clarification of values
   Respect for life

Note: [a]Selected examples only

Content selection

One of the first tasks facing a curriculum developer, armed with a set of objectives and recommendations from a situational analysis, is to select appropriate content to meet those objectives. When curriculum developers undertake the actual selection of content, the stance they take on what content to include may be seen in terms of a continuum. Figure 7.1 suggests that the approach towards selecting content varies between one emphasising a knowledge-based approach where the learning of factual material is of paramount importance, and one emphasising the process approach where skills are highly valued and seen as integral to effective understanding.

Subject-knowledge approach

This perspective claims that content has its own intrinsic value based upon human knowledge as determined by the academic disciplines. In other words, the real value of subjects is the human knowledge accumulated over time and the most effective expression of this knowledge lies with the academic disciplines. Thus in creating school curricula, content for subjects should be drawn from the various academic disciplines as this knowledge from the depositories of human wisdom is perceived to be of value to students in later life. Many leading educators have supported this viewpoint including R. S. Peters (1966), Paul Hirst (1968) and Jerome Bruner (1965).

An understanding of the accumulated wisdom of the academic disciplines provides a starting point for understanding the world as well as one's role within it. A subject-knowledge based curriculum also provides a sound sense of perspective for learning as it draws upon the knowledge base of the disciplines. Furthermore, in a constantly changing world the

Figure 7.1   Content selection continuum

SUBJECT APPROACH		PROCESS APPROACH
(Intrinsic value of content)		(Content is irrelevant)

knowledge, skills and values of traditional subjects may produce a sense of strength and security for learners. Finally, human wisdom is constantly accumulating and so an updating of content is a continuous phenomenon. Thus a grounding of learning in the academic subjects has logical value for learners.

Process approach

At the other extreme of the continuum is the view that process really is the content and that knowledge is simply a fabric to place over the framework of skills (process). Knowledge, it is contended, has little intrinsic value, particularly as it is constantly changing and expanding. The knowledge explosion of recent decades has effectively prevented people from coping with knowledge adequately and therefore what should be acquired is the means to obtain and process knowledge, that is, skills, both conceptual and physical in nature. Research skills such as conducting library searches, using indexes, collecting data, analysis, synthesis, generalising and so forth are an example, as are the range of skills integral to the problem-solving process.

This approach is particularly appropriate in a society where the information-technology paradigm has gained such credence in recent years. It has been argued, for example, that half the types of jobs people will be employed in within the next two decades have not as yet been invented. Similarly we are developing our knowledge base at an exponential rate and consequently cannot possibly maintain a learning pace with it. What is required, therefore, is an approach which emphasises the accessing of knowledge rather than storing it personally.

The process approach argues that content in the form of past knowledge is essentially moribund. Such knowledge is outdated even before it is disseminated in common public forms such as books. You might reflect, for example, upon those who learnt or are still learning lower-secondary school geography. In the 1960s this consisted in large measure of learning the nations of the world, their capital cities, their main products, exports and imports as well as their population statistics. Since that time the nations of the world have doubled in number and many have changed their name. The learning of this form of content, it may be argued, is therefore of little use. Rather, the skills for acquiring information are of value, as they allow one to locate current data and maintain relevancy.

Both approaches have strengths and weaknesses and it can be argued that neither is suitable in its extreme form. In this chapter we have taken a balanced approach, realising the importance of both skills and knowledge. At this point it may be useful to reiterate the *definition of content*— it is considered to be the subject matter of the teaching–learning process which incorporates the knowledge, skills and values of subjects. One needs knowledge to establish one's perspective and provide background, but it is also essential to be able to acquire more relevant information through the use of appropriate skills.

Content selection criteria

Michael Apple (1990; 1992; 1993) contends that the selection of content for a curriculum, and its subsequent organisation, is an ideological process, one that serves the interests of particular social groups and classes. While this ideological process may be less obvious in an Australian context it is, as seen in the chapter on curriculum presage, ever present. Those involved in the selection of curriculum content should, therefore, be well aware of what they are doing.

When selecting content specifically for a curriculum, the developer requires guidelines to ensure that the content is appropriate. The following criteria provide a framework for facilitating the selection of content. They are not presented in order of merit or worth, and not all would be applied equally. Nevertheless, they provide a useful guide for the selection of appropriate content. These criteria are particularly appropriate where a group of curriculum developers must decide upon the appropriate content to meet the needs as stated by the curriculum intent. What we all too frequently find is developers arguing for content inclusion based upon personal preference rather than substantive criteria as discussed below.

There is no doubt that the selection of subject content is a highly political activity, in that curriculum developers argue, negotiate, debate, and caucus each other in an attempt to control the content included in the curriculum. Nowhere is this more obvious that in the contestation created in subject syllabus committees which must decide the curriculum, and its content, for schools. Yet even here, the argument for certain content may prevail if the following selection criteria are employed. Certainly teachers may apply these criteria to analyse the content of draft-syllabus documents when they are released for discussion.

Significance

The criterion of significance applies where content is judged in terms of how essential or basic it is to the discipline or theme under study. Where content is considered to be of value to the subject area, it is deemed to be significant and thus worthy of inclusion in a curriculum. For most curriculum developers this criterion involves an appropriate balance between concepts, ideas and facts. As Nicholls & Nicholls state:

> If study were to be based on a number of carefully selected principles, concepts or ideas, facts would be learned to illustrate these and would be

included only in so far as they contributed to an understanding of these. This would reduce the problem of learning the large bodies of facts which seems to be the bugbear of so many courses at the secondary level. (Nicholls & Nicholls, 1978:52)

The significance criterion may be applied to any body of content considered for inclusion in a curriculum. For example, it may be used where content is based upon themes, problems, activities, such as in primary schools, or the most common form—subjects and disciplines. Certainly the criterion has greatest applicability where content is '. . . perceived as a logical structure and finds its widest application in curriculum development situations that involve experts and scholars in those disciplines which the curriculum includes' (Zais, 1976:344).

Nevertheless, this criterion is somewhat problematic when we pose the question 'Significant for whom?' At this point it is useful to reflect upon the discussion raised in the chapter on curriculum presage. Certainly those who are involved with the curriculum development process will bring differing perspectives to that task. Many argue that nowhere is the impact of that decision more important that in deciding what is significant content for inclusion into a curriculum.

Validity

An important criterion to apply when selecting content is that of validity. Content may be regarded as valid when it is authentic or true, and to a large measure this means whether the content is accurate. Accurate or true information says what it is supposed to say. For example, content that purports to cover the geography of Australia should do just that and not include New Zealand geography or Australian economics.

A significant test of the validity of content is to determine the degree of its obsolescence. In this rapidly changing world, the obsolescence of content is a continual problem faced by curriculum developers and those who implement curricula. Some school subjects, such as maths, science and social studies, appear to be in a state of almost constant flux. The recent plethora of Eastern European, African and Oceanic nations changing their names and the names of their cities is a nightmare for social studies curriculum developers.

The criterion of validity of content may also be measured in terms of the relationship between content and objectives. For content to be valid it must reflect the stated objectives. If objectives claim one thing while the content selected for the curriculum teaches something different then it is regarded as invalid. For example, if an objective seeks to achieve student understanding of Australia's political structure, and the ensuing content deals only with one political party, then the content would be invalid (let alone biased!).

This use of the validity criterion is particularly important for practising teachers who implement syllabuses developed by those external to the school such as state educational authorities. Exact congruence between explicitly stated intent and evident content should not always be taken for granted. Situations may arise where a subject-syllabus committee agrees on the intent of the curriculum and then proceeds to develop content more in line with the results of political pressures amongst committee members rather than the agreed objectives.

Social relevance

A somewhat controversial criterion for content selection is that of social relevance. This criterion suggests that content for inclusion in a curriculum should be selected on the grounds of its relevance to the social development of the individual, but within the context of a community-oriented perspective. Thus this criterion is concerned with content relating to moral values, ideals, social problems, controversial issues and so forth that would assist students to become more effective members of their society.

But what content would be included on these grounds? In a thinking, responsible society, curriculum developers may well incorporate content that reflects:

1 Democratic principles and values.
2 Understanding of cultural groups.
3 Social awareness and criticism.
4 The facilitation of societal change.

The *Common and Agreed National Goals for Schooling in Australia* (AEC, 1989) provide such a base for determining socially relevant content (see appendix). These statements of curriculum intent and direction have been phrased in such a way so as to provide social relevance, in a community context, for students in Australia's schools. Thus Goal 7 states the intention: 'To develop knowledge, skills, attitudes and values which will enable students to participate as active and informed citizens in our democratic Australian society within an international context.' This statement suggests the basis for content selection which would produce socially relevant content for students. Which other statements provide this direction?

One of the interesting, and problematic, aspects of the current development of national curriculum statements (in the areas of mathematics, English, study of society and the environment, science, technology, the arts, languages other than English, and health) is the degree of congruence between the agreed goals and the statements of content in these pseudo-national curricula. If these curriculum statements form, or could form, the basis of a de facto national curriculum, as many educators believe (Kennedy, 1989; Hughes, 1990; Piper, 1991; Print, 1991; Ruby, 1992), will they maintain consistency with the national goals? If not, then have they become the driving force in the national curriculum movement? And if so, who has the mandate for determining their direction?

Similarly, it will be interesting to ascertain the degree to which subject syllabuses developed at state level take cognisance of the national goals. In a recent review of social studies in Western Australia (Print, 1990) it was found that the criterion of social relevance was important to teachers and parents as a factor for including content within the curriculum. Similary in many states, such as New South Wales with its KLAs, recent curriculum development may have to be undone in order to be consistent with the national curriculum statements.

However, it is also possible that a particular group of developers would prescribe content that was dogmatic, slanted and furthering the interests of a sectional group. This potential problem reinforces the significance of the selection of curriculum developers, as argued in the case for curriculum presage (chapters 2 and 3), in any curriculum-construction activity.

Utility

A related criterion to consider when selecting content is that of utility. This criterion appears similar to the criteria of significance and social relevance but the term is defined in a rather specific manner in terms of of individual learners. When employed to select content for a school curriculum, the criterion of utility applies to the usefulness of content in preparing students for *adult* life. As such it implies a very directly relevant and functional approach to the selection of content that will lead to a desired outcome on behalf of the learner.

This criterion is also individually oriented, reflecting the concept of the value or usefulness of the content to individual learners experiencing the proposed curriculum. This is compared with the notion of value to learners in a social sense as discussed in the social relevance criterion. Together with the notion of usefulness for adult life, the utility criterion is an important consideration to be made when content is included in a curriculum.

As a criterion, utility is extremely valuable to those who favour a more functional school curriculum because it can be instrumental in maintaining real-world relevance in schools. Nevertheless, some schools and colleges, and many universities and other educational institutions, are perceived to take an excessively theoretical stance when selecting content for their curricula. By applying the criterion of utility to the content-selection process, developers can expect a curriculum to be more relevant and hence valuable to the real world.

Recent policy documents dealing with post-compulsory schooling in Australia—Finn (1991), Mayer (1992) and Carmichael (1992)—have sought to address the issue of a relevant curriculum for non-tertiary-bound students in schools by creating, based upon the utility criterion, general directions for appropriate content in the post-compulsory schooling curriculum. The result of these initiatives is the Australian Vocational Training Certificate, a utility-based approach to addressing the needs of this rapidly growing group of students.

At an extreme position, however, a rigidly applied utilitarian criterion could well perpetuate the status quo or provide a limited perspective on available content. This approach may cause difficulty within departmentalised institutions (such as secondary schools) as the utilitarian needs of adulthood may suggest that family life, career education, interpersonal skills, personal health, personal finances and so forth be included in the curriculum. Such topics, however, tend to be thematic or problem-oriented and hence cut across the traditional subjects and subject departments found in secondary schools. This specific issue has been raised many times in schools over the past few decades and is yet to be resolved, principally because educators have been unable to successfully address the problem of the overcrowded curriculum (see below).

A recent adaptation of the utilitarian criterion suggests that content should be selected to meet students' present needs. Students may well require content that deals with drug education, personal problem solving, multicultural understanding, financial awareness and so forth. While these approaches to the utilitarian criterion may cause some dissension amongst curriculum developers, the criterion itself is useful when selecting content. This criterion is particularly appropriate for curricula devised for non-tertiary-bound students.

Learnability

While it may appear obvious to select content that students are able to learn, this criterion has not always been applied in the past. The learnability criterion is particularly appropriate to curricula that have to meet the needs of large numbers of students with diverse backgrounds and a wide range of ability (Young, 1989; Kennedy, 1990). In these cases, if the content is to be acquired by all students, then consideration must be made not to make the content too difficult for this group of learners.

By contrast, there may be times when a curriculum developer is unsure just how able the learners may be. Creating a curriculum for high-ability learners, the so called gifted and talented, demands that content challenge such learners and so the learnability criterion would be used in a different manner. In the more general context, however, it is often difficult to take account of individual differences and hence aspects of content may not be learnable by some students. To lessen this problem and make content suitable to the ability levels of all students involved could reduce the content to the level of the lowest common denominator. This, in turn, would create an inane, pointless curriculum for many students. The answer to this problem lies, in part, in creating multiple content material, or variations of the basic content material by adding more advanced content for abler students, in order to meet differing student abilities or levels within a single curriculum.

An associated aspect on the learnability criterion is that of student readiness. It is extremely difficult for curriculum developers to predetermine curriculum content that takes account of learner readiness, beyond rather broad parameters. However, the classroom teacher, acting as curriculum implementer and curriculum adapter, is in an appropriate position to consider learner readiness. Thus it is a professional judgment by the teacher which will determine whether or not certain content should be included in the presentation of the curriculum based upon the readiness of the learners to accept that content. Effective teachers have been making such curriculum decisions for many years.

Interest

The interest of learners in the curriculum's content is generally considered to be an important criterion in the selection of that content by curriculum developers. After all, this is good sense. However, it appears to be one of those criteria more valued in the theory than in the reality. Certainly curriculum developers have accorded this criterion the lowest priority in practice. One of my postgraduate students noted a comment of his students that what they were learning '. . . bored them spitless'.

The problem associated with the student interest criterion is the dilemma it causes when determining just how significant a role this criterion should play. At one extreme curriculum developers could ignore student interest as a selection criterion. They could argue, perhaps justifiably so, that they know what content students should learn. However, this extreme position loses the potential of a strong student motivational force and hence may be counterproductive.

Alternatively, curriculum content selected largely upon a student-interest criterion possibly suffers from whim, immature development, and individualistic emphasis. The range of students' interests may appear to be unlimited and they are frequently of a transitory nature.

Obviously some accommodation of both arguments must be taken into account when constructing curricula. In Australian primary and secondary schools today one of the significant causes of student disruption is their belief in the lack of content interest and relevance of schooling. Curriculum developers would do well to ascertain a greater understanding of student interests and perceived needs. While maintaining the role of arbiter, curriculum developers must take greater cognisance of student interests.

One development which has been remarkably successful in recent years are the various courses created for non-tertiary-bound students in upper-secondary school. As the number of students continuing to upper school has increased, teachers have found that existing, tertiary-oriented courses are frequently inappropriate to student needs and interests. Arguably some of the most relevant curriculum development in schools has occurred, and is still occurring, to accommodate the interests of these students.

The criteria—significance, validity, social relevance, utility, learnability and interest—should be applied by curriculum developers when selecting content for a curriculum. Teachers will find these criteria useful when selecting content from within a curriculum document, particularly when decisions are required for their classroom programs. Where possible, all criteria should be considered, although it appears that the criteria of significance, validity and utility are accorded greater priority.

The overcrowded and finite curriculum

When selecting content for a curriculum, developers are faced with a fundamental problem—what content to include and what to exclude. As mentioned previously, this must be addressed by asking the question: What content is of most worth? All curriculum developers answer this question in their own way, either wittingly and deliberately or unwittingly and unknowingly.

In recent years, however, society has also placed increasing demands upon the content of the school curriculum. Social agencies argue, quite logically, that their needs should be met by including content on their activities in the school curriculum. In this way students would learn about these issues and such learning would make them a better person or reduce the possibility of something unfortunate occurring. Pressures for additional content have come in recent years from industry, health organisations, environmental groups, employers, multicultural groups, feminists, peace groups, Aboriginal organisations, parliaments, road safety organisations and many other groups.

The problem arises when these content demands are placed in addition to the existing content in the school curriculum. Typically few teachers and curriculum developers wish to see the demise of subject-based curriculum content. Some developers, particularly those acting in subject-syllabus committees, are aware of the need to change content from time to time on the grounds of social relevance, utility, interest and so forth. Indeed, many curriculum developers spend considerable time *adjusting curriculum content*. But few, particularly those in subject-syllabus committees, wish to *reduce* that content. Battles have been waged long and hard, especially in secondary schools, as subject departments seek to increase their influence over the school curriculum.

Yet to accommodate the demands of new content, the only way is for existing content to be removed and replaced. The reality of educational organisations is that a *finite curriculum* exists and few educators wish to change that situation. We see few demands by educators for a longer school day, or a longer week (e.g. school on Saturday), a longer year (e.g. 45 weeks rather than 40 weeks) or a longer school education (e.g. a fourteenth year). The result is a highly political activity as curriculum developers, curriculum organisations and schools interact to address the pressures of external groups.

A clear example of the general pressure on the school curriculum may be seen in New South Wales where the Board of Studies, the statutory authority responsible for K–12 curriculum development and assessment, has sought to meet school demands for new subject curricula. In 1991 it planned to release fourteen new syllabus documents for various years of secondary schooling. Further it planned to release another nine syllabuses in 1992. Not surprisingly it has not been able to meet its intentions, particularly considering the increased politicisation of secondary school curriculum development.

Meanwhile the demands of pressure groups for greater access to the content of the school curriculum continues unabated. Table 7.2 indicates some of those pressure areas in the past decade, the form that additional content has taken and the level of impact generally found (though this varies from state to state) of those pressures upon the school curriculum. The list of content areas is meant to be illustrative rather than comprehensive.

The architectonics of content

What happens to content once it has been selected? Where is it placed in the overall curriculum? Why is it placed there? Curriculum developers faced with the enormity and bewildering array of content available have sought refuge in various criteria to assist them in arranging content appropriately for learners. An orderly and rational scheme of *organising* content facilitates effective curriculum development and to this end we shall analyse the architectonics of content as they apply to a school situation. The organising principles could, however, apply equally well to any other learning situation requiring the structuring of content for a curriculum.

Table 7.2   Curriculum response to content pressure

Content area	Pressure sources	Content form	Curriculum impact
Environment education	Environmental groups e.g. Greenpeace, Conservation Foundation	Across curriculum; subject integration—geog., science	Selective impact, but very successful; policy documents
Multicultural education	Ethnic groups, multicultural councils, political parties	Across curriculum, ranging from special days to integration in subjects	Some evidence of curriculum integration, faded in 1980s
Girls' strategy	Feminist groups, Commonwealth govt	Attempts to integrate across curriculum	Major policy impact, little change in content
Peace education	Peace groups	Integration into subjects	Negligible impact in 1980s
Health: —AIDS —heart —drugs —anti-smoking	Medical groups	Selective integration in subjects, e.g. health education	Some impact e.g. drugs, anti-smoking, AIDS. Little for heart, cancer nutrition, etc.
Parliamentary education	Commonwealth govt, state govts	Selective inclusion, some subjects and special days	Variable impact related to schools and states
Technology	Commonwealth govt; state govts; ACTU business groups	Some subject integration, resource support	Variable impact at this stage. Substantial use of resources
Foreign languages	Commonwealth govt, Asian Studies Council, ethnic groups, business	New courses created, mostly in high schools	Small but rapidly increasing impact.
Road safety	Commonwealth and state agencies	Curriculum packages; medical, school visits	Minimal impact
Gifted and talented	Some state govts, parental groups	Special programs, selective schools	Negligible impact except in NSW

The architectonics of content may be defined as those principles responsible for ordering and arranging content into systematic categories for the purpose of facilitating learning (Phenix, 1964; Zais, 1976; Print, 1988). The term 'architectonics' relates to the structures needed to present a curriculum and the principles which assist the curriculum developer to organise the content of a curriculum in such a way so as to achieve maximum effectiveness for students. For our purposes we will concentrate upon the two most important principles of the architectonics of content, namely:

1 Scope of curriculum content.
2 Sequence of curriculum content.

Scope of curriculum content

The term 'scope' refers to the breadth and depth of content to be studied in the curriculum at any one time. That is, how the content is arranged at a specific point in time and the degree of depth of that content to be covered at that particular time (usually one term, semester or year in a school). To Zais, 'The word refers not only to the range of content areas represented, but to the depth of treatment each area is accorded' (1976:338). Sometimes scope is referred to as horizontal organisation or horizontal integration, although we shall use these terms slightly differently, as seen in chapter 4 where curriculum design and planning are discussed.

A useful starting point when dealing with the scope of content in a curriculum is to pose questions about the nature and balance of that content. For example, in the context of a school curriculum we might ask the following questions:

1 How much of each content area should students study at any one time? That is, what should be the ratio of time spent on maths, science, English, social studies, physical education, music and so forth?
2 Is there a body of common content that all students should know? Should all students leave school being exposed to a set of common learnings?
3 If one supports the notion of a core plus electives approach to content, what should be the role of elective content?
4 And an increasingly relevant question facing curriculum developers today—What content should be *excluded* from the curriculum? Given a finite school curriculum, with pressures to add more learning, what content do we excise?

In recent years these questions have been posed by the developers of the national curriculum statements in the areas of mathematics, English and study of society and it is interesting to see how they have been addressed. In the near future all of the eight areas designated by the AEC will have national statements available and in each case the curriculum developers have had to pose the above questions. Perhaps even more interesting to see will be how the various state education departments and the curriculum agencies relate these national statements to their respective subject curricula.

Unfortunately, there are few educational principles that can provide guidance when making decisions about the scope of content in a curriculum. This situation might help explain why such vigorous political activity occurs in schools when the distribution of time for individual subjects is made. There never seems to be sufficient time within the school week to treat all subjects adequately. Some schools attempt to resolve the problem of limited time and competing content by using differing cycles of time, e.g. six-day cycles, seven-day cycles and so forth. In reality they do little more than disguise the problem and simultaneously cause many difficulties with timetables. How the time is distributed, when subjects are taught, what rooms are used and so forth, become issues of considerable importance and are decisions resolved in a political manner (that is, by power in a typical secondary school). Nevertheless, the following concepts are helpful in determining the scope of content for a curriculum:

1 *Time* is a major constraint when determining the scope of content. Breadth of content is always bought at the expense of depth, and the reverse is also applicable. Breadth may be greater time spent on a particular subject theme or may represent more subjects to be taught in a given time period. The balance that occurs between breadth and depth will be resolved by the political forces in the school and the curriculum forces found in the head office of systemic curricula.

2 The notion of a *core or common* content appears acceptable to educators and society. The core concept suggests that there *is* a body of content that all students should acquire as a result of their schooling experience. Just how much the core should constitute (50 per cent, 75 per cent, 90 per cent . . .) and exactly what should be included in the core content are subject to debate.

As a generalisation, most core content would constitute a minimum of 50 per cent of the total content and would consist of at least the following—reading, writing, English, mathematics, science, understanding society and physical well-being. Somewhat different notions of the core curriculum are forwarded for the nine core areas in the *Core Curriculum for Australian Schools* (CDC, 1980), the seven curriculum components in the Beazley Report (1984), and the six (primary) and eight (secondary) Key Learning Areas in *Excellence and Equity* (1989).

3 The scope of content may also be influenced by the notion that schools should provide content to meet the *special needs* of children and adolescents. This might take the form of electives or options to

accommodate student interests and social contexts. Alternatively, special content might be devised to meet the needs of less able and more able students.

4 *Integration* of content is to be encouraged in order to provide some sense of reality to the learner. While schools provide specialist content through the form of subjects, the fundamental purpose of these subjects should not be overlooked. In the end, however, the ultimate responsibility for integration of content lies with the learner.

5 A final point to note when considering the scope of curriculum content is to reiterate a previous question. What content should be *included* and *excluded* from the curriculum? In a society which appears to abrogate many of its educational responsibilities, can we expect the formal educational institutions simply to include additional learning in an already overcrowded curriculum? Furthermore, are formal educational institutions such as schools the most effective organisations to teach these learnings?

It would appear that systems and schools have taken on additional content in recent years (such as multiculturalism, career education, transition education, values, sex education, gender equity and so forth). In large measure this has been by default—there simply was no other structure available, or perceived as effective, to undertake this teaching task. But are the schools the most appropriate places for such learning? And what happens to the traditional content? We have witnessed, and will continue to do so, considerable disruption and turmoil within the content of the school curriculum until this matter is addressed by teachers, systems, agencies and academics.

Sequence of curriculum content

Sequence is defined as the order in which content is presented to learners over time. In other words, content is broken down into manageable sections that can then be presented to learners over a period of time in varying arrangements or order. The order in which those parts are presented to learners is called sequencing.

How should content be arranged for learners? In attempting to answer this question, several important, related questions need to be posed, as suggested by Robert Zais (1976:340):

1 What criteria should determine the order of content?
2 What should follow what, and why?
3 When should learners acquire certain content?

Traditionally, subjects have been sequenced according to a logical criterion, that is, the 'logical' approach of the decision-makers involved. However, in reality this was little more than an intuitive response to past practices and the nature of the subjects involved. Thus arithmetic was studied before geometry and grammar before literature. While this approach seemed to work it was rarely challenged and was perceived by teachers as a natural sequencing of content to learners. In the past two decades four principles have become increasingly acceptable as criteria for sequencing content:

1 *Simple to complex:* This approach to ordering content is traditionally found in sciences, mathematics, grammar, music, foreign languages and many other subjects taught in schools. In this situation, sequence is seen as a progression from simple, subordinate components to complex structures, which in turn are the subordinate components of even more complex superordinate structures. To understand long division, for example, you need to understand multiplication, subtraction and addition at the very least. To understand multiplication, you need to know . . .

2 *Prerequisite learnings:* This principle is followed in subjects which consist largely of laws and principles such as physics, grammar and geometry. To understand one set of laws or principles, the learner must acquire the prerequisite learnings. To apply a law of motion in physics to a practical problem, for example, one must first know the law. It is difficult to deny the need for some consideration of prerequisite learning in any educational activity. Indeed much of the primary school curriculum in Australia is based upon the notion of prerequisite learnings. Gagne's (1970) concept of hierarchical learning is consistent with this approach.

3 *Chronology*: This principle suggests sequencing content according to the chronology of recorded events. This is particularly important if one accepts a causal relationship between events such that to understand an event you need to understand what preceded it.

History, music and literature use this approach, as does any subject that examines its own history, such as the history of science. To understand our relationship in the universe, most scientists first examine the chronological developments whereby we have come to acquire the knowledge and understanding we have today of our universe. The chronological principle can be applied forward or backward from any particular point in time.

4 *Whole-to-part learning*: The rationale for this principle is that understanding the whole makes possible the understanding of partial or constituent phenomena. In literature it is useful to study a novel as a whole before an analysis of its constituent parts. Typically a literature curriculum would recommend students read a novel as an entity before undertaking character and plot analysis. Commonly used in geography, for example, this principle suggests that the learner first examines the

Figure 7.2   Physical education spiral sequence

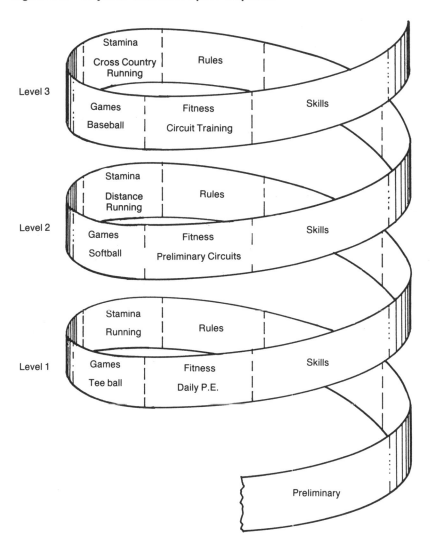

globe, then associated global concepts (time, seasons), followed by specific local topics such as weather. Similarly in biology, the student learns about the whole animal before one learns about its parts.

More recently these four guiding principles have been expanded to include two additional approaches to sequencing:

5 *Increasing abstraction*: Content can be sequenced according to the idea that one learns most effectively what is closer or more meaningful to the learner. Thus, we can commence ordering content with one's own experiences and proceed to more remote learnings. For example, content can be ordered to study one's own family unit, then similar cultural structures before studying social structures from different cultures. This principle is often applied to the sequencing of content in primary schools.

In a similar manner, content may be sequenced from concrete to abstract, that is, understand concrete concepts before moving into abstract, idealistic or theoretical concepts. For example, understanding distance on the ground before studying scale in geography or technical drawing.

6 *Spiral sequencing:* This term was described by Bruner (1965) in connection with whole curriculum organisation, but most often it is applied to smaller components of a curriculum. In the *Process of Education,* Bruner noted that students should be exposed to the content's basic ideas repeatedly, thus building on basic understanding until the whole concept or lot of learnings has been acquired. In figure 7.2 we can see how the content of a hypothetical physical education curriculum can be spirally sequenced. Level 1 might cover Years 3 to 5 of a school, level 2 Years 6 to 8 and level 3, Years 9 to 12. At each level the basic learnings are covered and then built upon at a higher level. In this way a thorough grounding in the required skills is obtained at the same time that physical maturity occurs.

We can also see how the components of the curriculum at level 1 are continued at levels 2 and 3. As a student progresses through the curriculum, the spiralling process allows the content (knowledge, skills and values) to be reinforced and extended. The end result is a student thoroughly familiar with the requirements of the curriculum.

Application of scope and sequence

Every curriculum developer is faced with the same dilemma when organising content—what content do I place where? If I place this here, what impact does it have? And if placed there, what effect will it then have? This dilemma may be resolved through the application of the architectonics of content, namely scope and sequence.

By examining the content selected in accordance with the curriculum's objectives, and the previously mentioned criteria, developers are faced with a jigsaw-type problem. Which parts should go where? If this jigsaw is represented *diagrammatically,* the visual result provides a clear image of what has occurred to the content organisation. This facilitates the process of arranging content. Few developers depict their content organisation pictorially and, as a result, they often suffer from an imbal-

Figure 7.3   Curriculum scope and sequence

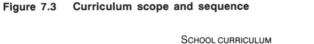

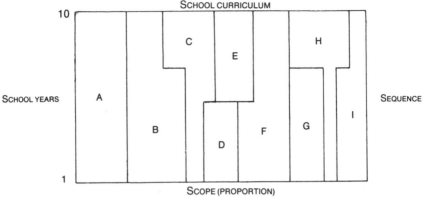

ance between different content components and hence disorganisation. It is strongly recommended that curriculum developers create a pictorial/diagrammatic representation of their scope and sequence arrangements for content.

In figure 7.3 the forces of scope and sequence illustrate *what* each learner will study *when,* and in what *depth.* Given the context of a school curriculum Years 1–10, the diagram depicts subjects that are constantly required (for example subject A, perhaps English), while others are deemed important at a later stage in the learner's development (E, or science). Still others, such as reading (F) and writing (I), are emphasised at an earlier stage and receive less time in later years. Subject H might be computer studies or perhaps a language, where it is considered important to have minimal experience in the primary years and rather substantial exposure in lower secondary school.

While figure 7.3 represents a scope and sequence matrix or chart for an entire school curriculum (Years 1–10), a similar representation could be made for any curriculum. It is worth reiterating that anyone involved in curriculum development should contruct a scope and sequence content matrix in order to better understand the nature of that curriculum. It is quite probable, for example, that you would want to devise a scope and sequence chart for a single subject area, say Year 11 and 12 history or home economics, or even an integrated course such as life skills, panel-beating, hairdressing and so forth, rather than an entire school curriculum. Figure 7.4 is an example of a scope and sequence chart for Year 9 social studies that depicts the relationship between the component parts of that subject's content.

Figure 7.4 illustrates the balance between the various content com-

Figure 7.4   Single subject curriculum matrix

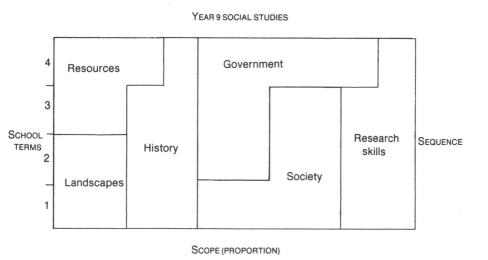

YEAR 9 SOCIAL STUDIES

SCOPE (PROPORTION)

ponents in Year 9 social studies clearly. In this way developers can reflect if indeed this was their intention for learners. Was it intended, for example, that the study of government cover such a large proportion (about half) of fourth-term social studies? Have research skills received enough emphasis? These are but a sample of the questions that developers can pose and resolve through the use of scope and sequence diagrams.

Cognitive development

While these organisational principles have an essential role to play in sequencing content, some educators have demanded a more empirical base to help devise the arrangement of content. The work of numerous psychologists, particularly those involved with cognitive development and learning, has provided a useful theoretical base for many of these principles. By examining the growth of learners' abilities, cognitive and developmental psychologists argue that we can determine when a learner should be exposed to particular content. Among the more influential learning and developmental theorists are R. M. Gagne, Jean Piaget, E. Erikson, R. J. Havinghurst and L. Kohlberg. Only one theorist is examined briefly here, but it is useful if curriculum developers read other theorists and so broaden the base for their curriculum considerations and deliberations.

The cognitive development theory argued by Jean Piaget (1963) implies that the sequence of curriculum content can be coordinated with the learners' stages of intellectual development. This position is based on

Piaget's theory that children's cognitive growth occurs in a sequential pattern through four related stages. In this way, what and how a child learns is determined largely by the child's present stage of development. David Pratt (1980) has summarised Piaget's theories and their application to the sequencing of content:

Stages of intellectual development

Jean Piaget, the dean of developmental psychologists, identified four main stages in intellectual development (1962). The sequence of these stages is inviolable; although an average age for each stage can be stated, the age at which each stage is reached will vary the social and cultural environment of the child: that is, intellectual development can be accelerated or retarded by environmental enrichment or impoverishment.

Sensorimotor stage (birth to two years)

Actions are at first random and reflex, with gradual development of coordination and sense of space. The child reacts at first only to perceptual signs: if a toy is removed from sight, the child is not sure that it still exists. Increasingly the child is able to apply actions to new situations and to experiment with new means to desired ends: for example, by pulling a blanket on which a toy rests. By age one and a half to two, the beginning of memory and planning is evident, as the child invents new means by mental combination; symbolic thought becomes apparent in representational play.

Preoperational stage (two to seven)

The development of language gives great flexibility to intelligence. At first, children centre their attention on only one aspect of an object or situation; later they can perceive relationships among parts. At this stage they reason from what they see, not from abstractions. Classification is undeveloped; if shown a bunch of flowers, half of which are daisies, they cannot say whether there are more flowers than daisies. They begin to use space and time and to observe rules of social behaviour by age seven, but cannot explain them. From two to four the child's social view is entirely egocentric; from four to seven this gives way to socially directed thought and action.

Stage of concrete operations (seven to twelve)

Ability to classify and serialise, to arrange objects by size, and the concept of reversability develop between about seven and eight. The child's social competence is increased with development of language and an understanding of the relativity of viewpoints. The child is concerned with the actual, and characteristically solves problems in terms of direct experiences.

Stage of formal operations (twelve to sixteen)

Preadolescents begin to solve purely verbal problems, to understand the concepts of proportion and reciprocity. They are able to integrate their new intellectual capacities for explanatory purposes. They can manipulate abstract ideas, and they become concerned with the possible rather than the actual. They are idealistic and tend to believe in the omnipotence of thought. The ability to distinguish between what is conceptually possible and what is attainable in fact comes after adolescence as a result of experience in the real world (Pratt, 1980:272).

Summary

- Curriculum content is the subject matter of the teaching–learning process and, as such, includes the knowledge, skills and values associated with that subject.
- Content selection tends to emphasise either a subject approach (knowledge) or a process approach (skills).
- The criteria for selecting effective content for a curriculum are:

  1 Significance: how essential it is to the subject.
  2 Validity: how accurate or true it is.
  3 Relevance: whether it is worthwhile to society.
  4 Utility: how useful the content is to adult functioning.
  5 Learnability: whether the student can acquire the content.
  6 Interest: whether it has intrinsic interest to learners.

- Current school curricula are finite in capacity and have increasingly become overcrowded due to pressures for additional learnings to be included.
- The architectonics of content include scope and sequence and serve the function of ordering content into systematic categories for the purpose of study.
- Scope refers to the breadth and depth of content within the curriculum at any one time. Scope may be influenced by time constraints, a common core, special-needs integration requirements and the total amount of content required.
- Sequence is the order in which content is presented to learners. It is influenced by principles such as simple to complex, prerequisite learnings, whole to part learning, chronology, increasing abstraction and spiral sequencing.
- Learning and developmental theorists have increased their influence in recent decades over the scope and sequence of content. Among the more significant contributions have been Piaget's four stages of intellectual development.

8 Learning activities

Good intentions, fine goals and objectives, excellent content, flawless evaluation procedures, then, are all for naught if the learning activities in which students engage do not provide them with experience whose consequences are educational. (Robert Zais, 1976:350)

This chapter will define the term learning activities, examine a range of appropriate teaching–learning strategies available for inclusion in a curriculum; outline a model for selecting learning activities, and analyse how learning activities may be organised within a curriculum. In undertaking these tasks it is important for curriculum developers to reflect upon the model of curriculum development being used (such as that advocated in chapter 3), and to integrate the curriculum elements of intent and content with learning activities.

Learning opportunities, learning activities, learning experiences, teaching–learning strategies and method are terms frequently used interchangeably to explain what the teacher does to facilitate learning within the student. That is, how the teacher imparts content and provides opportunities for learners to acquire that content. A slightly different way of expressing this concept is to see it as those opportunities offered to learners to achieve the stated objectives.

While educators often use the above terms synonymously, a distinction is becoming increasingly apparent within the literature, emphasising the difference between *intent* and *result*. Learning opportunities and learning activities emphasise what *is offered* to learners, while learning experiences suggests what *results* from those activities. It is hoped, even desired, that there is complete congruence between opportunities, activities and experiences, but this may not always occur. As well, students may learn something that was not planned, something that could even be in contradiction to the stated objectives. As Zais suggests, ' . . . planners can readily prescribe the learning activities that students will be engaged in, but they can only hope that these activities will result in the desired experiences' (1976:352).

Learning activities in the curriculum process

Learning activities may be defined as those activities offered to learners in the teaching–learning situation which are designed to enable them to acquire the designated content and thereby achieve the stated objectives and more broadly, the curriculum's intent. This definition incorporates all teaching or instructional strategies planned by teachers as well as those methods by which students may learn by themselves within the context of the classroom or learning environment (such as independent study, fieldwork and excursions).

In the cycle of the curriculum process, learning activities are integrally related to content and curriculum intent. Just as content is derived from statements of aims, goals, and objectives, so curriculum developers seek to implement that content effectively through the use of appropriate learning activities. In this way the various methods not only teach the content but also help achieve the initially stated objectives.

This relationship may be seen better in terms of an example. In a primary school, a group of teachers acting as curriculum developers want upper-primary students to become more aware of science concepts and principles (statement of objectives). Appropriate knowledge, skills and values (statement of content) have been developed to extend the primary science syllabus and to match the level of student cognitive development. The curriculum developers have suggested that students acquire content to understand base metals and their properties. The question now arises: What do we know about the learning process and our learners so that we can facilitate student acquistion of the curriculum's content?

This is a very real problem for both the curriculum developer and the classroom teacher to resolve. After all, the developer's intention is to provide the best possible guidance to teachers who will implement this curriculum. Consequently curriculum developers who are in close contact with current school practice are more likely to incude appropriate teaching–learning strategies in their curricula.

Continuing the above example, the curriculum developers have suggested, given the situational analysis undertaken and the curriculum intent stated, that a combination of interactive teaching and practical experiments would be appropriate methods for upper-primary students to learn about base metals. It may have been that demonstrations and audio-visual presentations were appropriate or, under certain conditions, perhaps even an inquiry approach. The selection of appropriate teaching–learning strategies reflects the curriculum developer's professional understanding of the task at hand and the needs of students, given the directions from the earlier curriculum elements. Later in this chapter a model is recommended for the selection of appropriate teaching–learning strategies.

The example above may be extrapolated to any curriculum being developed. While in certain areas of formalised learning some methods have become commonly accepted, there may be good arguments for students learning in other ways. An excellent example of this was the way in which business was taught in tertiary institutions. Traditionally, this was by means of formal lectures and some discussion groups. However, a more effective approach was introduced by institutions such as the Harvard Graduate School of Business. Techniques that have subsequently become familiar in business education involve case-study analysis, simulations, small group inquiry, role-playing as well as interactive teaching sessions. These methods have had the effect of making the task of learning business management more realistic and more valuable.

Teaching–learning strategies

There are numerous ways whereby a teacher may facilitate learning in schools. Several of these will be examined here briefly, although a more detailed and broader analysis may be obtained by consulting other sources. J. G. Saylor, W. Alexander and A. J. Lewis (1981:271–94) have a very comprehensive catalogue of teaching models and include such strategies as lectures, discussion–questioning, viewing–listening, inquiry, instructional systems, programmed instruction, practice and drill, role-playing, simulations, community activities, group investigation, jurisprudential, independent learning and synectics. In many ways, this group of strategies is similar to those analysed in some depth by B. Joyce & M. Weil now in the fourth edition of their well-known book *Models of Teaching* (1992).

Experience and research indicate that a *variety* of methods is important for effective teaching and therefore all teachers should have an effective repertoire of teaching–learning strategies. Unfortunately, there is also evidence to suggest that teachers use a narrow range of strategies, even though their teaching could be enhanced if they were to employ more methods.

The need for variety of teaching–learning strategies is taken up by numerous curriculum writers and educational researchers (Zais, 1976; Pratt, 1980; Joyce & Weil, 1992; Brady, 1992; Saylor, Alexander & Lewis, 1981) and the literature suggests that three arguments support this position.

1 Not all students learn equally well when the same strategies are employed. For example, some students prefer to learn through an inquiry method, while others favour an expository approach.
2 Certain teaching–learning methods are more applicable to particular situations. Lectures, for example, are not as appropriate when one is trying to develop student self-concepts as small group work or individualised tasks. No one strategy is appropriate, or can hope to be appropriate, to all learning contexts.
3 No single method is superior, particularly in terms of student performance, to another in all learning situations. One may be more efficient in one situation and less effective in another. For example, lectures

are very efficient use of teaching resources and may assist an educational institution to distribute resources more efficiently. But lectures may not produce effective student understanding and application of certain skills, as in a science experiment. Consequently, strategies must be matched to objectives so that the most efficient and effective one is selected.

The following are some of the more significant teaching–learning strategies available to teachers in schools. When examining each category of method, consider the advantages and disadvantages of each approach as well as the essential features involved. Furthermore, it is useful to view this variety of strategies as a problem-solving device to overcome the difficulties experienced in classroom teaching. If, for example, a teaching strategy is not working effectively, you should reflect upon whether it is appropriate to the learning context. Using the model (figure 8.3) outlined later in this chapter, you may locate a more appropriate teaching strategy. Using that model, or a simailar procedure, is the way by which curriculum developers should have selected appropriate teaching–learning strategies to meet their curriculum's intentions.

When considering a variety of teaching methods one should also distinguish between different categories, as well as within the same category in order to locate the most appropriate strategies. The principal groupings of teaching–learning strategies are:

1 Expository teaching.
2 Interactive teaching.
3 Small group teaching/discussion.
4 Inquiry teaching/problem solving.
5 Individualisation.
6 Models of reality.

Let us briefly examine each of these categories of teaching–learning strategies in terms of their nature, examples, advantages and disadvantages. However it should be noted that this is but a cursory analysis and is undertaken to assist the curriculum developer to be more effective in recommending an appropriate match between content and learning activities. An extensive literature and research base exists to provide more information on effective teaching–learning strategies which should be consulted. For the beginning teacher useful sources include Cole & Chan, 1987; Barry & King, 1988; Reynolds, 1989; Saylor, Alexander & Lewis, 1981; and Joyce & Weil, 1992.

1 Expository teaching

This method involves the transmission of information in a single direction from a source to learners. The source may take a variety of forms (books, television, persons), although it is commonly a teacher in a classroom. Learners are essentially passive receivers of information in this strategy. Common examples of expository teaching are lectures, demonstrations, set reading tasks and audio-visual presentations.

Efficiency and effectiveness of resources are hallmarks of expository teaching. A single source, a lecturer, for example, could provide the necessary information to groups of several hundred/thousand students simultaneously. The space available and the level of technology would be the controlling factors. Continuing the above example, a person could lecture to a group, of say 400 students, in a large lecture theatre. Through closed-circuit television this same lecture could be transmitted to students in nearby lecture rooms and through satellite or cable to students in distant places.

The new open learning university-level programs (TVOL) transmitted through the ABC are an excellent example of this method. Early analysis of student participation suggests that this is a significantly more popular approach to university education than was previously believed. This approach may also assist the Commonwealth government address the large numbers of students currently unable to obtain places in our universities. Indeed we have witnessed the Commonwealth government allocate substantial funds to create what will become, in effect, Australia's open university primarily utilising the technology of television.

Students receiving this information should be observing and listening to the best information synthesised from various sources and research and, hopefully, presented in an easily learnable way. The interesting and challenging television lectures on science that Professor Julius Sumner Miller used to provide were a specific example. Certainly some teachers are more effective lecturers than others in their ability to engage learners and enhance effective learning.

It is quite possible that the person delivering the lecture, giving the demonstration or providing the audio-visual presentation, is the most knowledgeable person available on that subject. In a one- or two-hour presentation, a student could acquire material that would take many hours of searching and reading in the library and hence this is very efficient for the learner as well for the curriculum provider.

Finally, through the use of expository teaching, instructors may feel confident that they have covered the course. When they are in control of the dissemination of content they know that, at least in terms of information dissemination, the curriculum's objectives have been met and students have been exposed to the curriculum's intent. The final effectiveness of the learning, of course, rests with the learner.

However, expository teaching does have many limitations as well. These methods emphasise passive learning behaviour on the part of students. Psychological studies suggest that passive learning methods may be relatively ineffective as the student may lack close association with the material to be learnt. Similarly, psychological experiments have also demonstrated that the retention rate of information from these sources, particularly lectures, tends to be low over periods of time. And where the information is presented poorly, expository teaching suffers greatly in terms of learning effectiveness.

Finally, students receive minimal immediate feedback and hence are not aware of the accuracy of their learning. Students who participate in forms of distance education have shown they prefer those forms of external study that provide opportunities for quicker feedback and interaction with teachers. Recent research (Hattie, 1992) shows that feedback to learners has one of the most powerful effects upon student learning.

> . . . the most powerful single moderator that enhances student achievement is feedback. The simplest prescription for improving education must be 'dollops of feedback'. (1992:9)

Overall, expository teaching is very efficient in terms of the use of teaching resources and addressing the curriculum, but generally less effective in terms of student learning.

2 Interactive teaching

Similar in nature to expository teaching, the essential difference with interactive teaching is the deliberate encouragement of interaction between learner and teacher. This usually takes the form of question–reaction episodes interdispersed with expository information. Sometimes known as the discussion or question–discussion technique, it incorporates the successful features of expository teaching with interactive and feedback elements. Essentially learners are more active in this approach and thinking skills are enhanced through the interactive element.

This teaching approach is found commonly in Australian classrooms and examples include classroom teaching, tutorials, seminars and group discussions. A typical example of interactive teaching is a teacher, with a class of 20–35 students, providing information through verbal and audio-visual means and interacting with students. At appropriate times question–answer episodes occur, invariably initiated by the teacher but also by students. In these instances feedback is given to learners and judgments are made by both teacher and learner as to the effectiveness of the learning incident.

The advantages of interactive teaching usually overcome most of the disadvantages of expository teaching while retaining many of the advantages of the latter. Interactive teaching incorporates effective and efficient use of resources, provision of immediate feedback, more active learner participation and more opportunities for remedial and extension work. The immediacy of feedback assists effective learning and is further enhanced when it can be initiated by the learner and is consequently particularly powerful (Hattie, 1992). Thus the opportunity for teacher–learner interaction is the major advantage of this category of method.

This method is extremely popular in schools for it allows classroom teachers not only to address curriculum requirements and to enhance student learning, but also to control students more effectively. Interactive teaching is also a mainstay of schools as some strategies, such as lectures, are largely inappropriate teaching–learning strategies for some learners. For example we would not expect Year 2 students to learn about family and societal roles through lectures, though television may be an appropriate medium.

However, interactive teaching is less effective in the utilisation of resources. For example, smaller groups of students are taught in the one venue and at the same time than by the lecture method and hence more resources—teachers, rooms, audio-visual machines—are required for interactive teaching. If a teacher were to have several classes in the same subject and at the same level, then the interactive method requires repeat teaching. This is clearly inefficient use of time and labour even if preparation time is saved through repeats. Where repeat sessions do not occur then high preparation time is also a disadvantage. Consequently interactive teaching is less efficient in terms of teaching resources, but for most educators this is more than offset by the enhanced quality of student learning and the nature of teacher–learner interactions.

3 Small-group teaching/discussion

The principal feature of this strategy involves the division of a class into small groups which work relatively independently to achieve a goal. In most cases this task is addressed through a group discussion procedure. Here the role of the teacher changes from one of transmitter of knowledge to coordinator of activities and guide to information and its processing. In small groups students are usually set learning tasks within the classroom context. This may involve, for example, students discussing a topical issue in social studies, resolving a problem in science or raising questions about a novel's main character. Through the interaction engendered by group discussion students acquire the skills of planning and organising work, developing arguments, sharing knowledge, dividing tasks, adopting compromise positions and so forth. Examples of small-group teaching include group discussions, some tutorials, some seminars, 'buzz' groups, brainstorming groups and so forth.

The advantages of small-group teaching revolve largely around the interactive benefits acquired by students. The skills mentioned above are learnt through student–student and student–teacher interaction. For many students, small groups are the only school opportunity for them to acquire these skills effectively. Students have much to learn from each other and as such this strategy should not be dismissed lightly. Similarly the ability to learn cooperatively, especially to solve problems through working in groups, is an extremely valuable skill.

One of the more significant lessons educators have learnt from the 1980s is to move away from excessively competitive, individualistic approaches to learning towards more cooperative, group-based learning approaches. Small group activities, particularly discussion groups, are an excellent way to achieve this goal. Curriculum developers should be deliberately finding ways to include this type of strategy in the curricula they are devising.

While many teachers use small-group teaching, particularly at secondary and tertiary levels in subjects such as English, social studies, history and legal studies, there is nevertheless considerable resistance to utilising this strategy in many school subjects such as mathematics and science. Apart from requiring a changed teacher role, the strategy is invariably time consuming and appears to cover little content, particularly that which is set in the curriculum. However, more up-to-date curriculum developers have realised the value of group work, both in terms of skills and the values they engender, and incorporated such activities deliberately within their curriculum.

Some teachers have expressed concern at the apparently unproductive nature of small-group work, especially when measured by the volume of noise generated. While students don't require complete silence in order to learn, and they can't participate unless they talk to each other, more effective group work is kept task-oriented by teachers. As well, teachers need to watch that student attitudes, expressed effectively through interaction in the small group, do not become little more than the pooling of ignorance. As well this strategy is invariably disruptive until students are experienced, somewhat haphazard in progress, often boring for many students, frequently non-task-oriented and certainly conducive to creating classroom disruptions.

Nevertheless, recent developments suggest that one thing we can learn from other countries is the ability to cooperate more effectively and to solve problems in groups. Perhaps, it is suggested by many, our society, and our educational system, have promoted excessive individualism and individualistic competition at the expense of solving problems together. Business and industry are moving in that direction and now it is time for our school system to promote the virtues of cooperative group work. Teachers may find some opposition from students but this largely reflects their inexperience with this teaching–learning strategy.

4 Inquiry teaching/problem solving

The hallmark of this strategy is that learners are actively engaged in determining answers to questions or resolving problems. Instead of teachers providing information for learners to digest, students are first posed a problem, a question to solve, a dilemma to resolve or an issue to address, which they learn about through the process of finding an answer. A variety of inquiry strategies are available and the inquiry approach may be used in almost any teaching–learning situation and with any subject matter. Inquiry teaching typically involves learners in four stages of activity which may be conducted relatively independently, in pairs or in larger groups.

1 Problem awareness: creation of doubt in students' minds.
2 Forming tentative hypotheses or possible solution to the problem or issue by the learner.
3 Research and collection of data to test those hypotheses.
4 Forming conclusions based on the evidence collected and accept or reject the hypothesis/possible solution.

A fifth stage, generalising conclusions and applying them to new data, is sometimes included in this strategy. In all of these stages, the essential feature is that the learner is actively involved in resolving the problem while the teacher serves more as a facilitator to enhance the problem-solving process.

Sometimes called enquiry teaching, discovery learning, problem solving, inductive learning, or even the scientific method, inquiry teaching has received remarkably and surprisingly little support in Australia's classrooms. This appears to be mainly because it is so different from interactive teaching, the staple teaching–learning method of Australian schools and because it appears to involve more work for teachers. However, this should not be the case for there are numerous advantages for both learners and teachers when using inquiry/problem-solving methods.

Inquiry teaching–learning is equally appropriate to a wide variety of academic subjects and themes in school. One could, for example, apply this method to social studies (Why was Australia settled by the British?); English (What impact did Tom Collins have upon Australian literature?); science (what happens to sugar when it comes in contact with heated nitric acid?); maths (What is the height of a building given certain information) and so forth. In all of these cases the role of the teacher changes to become more of facilitator and provider of resources, while the learner becomes more actively engaged in resolving the problem. And therein lies its main advantage and disadvantage.

The main advantage of inquiry teaching is the pervasive nature of the learning that occurs within students. Learners participating in the inquiry/problem-solving approach are more likely to associate closely with their learning task and, by so doing, enhance the depth of their understanding. That is, learners who resolve problems for themselves retain that understanding more effectively because of the close identification with acquiring that information. In this way students develop a range of inquiry-based skills which may be translated to realistic situations in later life. Finally, the inquiry strategy promotes a logical, rational way of thinking, a positive approach to problem solving and more systematic approaches to decision-making. Where this strategy is linked with groups of learners, the problem solving approach is potentially more effective.

Nevertheless inquiry teaching/problem solving is clearly not popular in schools, at least with many teachers, and this may be attributed to its numerous perceived disadvantages to teachers. It is an extremely time-consuming procedure when undertaken in classrooms and this places it in direct competition with other strategies attempting to address the demands of heavily knowledge-based curricula. The amount of content covered in, say, science using the inquiry strategy would be but a fraction of that completed using expository or interactive strategies. Initially it would also be more time consuming in terms of teacher preparation and student lack of familiarity with the procedure.

Classroom teachers often reject the inquiry strategy because it requires a changed role on their behalf. No longer are they the source of knowledge, the arbiter of right and wrong, but more the provider of materials and advice. In this transition, control of learning changes from teacher to students and this may be perceived as a threatening situation for many teachers. Research has shown us that change, even perceived change, is often regarded negatively if only because it requires us to do things, and think about things, differently from current practice. We tend to prefer the security of what we know and are familiar with and hence our resistance to change.

Furthermore, some school subjects are clearly not suited to an inquiry approach. Elements of curricula within industrial arts, home economics, physical education, science and so forth are obviously inappropriate to student experimentation if only for concern of student safety. Allowing students to inquire into the use of power saws in an industrial arts class on woodwork, for example, would clearly be inappropriate. Nevertheless many subjects are appropriate and teachers could well give greater consideration to the inclusion of the inquiry strategy in the repertoire of teaching–learning strategies found in their curricula. Curriculum developers should take a proactive position with this strategy and, as with the small group strategy, incorporate it, where appropriate, within the curriculum they are developing.

A variation of inquiry which emphasises a team or group approach to problem solving is known as group investigation (Saylor et al., 1981:288).

Less emphasis is placed here upon the scientific approach to data collection, although data analysis is important, while its strength lies with group cooperation and teamwork to investigate the problem. As mentioned above, this type of activity offers much for the future when extrapolated to adult, working environments.

5 Individualisation

The essential features of individualised learning are that learners complete tasks appropriate to their ability level and proceed with this learning at their own pace. The focus of responsibility for learning changes from the teacher to the learner and considerable learning is undertaken independently of others. Two forms of individualisation have been quite commonly found in schools in the past (though less evident recently) and they are equally appropriate to curricula in other educational situations such as TAFE and adult learning situations.

    a   Highly structured individualised learning kits. These offer learners the opportunity to proceed through a set sequence of learning tasks at an individual pace and at an appropriate level of complexity and difficulty. Diagnostic tests are frequently employed to determine the level of entry behaviour. Feedback is obtained by tests undertaken throughout the set tasks. Programmed instruction of various forms are examples and even the well-known and long-established Science Research Associates (SRA) materials used in primary schools could be included. The self-paced learning modules developed at many TAFE colleges, such as panel-beating skills, spray-painting and word-processing skills, are also examples. Students in hospitality studies programs within TAFE often experience some form of structured individual learning.

        One important feature of programmed instruction is the division of the learning tasks into small, sequenced units of study. Students working through these units receive immediate feedback as to the effectiveness of their learning. In this way the stimulus–response nature of programmed instruction carefully controls learning. More recently a push has been made to develop competencies for many areas of learning and the relationship between programmed individualised instruction and competencies is close.

    b   'Unstructured' or independent learning. In this situation, the focus is upon learners resolving problems of interest by essentially finding out for themselves and using the teacher as a facilitator in a relatively unstructured context. Little formal structure and minimal stimulus input are usually evident, although they may vary considerably with teachers. Learning contracts are typically used to provide some form of structure to the learning and to guide students as they work. In this strategy, intellectual independence is a desired goal and is enhanced through practice.

An example of an unstructured learning situation in a primary school might involve a teacher seeking to facilitate independent learning skills in social studies. Instead of teaching a section of content through an interactive strategy, a curriculum developer might suggest students learn by studying the topic through an individualised learning contract. Students could be given an individual learning task to resolve the problem 'Where do I come from?'. They would be encouraged to develop a four-generation family history through a learning-contract approach that requires them to investigate the problem for themselves. The nature of their learning would be set by the conditions agreed to in the individual learning contract.

Alternatively, a teacher may use individualisation to meet the needs of a particular group of students, perhaps the very able or those in need of specific subject-based remediation. Able students, for example, may be given an unstructured task to investigate cell microbiology as an extension to a biology lesson on animal development. Individual learning contracts are most appropriate to include in a curriculum where the developer believes, perhaps through data from a situational analysis, that the users of the curriculum will include many highly able (sometimes called 'gifted') students.

The advantages of individualisation as a teaching–learning strategy are vested almost entirely with the learner. Student learning is powerful where individualisation is perceived as personal resolution of interesting problems. Some of the highly structured materials are not seen as personalised, although they may still be highly relevant to student needs. Unstructured individualisation, however, is invariably highly personalised and problem-oriented and, as such, very effective. In many gifted and talented programs, for example, unstructured individualisation is both commonly used and highly desired as a means of enhancing student skills and knowledge.

Individualisation has the additional advantages of meeting student needs more appropriately and allowing for students to progress at their own pace. Such tasks may even be undertaken outside of school hours and location and student self-direction may be enhanced considerably.

Many teachers resist introducing individualisation into their classes as it requires substantially more teacher time for organisation and preparation. As some of my students, who are practising teachers, have said, 'But this means writing 30 programs instead of one!' While individualisation does not have to be taken to that extreme, it certainly will involve the teacher in more initial course restructuring and lesson preparation. If individual learning contracts are used, in conjunction with other teaching–learning strategies, this may overcome some teacher objections.

Furthermore, teachers have expresed some concern about individualisation as a teaching strategy as they have less direct control over student learning, particularly student exposure to content. In this situation the teacher may be unsure as to the appropriateness and breadth of the content material acquired by the learner. For extension work this may be less of a disadvantage, but if teachers were to divide content into sections for individualised work, concern may be evident over the students' total coverage of designated content.

Finally, individualisation appears to be the very antithesis of group or collective work appproaches and excessive emphasis on an independent, individual approach to learning may well prove counterproductive to effective learner outcomes. Here is a role for the curriculum developer to judiciously determine which teaching–learning strategies are the most appropriate given current conditions and contexts.

6 Models of reality

An alternative way to facilitate effective learning within students is to involve them in learning situations that are as real life as possible. Sometimes it is preferable to participate in 'real life' activities (such as work experience), but for many reasons this option is frequently not available in schools. Yet we know that most students will learn certain things very effectively if we can expose them to learning activities that are as life-like as possible. In these situations we need to replicate the real world by creating models of the salient features of that world, i.c. create models of reality. Simulations, physical models, games and role-playing are examples of these models. By involving students in experiences that they might encounter in the real world, albeit simplified for pedagogical purposes, learners have the opportunity to obtain a powerful understanding of the situation.

Examples of models of reality (see figure 8.1) range from physical simulations (flight simulators, home economics kitchens) through work models (practice teaching) through simulation games (Monopoly, Starpower) to role-playing exercises of various forms (perhaps involving students in a racial discrimination exercise so that they feel what it is like to be discriminated against). Figure 8.1 also illustrates the wide variety of models of reality, ranging from high reality, physically based models to low reality, abstract models, that are available to teachers.

In those models that have a high degree of reality structured within them, students learn in a situation that is as close as possible to a real life situation or context. Airlines, for example, have both flight-deck and

Figure 8.1 Models of reality

High reality ————————————————————————— Abstract reality

Physical models	Work Models	Games/simulations	Role-playing
Flight simulator	Practice teaching	Starpower	Students adopt roles
Architectural model	Articled clerkship	Monopoly	and act out situations
Ship simulator	Apprenticeship	Test cricket	to reflect: poverty, job
			interview, share
			trading.

cabin simulators that can replicate any known flight situation including crashes. Cabin crew and flight crew experience regular training and testing situations using the simulators so that they will know exactly what to do, particularly in cases of emergency. Many police and military forces have constructed simulation activities for combating terrorist attacks and similar emergency situations.

In schools, physical models of reality are relatively uncommon, usually because they are very expensive to provide. One example, however, is a kitchen set up in a home economics classroom. Here teachers have attempted to replicate a household kitchen in order that students might learn to cook in as real a context as possible. Similarly a business studies class may be set up as an office, serving counter, computer station and so forth. However, these are expensive options and many schools cannot afford such luxuries.

At the other extreme, a classroom teacher may wish to develop empathic attitudes in students by involving learners in a role-playing exercise based on people with physical deformities. Similarly an economics teacher might wish to familiarise students with the workings of the Australian Stock Exchange by simulating share-trading activities.

The essential procedural steps in models of reality commence with the teacher establishing a scenario (what is happening), students agreeing to abide by the rules of the model, and then a lengthy period of participation. All forms of simulations and role-play should also finish with a thorough debriefing session. Debriefing is a very important feature of any model of reality (especially role-play and simulations) and must be incorporated within the curriculum. And as part of the learning exercise students can be involved in researching the nature of the models they are using. In a simulation on share trading, for example, students could research what it means to be defined as a trader, what shares are, how they are traded in a modern computer system, what sorts of experiences people might encounter when moves are made on the exchange, and so forth.

modern computer system, what sorts of experiences people might encounter when moves are made on the exchange, and so forth.

Models of reality are very powerful learning strategies and their advantages are numerous. Handled well, they involve the learner thoroughly in the situation concerned, and by attempting to deal with reality the student learns effectively and pervasively. Models of reality also provide learning situations that are often difficult to comprehend in other ways. Teaching values in a classroom, learning how to cook a sponge correctly or how to steer a super tanker are difficult to achieve effectively by lectures, discussions and so forth. For some forms of learning to be effective, the student simply has to *learn by doing.*

Some schools have developed simulation games to teach less cognitively able and less cooperative students by involving them in a more *'experiential' form of learning.* To be taught the medieval system in history, for example, through lectures, discussions or audio-visual material may well be very efficient, but for many students it would be quintessentially insipid and boring. But to create a simulation game which re-created knights, peasants, merchants and lords undertaking their daily lives many hundreds of years ago is quite a different learning experience. Such a simulation was created for a group of less able students who experienced considerable difficulties learning the curriculum through expository and interactive teaching methods. But a thoughtful teacher adapted the curriculum for students to participate in a medieval simulation and the result was one of the most powerful learning experiences those students had ever encountered.

Yet the disadvantages of replicating reality have meant that for many students in schools, models of reality are almost unknown teaching–learning strategies. Teachers often don't employ them because they are very time consuming, have questionable learner effects in terms of achieving curriculum goals, require substantial additional teacher preparation and usually demand teachers change their standard classroom procedures. Consequently many students have little exposure to models of reality, and when they do, they often act inappropriately.

While for many training situations these strategies are essential (for example, flight-deck and cabin simulators are an essential part of airline training before crew and attendants take to the air), in schools they are perceived more as optional and certainly as expensive and hence are employed rarely. School timetables often don't allow for role-playing and simulations to occur (it is usually difficult to start and stop a simulation within a 40-minute period) and many teachers are unaware how to conduct these strategies effectively. Consequently models of reality remain, in schools, one of the most underutilised, yet effective, learning–teaching strategies available.

Other teaching–learning strategies

Some writers distinguish *practice/drill* as a separate strategy (Saylor et al., 1981; Marsh, 1986), although they may be considered more a method of reinforcement than a learning strategy. Once a student has learnt something, through one of the above strategies, it may be deemed prudent to reinforce that learning through practice/drill. The important point here is that learning is usually acquired elsewhere and the practice or drill serves to consolidate that learning. In schools, practice and drill are continuously used in subjects such as maths, physical education, dance and so forth. The reinforcement role they serve is important though this is usually more the responsibility of the teacher, as user of a curriculum, than the curriculum developer.

A useful way of summarising the teaching–learning strategies discussed in this chapter is to place then in perspective with each other, such as in a continuum (figure 8.2). At one extreme of learning strategies on the continuum below we could include learning through reality. Learning by participating in a real situation is certainly a powerful way of acquiring information, skills and values. However, it is one over which curriculum developers and teachers generally have no control as it is beyond the domain of the educational institution concerned. While reality may be an effective teacher it is rarely an efficient, systematic and thorough teacher where learning through a specifically designed curriculum can be extrapolated from one context to another.

In recent years, therefore, we have witnessed a significant trend towards formalised learning situations in many institutions involved in some form of education. Take, for example, learning how to sail a yacht. One could learn through participating in real situations—through trial-and-error as we call it. But does learning to sail on a mirror or similar centre-board dingy prepare one effectively for sailing an ocean racing sloop? To some degree the answer is yes, but if one participated in a sailing school and learnt how to sail through learning the sailing cur-

Figure 8.2 Teaching–learning strategies

Low reality   High reality
High teacher participation ——————————— Low teacher participation
Low learner involvement   High learner involvement

Exposition   Interactive   Small   Individualisation   Inquiry   Models of
              teaching   groups   reality

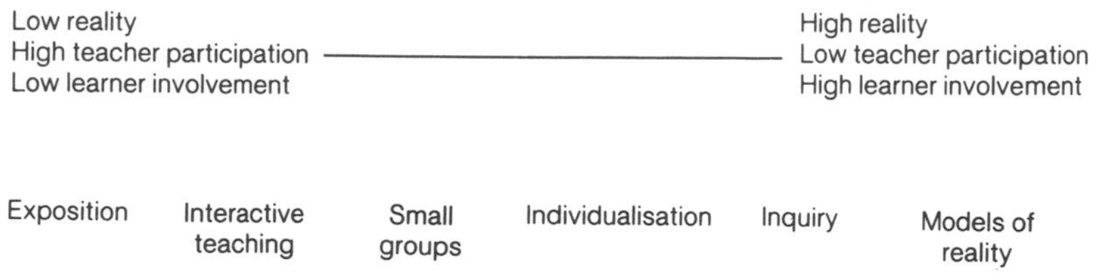

riculum, then one should have acquired generic and specific skills transferable to many different contexts.

Criteria for selecting learning activities

How does one select appropriate learning activities from this array of teaching–learning strategies to include in a curriculum? Obviously not all activities are equally applicable to all teaching situations. Yet it is equally obvious that teachers have preferred methods which they use constantly, almost to the exclusion of all others. At this point it would be useful to reflect on the arguments forwarded earlier in this chapter for using a variety of strategies.

It is my belief that curriculum developers have a responsibility to advocate appropriate teaching–learning strategies for a curriculum even if they believe that classroom teachers will make their own strategy selections based upon their own criteria. While teacher professionalism and autonomy should not be diminished, the curriculum developer may have very important reasons for recommending particular strategies. To achieve the desired empathic intent in a history curriculum, for example, a curriculum developer may recommend specific strategies which would achieve that intent, such as the use of simulations, role-play, small-group discussions and so forth. Using such teaching–learning methods would help history teachers achieve the desired intent of empathic understanding of a particular historical era and context.

If teachers wished to achieve the effect as outlined in a curriculum document they would employ the recommended teaching–learning strategies in the manner suggested, if that was possible, even if they clashed with the teacher's standard procedures. Ultimately, however, it is the teacher's professional decision as to which specific strategies will be employed to teach the content in the curriculum.

Several authors have posited criteria for the purpose of selecting appropriate methods in a school situation. McNeil (1985) argued for philosophical criteria, psychological criteria, technological criteria, criteria from pressure groups and practicality as a criterion in the procedure for selecting teaching–learning strategies. While these criteria are valuable, some of them lack direct practical application for school curricula.

Zais (1976:355–64) suggested aims, goals and objectives; foundation commitments; content; and students' experience as appropriate criteria. Brady (1992), however, argues for the selection criteria to include variety, scope, validity, appropriateness and relevance as means by which to judge learning activities.

When selecting criteria it may be useful to employ Wheeler's 'principles of learning'. Learning theory can provide an insight into how students learn and therefore help match appropriate learning activities.

However, there is probably more agreement amongst educators over the principles of learning than there is about learning theories. Wheeler's 'principles' are included below (1967:130):

1 Learning is an active process in which the learner must be involved.
2 Learning proceeds more effectively if, as well as being an active participant, the learner understands what he is learning.
3 Learning is considerably affected by individual goals, values and motives.
4 Frequent repetition of response to a class of situations is important in learning skills.
5 Immediate reinforcement promotes learning. Cognitive feedback is most effective when time lapse is minimal.
6 The wider the range of experiences presented to the learner, the more likely are generalisation and discrimination to occur.
7 Behaviour is a function of the learner's perceptions.
8 Similar situations may elicit different reactions from different learners.
9 While transfer does occur, it is usually much less than people think. What there is may usually be attributed to similarities between the tasks involved. Both likenesses between situations and possibilities of transfer should be pointed out specifically.
10 Group atmosphere affects both learning product and accrued satisfaction.
11 Individual differences affect learning. Such differences are both biogenic and sociocultural.
12 All learnings are multiple. Although focus may be on one particular (desired) outcome, other learnings take place simultaneously.

With these principles in mind, what is a useful procedure for selecting appropriate learning activities? Figure 8.3 suggests that a 'percolating' procedure is helpful to teachers seeking to select the most effective teaching–learning strategies for curriculum development and for the teaching of a curriculum's content in their classrooms. In this model, the process of percolating through the four levels is set within the broader

Figure 8.3   Selection of learning activities

Objectives
↓
Learners
↓
Resources
↓
Constraints

context of the curriculum conception favoured by curriculum developers. Thus those who prefer a more academic discipline/cognitive skills perspective to curriculum tend to favour more expository and interactive teaching–learning strategies. While this may appear logical, curriculum developers should take cognisance of preferred learner styles which will encourage teachers to balance the emphasis upon strategies. Certainly curriculum developers should encourage teachers to employ a variety of teaching–learning strategies in the application of a curriculum.

The model advocated in figure 8.3 suggests four criteria that curriculum developers may use which can serve the function of sifting through a range of learning activities to determine the most appropriate for a curriculum. Furthermore, teachers may wish to apply the same criteria to a curriculum when applied in a specific context. These criteria are objectives, appropriateness, resources available and constraints.

Objectives

The first barrier or sifting layer that curriculum developers must pass learning activities through is to determine if they can achieve the stated objectives. Many learning activities are available to the curriculum developer and the teacher to select from but only a few may be appropriate to facilitate the curriculum's intention. Thus the first of the four barriers to pass through is to determine if the learning activities can possibly achieve the curriculum's objectives.

For example, if a science curriculum's objective requires students to understand the operation of scientific equipment such as a Bunsen burner, then the interactive and expository strategies would be appropriate, although the inquiry would not. However, if the same science curriculum's objectives sought students to operate a pipette correctly and safely, then the interactive method, small-group methods, and perhaps individualisation would be applicable.

Similarly, if the curriculum objective seeks to emphasise cultural empathy in literature, then inquiry and models of reality teaching–learning strategies would be far more appropriate than expository and interactive strategies. In the end, it is important for the curriculum developer to determine exactly what the stated objectives seek to achieve when deciding the most suitable learning activities for inclusion in the curriculum. In turn, this process reinforces the need for well-constructed and clearly phrased statements of curriculum intent.

The major point to be made in applying the objectives criterion of the method-selection algorithm is that the type of method or techniques selected by the curriculum developer is primarily dependent upon the nature of the objectives involved. As there are many teaching–learning strategies available and many appear to meet the curriculum's intentions, it is important to limit the range of potential techniques to those which suit the objective as a first step. This selection process will further reduce the number of strategies as subsequent steps of the algorithm are applied.

Learner appropriateness

Having limited the range of potential methods to those which satisfy the needs of the curriculum's objectives, it is important for curriculum developers to consider which of the remaining methods are consistent with the characteristics of the students involved, namely, the students' interests, abilities and levels of development. In one sense this criterion will already have been considered when the objective itself was decided upon. In applying the criterion of attainability to the selection of objectives (see chapter 6), the astute curriculum developer would have taken such obvious characteristics as age, general ability and stage of intellectual development into account when deciding on the appropriateness of the objective for the group of students in mind.

It is also possible to relate learning activities to the concepts argued by developmental psychologists such as Jean Piaget. Here, some activities would be more appropriate to a particular level of learner development than others. Expository and inquiry strategies, for example, may be more appropriate to the formal operations level, although for different reasons. In earlier stages, drill and repetition may be more appropriate as might individualisation and small groups. After considering appropriateness of the strategies to the learner, the available pool of methods has been further reduced in number.

Resources

Having considered the nature of the curriculum's objectives and the characteristics of the learner, curriculum developers and teachers should apply the criterion of resource availability. Some methods will require access to hardware (for example, film projectors, computers, tape-recorders) and software (for example, films, computer programs, tapes). But do these resources exist within the institution and are they available at the required time? An objective that required students to observe the action of the ocean waves in practice is extremely difficult for students in Alice Springs! Clearly, the availability of needed resources is a significant criterion to be applied to the selection of methods. When each potential method is assessed in terms of this criterion, the number of viable methods remaining is likely to be reduced substantially further.

Constraints

Closely allied to the criterion of resource availability is the notion that in all teaching–learning situations there is a number of constraints that operate to further reduce the choice of the ideal (or most appropriate) methods. Perhaps the most significant constraint in schools is time. For example, after having considered all the earlier criteria, one may have decided that an excursion or field trip is the best way to put across your objective(s). However, an excursion may take half a day and antagonise some of your colleagues, while an audio-visual presentation may have nearly the same impact in just twenty minutes and with considerably less opposition.

Another constraint might be a teacher's recognition of his/her own limitations. For example, some teachers may feel uncomfortable with the noise generated by group discussions and simulations, or the seeming chaos resulting from individualised self-pacing. This, of course, further reduces the choice of appropriate methods available for a given objective. Other constraints to be considered when selecting learning activities in a school setting include:

1 Finances available.
2 Availability of staff (for example, for fieldwork, team teaching).
3 School policy.
4 Central organisation policy (for example, New South Wales Department of School Education policy, Catholic Education Office policy, Northwest Region policy).

This model or algorithm suggests how developers might proceed in selecting appropriate learning activities in their curricula. The model further suggests that developers have an intimate knowledge of the institution for which the curriculum is being developed in order to select methods effectively. And while the examples cited relate to schools, the selection criteria are equally appropriate to other organisations involved in curriculum development.

Organising learning activities

Little research or writing is available in the curriculum field that deals with the issue of organising or structuring learning activities. In part this is due to the strong tradition of classroom teachers determining the appropriate learning activities for their students. Teachers claim, quite reasonably, that their experience, their knowledge of the learners' abilities and the school context places them in a unique position to organise learning activities. Their professionalism, through their understanding of their students, the curriculum and the learning context, suggests to them the most appropriate organisation of learning activities.

As well, the situation is compounded by the complex nature of learning and the variety of influences that affect individuals' effective learning. Finally, learning is acquired over an extensive period of time and hence it is difficult to distinguish between influential variables. In all, then, the substantial number of variables and their complex interrelationships over time make it difficult to determine the precise effectiveness of single activities and how they should be organised in a curriculum. Nevertheless, three criteria proposed by Tyler (1949) have become accepted in the field as a rule-of-thumb basis for organising learning activities. They are useful for curriculum developers to consider in their planning and for teachers to incorporate in their practice. They are:

continuity
sequence
integration

Continuity

Tyler (1949) defined continuity as ' . . . the vertical reiteration of major curriculum elements'. This means that if an objective emphasises particular processes such as inquiry skills, then these skills require repetition at various points along the curriculum in order that learners may have repeated exposure to and opportunity to practise this activity.

Sequence

This concept is an extension of continuity. Sequence requires that the activity not only be repeated, but also that it progresses from simple to complex. This hierarchical organisation of learning activities may occur within a subject or theme over a period such as a year, as well as progress through many years of schooling. Thus, with reading the basic skills are acquired before complex vocabulary is added and later sophisticated comprehension is undertaken. Taba (1962:296) refers to sequencing as 'cumulative learning', a term which seems quite appropriate.

Integration

The third criterion suggested by Tyler refers to the horizontal relationship between learning activities. Tyler's intention was that at any point in time, the learning activities are so related that they provide a unified and integrated experience for the learner. For example, activities in English literature may involve associated mapping skills from geography as well as research skills from botany. Traditionally, educators have not performed well according to this criterion, claiming instead that the responsibility for integration lies with the learner. As well, it appears difficult to entice educators out of the shell of their subject areas and so promote integration.

Summary

- Learning activities include those specific activities offered to learners that will allow them to understand curriculum content and so achieve the stated objectives.
- A wide variety of activities, particularly teaching methods, is available and should be used appropriately.
- Curriculum developers should recommend the use of a variety of learning activities which are consistent with the objectives and content.
- Useful learning–teaching strategies include:
  — Expository teaching: flow of information from source to learner.
  — Interactive teaching: incorporating interchange between source and learner.
  — Small-group teaching: emphasises group participation.
  — Inquiry teaching: learners actively engage in resolving problems.
  — Individualisation: completion of tasks appropriate to learner's level of ability.
  — Models of reality: involving learners in replications of the real world.
  — Reality: involves learners, outside educational institutions, learning through experience.
- A model for the selection of appropriate learning activities considers in descending hierarchical order:
  — Objectives.
  — The learner.
  — Resource availability.
  — Constraints.
- The organisation of learning activities, unlike content, has few guidelines based on research and in the literature. Some suggestions include structuring learning activities according to continuity, sequence and integration.

9 Evaluation and assessment

An understanding of the role of evaluation in the designing and redesigning of curriculum . . . is central for the professional teacher who has the autonomy and responsibility to reflect and deliberate about curriculum. (Karen Zumwalt, 1989:179)

This chapter will examine the nature and function of evaluation; define the principal terms involved in the evaluative process; examine a range of measurement instruments briefly; consider two forms of assessment; distinguish between different types of evaluation and provide a model for evaluating curriculum materials. In so doing, this chapter will follow the recommended procedure used when making effective judgments in curriculum, namely, using measurement instruments to collect data, assessing that data and finally making evaluative statements based on the assessed data.

The nature of evaluation

In its broadest sense, *evaluation* is concerned with making judgments about things. When we act as evaluators we attribute 'value' or 'worth' to behaviour, objects or processes. In the wider community, for example, one may make evaluative comments about a play, clothes, a restaurant, a book or someone's behaviour. We may 'enjoy' a play, 'admire' someone's clothes, 'rave' about a restaurant and so forth. Invariably these are rather simple, straightforward comments of value or worth.

To be more effective, however, evaluation requires that judgments be based on appropriate and relevant data. Ineffective evaluation is made upon whim or fancy, even in the broader community context. To say, for example, that a film was 'good' or 'bad' says little unless the basis of these judgments is made. An enjoyable or good film may have a well-written script, tight direction, mood-enhancing music and so forth. These are characteristics of the evaluation upon which judgment can be made subsequently.

In education it is inexcusable to make fanciful evaluations, even if based on the so-called 'intuitive reaction' of experienced teachers. An abundance of data exists upon which evaluations can be made in education and it is incumbent upon all educators to employ such data when making their judgments, particularly about students. Thus, an effective evaluation of a curriculum or a student's performance will be based upon appropriate data and will reflect what that data reveal.

Evaluation in our schools is essentially concerned with two major approaches to making judgments:

1 *Product evaluation* is an evaluation of student performance in a specific learning context. Such an evaluation essentially seeks to determine how well the student has achieved the stated objectives of the learning situation. In this sense the student's performance is seen as a product of the educational experience. A school report is an example of product evaluation.

2 *Process evaluation* examines the experiences and activities involved in the learning situation i.e. making judgments about the process by which students acquired learning or examining the learning experience before it has been concluded. In most cases, process evaluation is used when making judgments about school effectiveness, classroom inter-actions, the curriculum and about the effectiveness of specific pro-grams. For example, process evaluation may be conducted upon the nature of student–teacher interaction, instructional methods, school curricula, a program for gifted students, and so forth.

The difference between 'product' and 'process' evaluations is some-thing of a fine line. Students usually pass through a school, experience a curriculum and then depart. In that sense we can refer to a product, just as we can refer to a student's progress as 'the proof is in the product'. Curriculum evaluation and program evaluation are conceptualised as process evaluations as the activity involved rarely comes to a conclusion in schools, i.e. the curriculum is ongoing. However, if a curriculum or a particular program had been terminated, for example, then a form of product evaluation would be conducted.

Three subcategories of process evaluation are frequently referred to in the literature—curriculum evaluation, teacher evaluation and program evaluation. *Curriculum evaluation* is a relatively recent term that has become well recognised in recent years. It applies the processes of evaluation to the context of the curriculum and, in so doing, somewhat different notions of the evaluative task have emerged, including the following. 'Curriculum evaluation is the process of delineating, obtaining and providing information useful for making decisions and judgments about curricula' (Davis, 1980:49).

> Curriculum evaluation differs from other kinds of educational evaluation in that it focuses upon how *teachers and students interact over a particular curriculum or syllabus* . . . curriculum evaluation involves an examination of the goals, rationale and structure of a teacher's curriculum, a study of the context in which the interactions with students occur (including parent

and community inputs) and an analysis of the interests, motivations and achievements of the students experiencing a particular curriculum. (Marsh, 1986:137)

In still another sense, curriculum evaluation may be seen as the final element in the curriculum process, as in the model of curriculum development advocated in this book. Many curriculum developers would agree that once the content and learning activities elements have been developed from aims, goals and objectives, and evaluation of student performance has occurred, the developer's task is to devise appropriate evaluation procedures to determine if the curriculum has been effective in achieving its intention and if it requires further modification (see figure 3.8 and chapter 3).

Teacher evaluation, the second subcategory of process evaluation, is concerned with an examination of the teacher's performance with a view to providing useful feedback. Often conducted as a self-evaluation, this approach provides an insight into the dynamics of the teaching–learning situation and, as such, can provide data to enhance teacher performance. In recent years, under the pressure of greater community accountability and driven by economic rationalism, school systems have been moving towards a performance-based approach to teacher evaluation. The 1990s will see further moves in this direction as educational systems respond to economically driven pressures.

Program evaluation may be seen as both a form of process evaluation and as something broader in the wider community. Outside of education, program evaluation is used as a means of determining the effectiveness, efficiency and acceptability of any form of program such as an AIDS awareness program, a poverty relief program, a group housing program and so forth (see McLaughlin & Phillips, 1991). Within education we can use the term in a similar way as in the case of evaluating the effectiveness of a new writing program in primary schools or a reading program for NESB students (non-English speaking background). Overlap with curriculum evaluation can, and does, occur as educators frequently do not differentiate between curriculum and non-curriculum programs in their evaluations.

In this chapter we shall concentrate upon the *evaluation of student performance*, as this is a fundamental task of any teacher as well as curriculum developers. To a lesser degree process evaluation will be dealt with, and some specific comments will be made about curriculum evaluation. Towards the end of this chapter specific attention is paid to *curriculum evaluation*, particularly as it forms an integral part of the curriculum development process. However, it should be noted that a vast literature exists in the area of curriculum evaluation which is not addressed here (though numerous references are cited) but which is recommended to be consulted.

Functions of evaluation

Why bother to evaluate in schools? Why be concerned about student performance or how well the curriculum is working? After all, teachers' intuitive understanding of how well students perform in their classes is often very accurate (or is it a self-fulfilling prophecy?). Certainly product evaluation is one of most teachers' least preferred activities and curriculum evaluation as well as teacher evaluation are positively resisted in schools, if only due to insufficient time and resources.

Yet all educators need to regard evaluation as both a necessary and integral function of their teaching. And for curriculum developers, there is no option to providing guidelines and directions for evaluation in the production of a final curriculum document. There are several powerful reasons for educators to become more familiar with and employ evaluation in purposeful, useful ways in schools.

1 Evaluation is essential to provide *feedback to learners*. Recent research (Hattie, 1992) has emphasised the valuable contribution evaluation makes to student learning through the provision of feedback on student performance. This means more than providing test and examination scores, project results and so forth, it involves useful information that addresses student strengths and weaknesses and how to improve their performance.

2 Evaluation is essential in determining how well learners have *achieved the stated objectives*. This is a prime function of employing evaluative techniques in any learning situation. Where objectives are not stated specifically as such, evaluation is concerned with determining the nature of student outcomes.

3 Evaluation provides information to *improve curricula*. Evaluative data, collected during a unit of study, will provide the basis for changes that will make the curriculum more effective in meeting objectives. Effective educators and curriculum developers constantly seek to improve their curricula.

4 Information from evaluation is employed by *students in personal decision making*. In particular, future courses of action concerning studies, employment, a career and the like are based on evaluative data given as feedback to students from their participation in a curriculum.

5 Evaluation provides useful information to curriculum developers to *clarify the stated objectives*. Feedback obtained through evaluative procedures indicates how realistic and effective the original objectives were and where change is required.

6 Those interested in how well students perform in schools—parents, educational systems, employers, universities, government planners and so forth, need constructive information on student performance to

enhance their *decision-making effectiveness*. Curriculum developers should ensure that provision is made for evaluative information that is meaningful and valid.

Types of evaluation

Evaluation may be conducted at several places or instances in the teaching–learning process, both for product evaluation and process evaluation purposes. Many teachers may not realise that they actually can, and frequently do, evaluate in ways other than to provide evaluative information for the end of a course of study. Three forms of evaluation are commonly accepted by educators as being important, particularly to student evaluation and curriculum evaluation, although these forms are not used equally well or frequently.

Formative evaluation

Formative evaluation is directed towards providing information on learner performance at one or more points during the learning process. For example, a home economics teacher is interested in determining the degree of mastery *during* a learning task (sewing a shirt) and to pinpoint that part of the task not mastered. Appropriate assessment activities would be employed to determine the effectiveness of student progress at particular points in that process and to provide them with feedback on their performance.

Within product evaluation, the purpose is to help both the learner and the teacher focus upon the particular learning necessary for mastery, that is, evaluate how well the student is progressing *during* the learning experience in order to determine if changes are required along the way. Formative evaluation may also be undertaken in curriculum, teacher and program evaluation in order to obtain evaluative information of the performance, at that time, of that curriculum, teacher or program.

Some would argue that most of the application of curricula is concerned with formative evaluation. This means that any evaluation we undertake is seen as part of a process of ongoing development and the evaluative information available will enable changes to be made. Thus a student receiving evaluative information in Year 10 is better placed to make decisions and to improve one's performance for Years 11 and 12. Similarly a program may be subject to formative evaluation with a view to providing feedback to participants on how well they are progressing.

Summative evaluation

Summative evaluation is directed toward a general assessment of the degree to which the larger outcomes have been attained over the entire course or some substantial part of it; that is, evaluation employed at the *end* of a learning experience to indicate student achievement. Major examinations (HSC, TEE, for example) provide data for end-of-schooling evaluation.

Sometimes it is difficult to determine if evaluation is summative or formative in nature and indeed some educators argue that all evaluation is essentially formative. However, there are times when the nature of the educational experience changes so significantly that the evaluative data collected may be used for a summative purpose. When students move from primary to secondary school and from there to university, TAFE or employment may be judged to be two occasions at which summative evaluation may be made.

Thus educators can, and do, make summative evaluations about student performance in primary schools, about their educational experiences in secondary schools and about their educational experiences in university and TAFE. Frequently these summative evaluations are manifest in certificates, reports, achievement statements and so forth.

In terms of educational programs, for example a reading program, a personal development program or an advanced science program, summative evaluation techniques may be employed to determine whether or not the program should continue. Summative evaluation is also frequently used with programs to determine the degree of their effectiveness in achieving their stated goals.

Diagnostic evaluation

Diagnostic evaluation is directed towards two purposes, either for *placement* of students properly at the outset of an instructional period (such as secondary school), or to discover the underlying cause of *deficiencies* in student learning as instruction unfolds. The essential feature of diagnostic evaluation, therefore, is to provide useful information on student performance in order to address a perceived problem.

Diagnostic evaluation may therefore be used when grouping students prior to instruction. In New South Wales, for example, it is common for students to take a battery of tests as part of the process to be chosen for selective primary school programs (opportunity classes) or entire selective schools such as Sydney Girls High School and Sydney Boys High School. Alternatively, diagnostic evaluation may be employed when modifying content in a curriculum by the exclusion or addition of material or in modifying the program of a student to meet individual needs.

Teachers constantly engage in all three forms of evaluation although often not in a systematic manner. Students coming into a new school year are often evaluated during a course of instruction and given feedback to assess them with their development. Finally, school reports at the end of term, semester or year reflect the summative evaluation undertaken by the teacher.

Table 9.1 features the main characteristics of formative, summative and diagnostic evaluation as outlined by Bloom (1971).

Table 9.1   Types of evaluation

	Formative	Diagnostic	Summative
Function	Analysis of learning units. Feedback to students and diagnosis of difficulties. Feedback to teachers and quality control. Forecasting summative evaluation results.	Diagnosis of prerequisite entry behaviour and skills. Diagnosis to determine the extent of prior mastery of course objectives. Placement diagnosis for alternative curricula.	Assignment grades. Certification of skills and abilities. Prediction of future success. Initiation of subsequent learning. Feedback to students. Comparing outcomes of different groups.
Emphasis	Cognitive entry behaviours. Affective entry characteristics.	Cognitive and affective behaviours. Physical, psychological and environmental factors.	Cognitive outcomes. Affective outcomes. Rate of learning. Type of achievement.
Time	At frequent intervals: whether or not preliminary instruction is complete.	For placement. Before commencing a unit of learning. During instruction when a student reveals repeated inability to profit from the learning experiences.	Generally, at the end of a unit of learning. More frequently at progressive stages in a course of study (i.e. continuous assessment of developmental stages in learning).
Types of instruments	Instruments constructed to test the essential elements of a unit: teacher-made tests, work samples, interviews, checklists, rating scales.	Standardised achievement tests. Standardised diagnostic tests. Teacher-made instruments. Observations and checklists.	Final summative examinations, unit progress tests, work samples, self-reports.

Source: After B.S. Bloom, 1971

Measurement, assessment and evaluation

Evaluation is a process which consists of the subprocesses of measurement and assessment providing adequate and useful data upon which the final judgments are made. In this way, an evaluation may be seen as a cumulative procedure. The relationship between the terms measurement, assessment and evaluation is hierarchical in nature, where one concept builds upon the other until an evaluation is achieved. Thus measurement and assessment are necessary conditions for evaluation to occur, although they have an independent existence as well. Figure 9.1 shows the interdependent relationship between the three concepts in the evaluation process. As Figure 9.1 illustrates, the starting point in evaluation is the collection of measurement data. These data are then interpreted and finally evaluative judgments are made.

Measurement

Measurement is concerned with the *statement of performance* usually represented in quantitative terms. Invariably measurement in schools takes the form of descriptive data obtained about student performance by using a measurement instrument in a given learning situation. For example:

the student . . . received 9/10 on a spelling test;
            . . . threw the javelin 100 metres;
            . . . completed all six steps in the science experiment;
            . . . obtained 72 per cent for a maths exam.

Measurement could also involve the collection of data about teacher performance or about the performance of a curriculum. However, regardless of what is being measured, the data obtained have little value by themselves and they require interpretation by someone skilled in evaluation procedures. Indeed, measurement data in the hands of unskilled persons may be grossly misinterpreted. For example, what does a student's score of 12/20 on a test indicate? By itself, it means very little and it

Figure 9.1   Evaluation Process

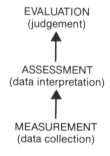

EVALUATION
(judgement)

ASSESSMENT
(data interpretation)

MEASUREMENT
(data collection)

requires interpretation before it is considered meaningful. It could mean that, on that test, the student has performed quite poorly as the mean score on the test was 15/20. Or perhaps it means that the student has performed quite well as the median score was 8/20. Thus the score by itself has little meaning and it requires interpretation through the use of assessment procedures.

Assessment

Assessment is broader in scope than measurement in that it involves the *interpretation and representation of measurement data*. It is essentially concerned with firstly making sense out of measurement data and then assigning a mark, a grade, a rank, or some form of qualitative comment to that previously collected measurement information. The assigning of a mark may be in quantitative or qualitative terms; quantitatively this may be 81 per cent, eleventh percentile, second decile, 81/100; qualitatively this may be 'distinction' or 'credit'.

Usually measurement data are interpreted in terms of whether or not an intended level of achievement has been attained. In turn, this achievement is expressed as a pass (or fail) or by some letter or numerical grade. Thus, in an examination a student's mark of 58 per cent may be interpreted as a pass or a B-level or grade pass.

An example of typical assessment in a school would be where a teacher analyses a student's test score of 12/20 to determine whether that student should pass or fail the test or what grade should be awarded. In determining this assessment, the teacher may consider the performance of other students (norm-referenced assessment) or how well the stated objectives have been achieved by the student concerned (criterion-referenced assessment). In this way the teacher has interpreted the raw data from the test and made an assessment of the student's performance.

In the example cited above the student's raw score of 12/20 (measurement) must be interpreted to make sense. It may be interpreted as a pass, a distinction (or an A-level pass) or perhaps even a fail! This will depend upon the use of norm-referenced or criterion-referenced procedures (see below) as well as the student's performance relative to others or the stated criteria. Thus the student may have performed relatively well compared with others and the score of 12/20 may be translated or represented as a 'credit' or B-level pass. Alternatively the student may have obtained the score in response to a criterion-referenced activity and achieved a sufficient score for an ordinary level or C pass.

In some situations, such as curriculum evaluation, teacher evaluation and indeed aspects of product evaluation such as student values and social skills, the measurement data collected may be of a qualitative nature. Such data cannot be interpreted quantitatively (as with test scores), but rather in the context of an educational setting and are expressed in the form of comments. A school, for example, may be concerned to assess the moral development of students after several years of school experience. Data based on observation, interviews, questionnaires or some other measurement device could then become the basis of evaluative comments set within the context of that school.

In times when accountability is prominent in society, pressure is evident to ensure that assessment plays a significant role in the educative process. In schools this usually means considerable attention is devoted to assessment procedures and to scoring well on measurement instruments. What has to be carefully considered by curriculum developers and teachers is that assessment does not overshadow the initial curriculum intent.

Where this occurs we refer to it as the *assessment-driven curriculum*. Examples of assessment-driven curricula are the Higher School Certificate, Tertiary Entrance Examination type courses found in all states in years 11 and 12. Here the original purposes of study (extended learning; preparation for university; employment preparation) have been overshadowed by the nature of circumstances (few tertiary places; extremely competitive faculty entrance; few jobs) which have forced the preparation and teaching of courses to be dominated by assessment considerations i.e. teachers manipulate the curriculum and their teaching strategies in order to enhance student performance on examinations and tests. High scores on these tests and examinations have become essential in order to achieve the desired university, faculty or employment position.

Evaluation

Undertaking evaluation, the highest level in the hierarchy of terms, is based upon assessment interpretations of the collected data. With the information gained from measurement and assessment, educators are in a better position to make *value judgments* which are invariably expressed as written comments. The important feature of educational evaluation, however, is that it is based upon assessment data and not upon whim or fancy.

In schools, teachers participate continually in product evaluation (i.e. making judgments about student performance) as well as curriculum, teacher and program evaluation. Typical product evaluation, or what most teachers refer to as simply evaluation, takes the form of evaluative comments on school reports and record cards. Evaluative statements could also be oral in nature and teachers often make these comments on student performance to parents. Alternatively, an evaluative report, based on interpreted data, may be written on teacher performance, on a curriculum or a program used in any teaching–learning situation.

The interrelated nature of the three evaluative components (measurement, assessment, evaluation) in the following example shows how the concept of evaluation may be conducted in schools. Using data from tests, student work samples and interviews, a teacher has determined that a student has achieved a final semester/year mark of 72 per cent in English *(measurement)*. When interpreted, using norm-referenced assessment, this information was translated into a grade of A as the student's mark was near the top of the class in English *(assessment)*. On the student's school report, the A grade was noted (as well as an interpreted score such as percentiles, stanines, or deciles) and judgmental comments made about the student's performance based upon the interpreted data (evaluation).

The assessment process

How should teachers go about the process of assessment and subsequent evaluation in schools? Most schools should have evaluation and assessment policies as part of standard operating procedures for the curriculum. However, should that not be the case it is important for teachers to raise the issue of evaluation policies and assessment procedures. The following is a guide upon which assessment procedures may be made, remembering that it is important to take into account both the educational system evaluation policies and the school context.

We commence by assuming such policies are in place within the school. Once measurement instruments have been used to collect data about student performance, behaviour, or perhaps attitudes, the educator is in a position to make valid assessments. It has been noted earlier that assessment may be defined as the interpretation of measurement data. In this task, assessment provides some sense to the raw data collected previously as they, in themselves, provide educators with little insight.

In terms of product evaluation, for example, a student may achieve a mark of 69 per cent in a test. But what does this mean? If the class mean on the test was 82 per cent, then the student is performing well below average. If the group mean had been 44 per cent on the test, the student's performance was outstanding. However, by itself the mark of 69 per cent tells us very little about the student's performance. Therefore we must resist making excessive use of such data unless they are interpreted. Similarly we must encourage inexperienced others, particularly parents, from making inferences based upon measurement data alone. Given in context, with explanations, and transformed through assessment procedures is even more valuable and meaningful.

In the process of translating raw data into meaningful information, the educator will use either norm-referenced or criterion-referenced procedures. The former compares individuals with others from a comparable group, while the latter relates the individual to a set of predetermined criteria. In schools, we usually refer to these as norm-referenced assessment and criterion-referenced assessment as we are mostly concerned with product evaluation (student performance). However, both forms are also used in process evaluation. When the measurement data have been tranformed they are then ready for the interpretative process associated with making value judgments and hence the final stage of evaluation.

Norm-referenced assessment

Norm-referenced assessment compares the performance of an individual with that of other students, using the same measuring device. This may be a test, an essay, an exam, a work sample, a performance checklist and so forth. The student's performance is then reported as a grade, mark, percentile, decile, quartile or whichever form has been selected in the school context. Additional information on means, medians or modal scores provides useful information for meaningful interpretation of individual performance against that of others in the group.

It is important to remember that norm-referenced assessment involves the comparison of a student's performance with the performance of other students in the same category, that is, comparing a Year 6 student's score in a science test with the scores of other Year 6 students on the same test. An individual's performance may then be assessed in terms of how well she or he has performed compared with the other students. For example, the student who receives 14/20 on a science test may be assessed as an A-level pass (if everyone else performed poorly), or ordinary pass (if others performed similarly), or a fail (if others performed much better).

What is reported is a student's performance relative to other students on that task, not how well the student has performed relative to himself or herself or against set standards. Thus a student may perform very well on a task and receive a relatively average grade as other students performed equally well, as seen in the above example. Similarly students may not feel they have performed particularly well on a task but compared with the performance of other students they have and consequently receive a high grade.

Therefore the basis of norm-referenced assessment is that the performance of any individual student can be related to any other student(s) where they have used the same test or had the same activity to perform. Standardised achievement tests are norm-referenced as they are designed to compare the performance of individuals with the performance of a normative group. The Basic Skills Tests, currently used in many states at the primary school level, are a form of norm-referenced assessment. Here the individual student's performance on a range of basic skills may be compared with that of others in the same school and between schools.

As well, most teacher-made tests have been constructed as norm-referenced statements when they compare the performance of one student with another, or one against the group. Similarly most work samples, performance checklists, examinations and other measurement instruments are used in a norm-referenced manner. They could, however, be employed in a different, though related, manner.

Criterion-referenced assessment

By contrast to the method above, criterion-referenced assessment compares an individual's performance with a predetermined level or standard of performance. It assesses whether a learner has achieved what is required to establish certain standards in the learning task. For example, a student learning to play the piano must achieve certain standards or reach certain criteria at a level in order to proceed to the next level. Once evidence of that standard has been achieved the student is able to proceed to the next stage, that is, to acquire the learning for the next criterion or standard. Similarly, a criterion-referenced approach to assesment may be used in learning languages, acquiring scientific understanding, learning a sport, acquiring computer skills, or learning the skills of panel-beating and spray-painting.

Criterion-referenced assessment in schools compares student performance against a set of predetermined criteria which are necessary to complete a task. In home economics, for example, a student's performance may be compared with a set of criteria or tasks for producing a sponge. In order to interpret that performance the student's work is assessed against the predetermined criteria for effective sponge-making. In this way the student competes against a set of criteria, not against other students. Consequently most, perhaps all, students may receive a top mark such as an A as they achieved the set criteria. Similarly most students may receive a C-level pass or a failing grade as they did not achieve the predetermined criteria.

In a primary school a teacher may decide to use criterion-referenced assessment in physical education. Where students are to acquire certain skills, for example, the skills related to netball, minkey, football or physical capabilities (that is, through daily physical education), the teacher tests student performance against predetermined standards or criteria. In these situations as well, the student competes not against other students, but against the standard.

Criterion-referenced assessment is commonly used in mastery learning situations, programmed instruction and instructional systems designs. It should be noted that the term standards-referenced assessment is being used increasingly by educators, although it means the same as criterion-referenced assessment.

However, it should be asked: Where does the concept of a standard come from? In most cases the reply is: What the average or typical performer can achieve at that level. Thus criterion and norm-refernced assessment should be seen more as two ends of a continuum rather that two independent variables. When criteria are set, they are created in the context of some known perform levels, while norm-referenced assessment has some appreciation of desired levels of achievement. Nevertheless, educators need to set their assessment procedures to be essentially criterion-referenced or essentially norm-referenced.

The issue of whether to adopt norm-referenced or criterion-referenced assessment procedures in schools has become particularly pertinent in recent years with demands for greater accountability in schools in terms of student performance. A number of countries have adopted national testing procedures and Australia is one of several countries becoming increasingly involved with international student performance comparisons (Wyatt & Ruby, 1990; Robitaille & Overgaard, 1991).

As the attention of policy-makers in many countries have become increasingly focused upon the outcomes of schooling in a time of contracting budgets and shifting ideologies, and simultaneously system and school-level administrators are being held more accountable for the achievement of these outcomes, so strong pressure has been placed to identify policy-sensitive variables which will have an impact in measured student learning. National and international testing programs are ways of meeting these demands.

Similarly within Australia there have been growing moves to adopt some form of national testing or national assessment procedure. Typically this would take the form of administering standardised tests to determine levels of student performance (as a Basic Skills Test might do) within and between schools. In such situations it is very important that the measurement data collected be interpreted validly so that the assessment reported to the community makes sense. Comparing the performance of a school with a low academic profile (say from a school with few resources, unmotivated and low-achieving students) with that of a high academic profile school (say a selective school with highly motivated, high-achieving students and typical resources) would be invalid unless the contextual factors are taken into account.

Outcome statements

Recent developments within educational systems around Australia, based upon the perceived need for greater curriculum accountability within schools, have witnessed the restructuring of reporting and assessment activities in terms of what are referred to as learner outcome statements and grade descriptors. The need for outcome statements has been said to be to assist in defining curriculum intent more precisely, clarifying student progress through more precise means, assisting schools to communicate student progress effectively and providing a focus for teacher assessment of student performance (NSW Board of Studies, 1992).

This development reflects not only societal demands for greater educational accountability but also the greater politicisation of the curriculum. In New South Wales, for example, the need for outcome statements can be found the initial committee of inquiry—the Carrick Report (1989), the minister's statement—*Excellence and Equity* (1990) and the Education Reform Act, 1990. From this base, the NSW Board of Studies now requires all syllabus committees to provide not only curriculum objectives but also statements of outcomes.

Outcome statements may be defined as the intended results of the teaching learning process as identified in a curriculum document (usually called a syllabus) and expressed as a set of broad, comprehensive, assessable and observable indicators of student achievement. Together, a set of outcome statements should cover not only the knowledge and skills domains of a subject syllabus but also the attitudes and values domain as well.

The relationship between outcome statements and curriculum intent may be seen in the following example. A general or unit objective (see chapter 6) in a unit of work in a geography/social studies curriculum may be expressed as: to develop practical skills in preparing maps and diagrams. In turn, this could be expressed in terms of such curriculum outcome statements as:

- constructs maps and diagrams accurately using conventional formats
- makes precise and accurate measurements
- uses equipment purposively and effectively
- presents maps and diagrams in clearly understandable ways.

Similarly, an objective which seeks to develop in students an understanding of life in a planned, urban environment in terms of transportation options and technology could produce curriculum outcome statements such as:

- identifies issues arising from the impact of different transportation forms on an urban environment
- understands and uses terms related to urban environments
- identifies and analyses evidence collected from a study on the impact of urban transport
- appreciates differing perspectives of indivdual transportation needs.

In what ways can the classroom teacher use curriculum outcome statements? As the teacher refines and translates the syllabus into a curriculum program, so the outcome statements will need to be refined into more specific and usable *statements of classroom-level outcomes*. Student performance should be assessed in terms of the achievement of these outcomes, though not all outcomes would be tested or measured. Educators generally agree that student attitudes and values should not be formally assessed.

These more specific outcome statements may then be used as *performance indicators* upon which to judge individual student progress. At the syllabus level, the outcome statements can provide more general performance indicators which are appropriate for reporting to the general community.

Measurement instruments

For asessment to be undertaken effectively and validly we have said that measurement data must be first obtained. Measurement has been defined as a statement of performance, usually that of the student but also possibly including the performance of the teacher, a program or the curriculum. But how do we obtain these data?

Teachers in schools have long been familiar with an array of tests, exams and other procedures for gathering data on student performance. The following section will examine a number of useful measurement techniques briefly, but a detailed analysis of those techniques will not be provided. Useful references for learning more about measurement instruments include the SET series from ACER (Australia Council for Educational research), Kerlinger (1986), Marsh & Stafford (1988), Fraser & Fisher (1983), Gay (1985), Davis (1981), Marsh & Print (1975), Piper (1976), van Dalen (1973), Ebel (1972). The list below is not exhaustive although it will be of value to educators conducting product and process evaluation.

> standardised tests
> teacher-made tests
> work samples
> oral tests
> systematic observation
> interviews
> questionnaires
> checklists and rating scales
> anecdotal records
> sociograms
> self-reports

Several references provide substantial information on the construction and use of these instruments as noted above. It should also be noted that there is wide support for employing a *variety* of measurement techniques when undertaking evaluation in schools. Not only is a more complete picture of student performance obtained, but with a diversity of measurement instruments in use, students have a greater opportunity to demonstrate their individual strengths. To use only one form of measuring student performance, say tests or work samples, provides a restricted range of information upon which to base subsequent evaluative judgments. Thus a student who performs poorly on a test would be disadvantaged if the teacher employed only tests in collecting measurement data. Most schools have policies, implied if not explicit, that a variety of measurement instruments is to be used in collecting data on student performance.

Standardised tests

Commercially developed and produced tests which have been normed against a standard population are known as standardised tests. Most of the commercially available achievement intelligence, readiness and ability tests are standardised. The Australiian Council for Educational Research (ACER) produces a range of tests standardised for Australian populations. Some of the more useful standardised tests include:

1 ACER Intermediate (A, G or 1).
2 Ravens Progressive Matrices.
3 Stanford-Binet Intelligence Scale (individual IQ).
4 Wechler Intelligence Scale for Children (individual IQ).

The strengths of standardised tests are the high degree of validity and reliability derived from the standardising process and the ability to project about student performance based on the results. Standardised tests are frequently used for student entrance (into a school or program) or for comparison between large numbers of students within an educational system. Standardised tests are typically used as a basis of selection procedures for entry into selective schools in New South Wales and for scholarship entry into independent schools throughout Australia. More recently, the Basic Skills Tests in Years 3, 6 and 9 are designed to provide information on student and school performance on a standardised basis.

However, there are substantial limitations to using standardised tests, especially by classroom teachers. The testing process is very expensive in any context, is rarely appropriate to specific curricula (particularly in Australia), very expensive to prepare, take lengthy periods to construct and standardised tests are often inappropriate for determining individual student performance if that test is the exclusive measure of that performance. Consequently most product evaluation in schools is based upon teacher-made tests.

Teacher-made tests

All forms of tests that have been devised by teachers to assess student understanding of stated objectives are called teacher-made tests. Included here are multiple-choice answer tests, essays, short-answer tests matching items, sentence-completion tests and the like. These tests rarely have any form of standardisation, let alone quality control, to ensure that they are valid and reliable forms of measurement.

Nevertheless, teacher-made tests are economical, flexible, highly relevant to specific curricula and can be written quickly. Some of the better teacher-made tests are the external examinations held at the end of secondary schooling such as the Higher School Certificate (HSC) and the Tertiary Entrance Examination (TEE). These have considerably more thought applied to them, have enhanced reliability and validity through using multiple exam constructors and past exam data and are constructed specifically for the curriculum being studied. They are quite different from, yet serve the same tertiary-selection purpose as, the standardised Scholastic Aptitude Test (SAT) used so widely in the United States.

Work samples

Actual evidence of student work is an important, and frequently undervalued, method for understanding student performance. It may take the form of a product (model, project, essay, practical workbook, sculpture, poem, composition, diagram) or a performance (dance, recitation, experiment, race, game). This form of measurement is often underrated by some teachers, although it can also be just as easily overused by others.

The value of a work sample is that it can depict what the student is capable of, usually in a non-threatening environment, at any one particular time. Unlike a test or exam, taken and studied for at strategic times, students tend to perceive work samples as less threatening, more realistic, and hence more valuable to them, and as an expression of their performance.

In schools, work samples are found commonly in writing, reading, home economics, art, industrial arts, craft, physical education and so forth. Greater use of work samples could probably be made in such subjects as geography, history, social studies, science and maths.

Oral tests

Apart from obvious areas of the school curriculum such as foreign languages, Australian educators tend to take little advantage of utilising any form of oral or verbal assessment. In other countries, in other institutions (such as universities), and at other times, oral examinations have enjoyed significant popularity and support. In medieval times, for example, oral exams were more commonplace in universities and even today many universities still use the oral examination as the final decision-making stage. It is common in American universities for doctoral candidates to experience an oral examination of their qualifying examinations on their coursework before undertaking their thesis. After their thesis has been examined in its written form, candidates are then typically subjected to a two-hour oral examination of the thesis by a panel of experts. Similarly, American schools continually employ different forms of oral assessment as an integral part of their assessment profile.

In Australian schools teachers could use oral assessment in a variety of contexts. As an alternative to writing a report on a topic or preparing a summary of a chapter, students could present an oral report to the teacher or the class. Students could opt to take an oral test rather than a written test. Groups of students might make an oral presentation to the class as part of a major project. History students might present a paper orally on a topic, while mathematics students might choose to explain the solution to a problem orally rather than in written form.

Oral assessment is useful as it adds another quite different dimension of measurement to the array available to teachers. This will assist many students who do not perceive themselves as having strong written skills and hence will be a more valid depiction of their performance. This form of measurement is also extremely person-oriented as every student could be treated individually. While this might lessen the argument of validity and reliability, it does enhance the case of finding out what the individual does know and hence providing effective feedback. Oral assessment is sometimes perceived negatively as being excessively time-consuming, but when a trade-off is made with marking papers the problem disappears. Similarly, if a set of criteria are used, oral assessment does not become excessively subjective in its assessment of student performance.

Systematic observation

Teachers continually observe student behaviour, although rarely in a systematic manner and with a view to measurement. To employ this technique effectively, teachers need to establish appropriate criteria for purposeful observation, systematically watch students and then record observations according to the predetermined criteria. In this way a written record of student performance will result which will assist in providing useful evaluative data.

Examples of systematic observation might be observing and collecting data as described above for a science experiment, completion of practical tasks in geography, a drama performance, handwriting exercises, problem-solving exercises in mathematics and so forth. More specifically, in a home economics class, the teacher may have a list of desired behaviours which should be present in the preparation and cooking of a three course meal. As students proceed with preparing the items, the teacher observes student behaviour according to the predetermined criteria. Comments are noted about student behaviour in a systematic manner and the information used for later evaluative comments.

This technique collects qualitative data about student performance as well as quantitative data. Such data are extremely useful when developing a more complete profile on student performance and hence are most valuable when writing evaluations.

Interviews

Australian educators tend to place little value on oral measurement techniques such as the interview, except where it is of obvious use such as in language assessment. Yet this is a technique that can, in the hands of a skilled interviewer, quickly determine the depth of a student's understanding. Also, it provides a viable alternative to typical pencil and paper forms of assessment.

An understanding of the interview technique is important before incorporating it within one's assessment repertoire. Interviews may be structured or unstructured, formal or informal depending upon their function (Marsh & Print, 1975). Classroom teachers could typically use a structured, informal interview to assess student performance and so provide additional breadth of information for evaluation. Furthermore, many students may give more realistic evidence of their ability through an interview. The references cited at the beginning of this section provide further details on conducting interviews.

Questionnaires

Questionnaires have a limited role to play in measuring student performance but they are far more helpful in gauging student attitudes to a wide variety of issues. To ascertain such information a teacher would undertake survey research, the basis of which is the collection of attitudinal and behavioural data using questionnaires. As such, the questionnaire has a wide applicability and it can be a particularly valuable tool for collecting data in product and process evaluations which involve large numbers of participants.

In schools, questionnaires are used principally to gather data on student perceptions of learning situations or to determine student behaviour in some context. Thus, a school may be interested in ascertaining student attitudes towards a new mathematics course or in determining student study habits. In these cases a questionnaire is an effective, efficient means of gathering data, particularly where large numbers of students are involved.

Questionnaires require careful construction, the selection of an appropriate sample (if required), reliable implementation and detailed analysis of resulting data. It is beyond our scope here to undertake a detailed analysis of a questionnaire, but the following points will be helpful with questionnaire construction:

1 Ask only essential questions.
2 Ensure anonymity of responses.
3 Avoid biased questions.
4 Use a Likert scale for measuring attitudes.
5 Ensure questions can be understood easily.
6 Emphasise closed questions, forcing respondents to choose amongst alternative responses.
7 Ask brief questions or pose succinct statements.
8 Briefly explain the purpose of the questionnaire at the beginning.

Checklists and rating scales

Both checklists and rating scales are instruments available for use by educators to measure student behaviour. They offer a systematic approach to ordering data so that they may be used more effectively in later analysis. As such they are useful methods for collecting data on student performance, and though have not been popular in the past they should be given greater consideration by teachers.

Checklists usually consist of a list of predetermined student behaviours which are then recorded or noted at particular times. To undertake this the educator must first determine which specific behaviours are of sufficient importance to be 'measured'. A list is then compiled, students observed and their behaviour 'checked' against the list. The observation and recording stages may be repeated on several occasions throughout a course or unit.

In a primary school, for example, a teacher may wish to measure student cooperation and participation in group activities. A checklist of desirable behaviour is then constructed. At the times when group work is undertaken, students are observed and their behaviour recorded on the checklist. The final step consists usually of a simple tick to indicate the presence of the desirable behaviour.

A secondary school example might be a science experiment which requires a student to perform a sequence of tasks. The teacher, in observing the student's behaviour, is able to indicate whether or not the required tasks have been satisfactorily completed. The opportunity would also be available, particularly if given space on the checklist sheet, to add qualitative comments which would facilitate the teacher's subsequent evlaluative comments.

A *rating scale* provides a quantitative dimension to the checklist technique and so provides additional measurement data. While rating scales may be generally used for measuring attitudes, they are equally applicable to measuring cognitive, affective and psychomotor skills and knowledge. The essential feature of a rating scale is that it offers a range of alternatives, or several points on a scale, as a means of measuring the perceived degree to which the behaviour is present.

Typically, the rater observes a student's performance or specific behaviour and then assigns a rating according to a predetermined scale, perhaps a scale of 1–10. The scale may have numerical values associated with each point or category and so an averaged numerical score over all traits can be obtained. Thus a student might achieve an average rating score of 7.3 based upon the summation of individual ratings made upon several traits.

An English teacher in a secondary school, for example, may wish to use a rating scale as a means to measure student performance in debates or to assess oral performance in the presentation of a verbal argument/defence. A scale would be constructed consisting of the significant characteristics or traits of debating/verbal presentation and perhaps a five-point scale assigned to each trait. The debate/presentation is then observed and the students' performance rated 1–5 on each trait. At the end of the activity the ratings from two or more observers may be averaged and a comparison between students made.

Rating scales are extremely useful measurement techniques for classroom teachers. Not only can they measure student performance that is difficult to undertake with tests, but they can also enhance the variety of measurements sources. It is not difficult to construct rating scales and they are invariably completed at the time of student performance and hence do not require marking at a later time. It is not difficult for teachers to create a rating score matrix (or a checklist matrix either), which has on one axis the rating characteristics and on the other the students in the class. Scores may then be assigned at the time of the student performance and a record maintained.

Anecdotal records

Another useful source of information on individual students can be found in anecdotal records. These are teacher-recorded statements of events or incidents that occurred in the classroom, playground, sports field and so forth. The recordings are more substantial than observational notes and are usually rewritten from earlier, quickly noted jottings. Written as soon as possible after the event, while the happenings are easily recalled, anecdotal records cover incidents that occurred at irregular, unanticipated or unexpected moments, as well as at regular, anticipated and expected times.

Such records are obviously subjective and provide qualitative data that can amplify the picture of student behaviour and performance. However, by being recorded at an appropriate time, these data may be used later when the event has probably been forgotten.

Anecdotal records are rather time-consuming to maintain on behalf of teachers. They may directed towards the class at large or towards particular individuals. In a class with a few uncooperative students, for example, a teacher may wish to keep anecdotal records on their behaviour. The records may be used later to analyse and evaluate student behaviour and so determine an appropriate classroom-management strategy. Similarly, data from anecdotal records may be used to expand evaluative comments in a school report.

Sociograms

Sociometric measures are useful for studying the organisational patterns of groups such as students in a classroom, play group, sports group and so forth. A sociogram can help to reveal popular students (stars) and unpopular students (isolates, rejectees) according to some predetermined criterion, and so reveal the fundamental social structure of the group.

The technique is based upon students being asked their preference for a companion to participate in specific activities. In schools, students may be asked whom they would most (and least) like to sit next to in class, do homework with, play with after school, work on a project with and so forth. The choices obtained are plotted on a sociogram and the patterns that emerge indicate the popular and unpopular students.

Those who are extremely popular in the designated activity (which may be different with other activities) have traditionally been called 'stars', while those who receive no choices are termed 'isolates'. Students who receive many negative choices, in the designated activity, have been known as 'rejectees'. At best a sociogram can provide an insight into student behaviour and assist educators in forming and reforming student groups. They are usually employed at formative stages of evaluation and provide a qualitative dimension to amplify evaluative data.

Self-reports

Measurement of student behaviour and performance does not always have to be conducted by an educator such as a teacher in a school. Indeed, in a process evaluation, particularly curriculum and teacher evaluation, it is very important to determine the participants' opinions about the process being evaluated. In product evaluation teachers have long undervalued student self-evalution, usually on the grounds of validity and reliability, and hence it is rarely used in schools. Nevertheless there are times when such data are useful, particularly in amplifying the teacher's overall perspective of student performance.

Self-reports may take the form of *self-report scales, diaries* or *logs*. A self-report scale provides the participant with a predetermined scale of selected behaviours and attitudes that relate to his or her situation, such as in a school. Participants simply react to the statement by selecting a point on the scale which best represents their thinking at that time. Some self-reporting scales have been produced commercially and thus the validity and reliability of the instrument are invariably enhanced. Alternatively, educators may devise their own instruments and this would be appropriate to teacher and curriculum evaluations particularly.

Other forms of self-reports are diaries and logs. Essentially these are records kept by participants in some reasonably systematic manner. These instruments should be maintained on a regular basis and should provide details of significant events. The principal value of these instruments lies in the qualitative data they provide over a period of time which serve to extend other information. They are particularly useful in teacher evaluation as well as curriculum evaluation.

With the availability of assessment data, the educator is now in a position to complete the evaluative process. The final phase is the formulation of evaluative comments based upon the previously collected data. This may take the form of a school report (student performance), a written report (teacher or curriculum evaluation) or a verbal and/or visual report. In these contexts assessment data are usually included as a reference point to facilitate understanding of the evaluation.

Curriculum evaluation

One important form of process evaluation is comprehensive curriculum evaluation. It it a procedure which seeks to make judgments about the operation and effectiveness of a curriculum. Curriculum evaluation has been defined earlier in this chapter and now we are interested to see how curriculum evaluation might be undertaken. In a time of increasing accountability, an understanding of curriculum evaluation will be a considerable advantage to teachers.

The process of curriculum evaluation is outlined below and is represented in form of the curriculum evaluation algorithm in figure 9.2. While this is but one approach to curriculum evaluation it appears to have considerable support in terms of other approaches available. Useful sources on curriculum evaluation include Parlett & Hamilton (1972), Eisner (1979), Stenhouse (1975), Davis (1980), Stufflebeam et al. (1971), Print (1990), Simons (1987), McLaughlin & Phillips (1991), Kemmis & Stake (1988).

Curriculum evaluation algorithm

This algorithm suggests that the process of curriculum evaluation consists of seven integrally related sequential steps. Teachers and curriculum evaluators may follow these steps in undertaking the evaluative task, regardless of whether that task is the evaluation of a class-level curriculum, a school curriculum, a system curriculum or somewhere in between. The seven steps of the algorithm are:

1 Evaluation presage: understanding of the evaluation context.
2 Task specification: delineating the scope of the evaluation (whom is it for, what is involved, relate to objectives).
3 Evaluation design: devise plan for conducting evaluation.
4 Data collection: obtaining data both from existing sources and by using techniques devised in design stage.
5 Data analysis: analysis, synthesis and interpretation of data as organised in design stage.
6 Conclusion: prepare conclusions based on results and prepare report.
7 Present conclusions and recommendations to audience.

The first task of the evaluator, on acknowledging the need for, or being given the task of, evaluating a curriculum, is to ascertain the nature of the evaluative context. Evaluations are not conducted in politically neutral environments, rather they are subject to pressures and agendas set by those involved, particularly the evaluation initiating clients (Weiss, 1988; Simons, 1987; Patton, 1988; Print, 1990).

Most importantly here, the evaluator must determine what the client *really wants evaluated*. In many cases the client is either not exactly sure or may have some apparently hidden motives for initiating the evaluation. This first phase involves the evaluator attempting to determine as much about the evaluation context as possible before physically commencing the evaluative task.

In the task specification stage, the second stage of the algorithm, the evaluator seeks to determine the precise parameters of the evaluation, i.e. what are the boundaries within which the evaluation will be conducted. Usually the parameters will be negotiated with the client, or initiating audience, before the evaluator commences any collection of information.

In addition, the evaluator would need to know the objectives or terms of reference for the evaluation. These are invariably translated into a number of what may be called task-specification questions which give the evaluator guidance and direction in undertaking the process of the evaluation.

A third stage in curriculum evaluation is frequently overlooked or assumed to have occurred. When an evaluator has accepted the task of evaluation, considered the context (evaluation presage), and specified the nature of the evaluation exercise through determining parameters, one must consider how the evaluation will proceed. In other words what sort of evaluative design will be employed in terms of data collection, data analysis and report presentation?

Will the evaluator choose to use more qualitative data collection techniques and employ an ethnographic or perhaps case study design? Or will the evaluator chose a design based on a cost-effective approach, requiring the collection of quantitative data? (See McLaughlin & Phillips, 1991 for alternatives.) In this stage the evaluator needs to decide which form of evaluation design is most appropriate to the curriculum under evaluation and the curriculum context.

In the fourth stage—data collection—the evaluator may follow one of two paths. In posing the question—What information needs to be collected to answer the task specification questions?—the evaluator will determine whether new as well as existing data will need to be collected. Many of the measurement instruments discussed earlier in this chapter are appropriate for this data gathering exercise.

The fifth stage in the evaluative process is data analysis, i.e. examining the data and then synthesising to determine themes, factors or areas of commonality. This produces the basis for making conclusions about the curriculum being evaluated. Some use of statistical procedures may be required but the most important part of this stage is the analysis of all data collected and its consideration in terms of the original evaluative questions or terms of reference. The exact approach used here will depend in large measure on the evaluation design chosen earlier.

Using the information from the previous stage the evaluator is then able to make well-balanced and justified judgments about the curriculum. These take the form of conclusions about the effectiveness of the curriculum, particularly in terms of relating the curriculum to its intentions, and consequential recommendations for action.

For many, the process of evaluation ends with the previous stage. However it has become obvious that evaluators need to proceed one stage further in order to enhance the effectiveness of their evaluation (Weiss, 1988; Patton, 1986, 1988; Simons, 1987). This involves the evaluator in presenting the evaluation's outcomes to at least the initiating audience (the clients) as well as other audiences, particularly the participants of the evaluation (Simons, 1987). The final stage is somewhat precarious for it involves the evaluator in an attempt, not always successful, to ensure that the evaluation report is implemented (Weiss, 1988; Patton, 1988; Simons, 1987; Print, 1989, 1990). These seven stages of the evaluation algorithm may also be represented by means of a diagram (figure 9.2).

Evaluating curriculum materials

Educators are constantly presented with curriculum materials that may be used to facilitate their teaching. Classroom teachers in particular are

Figure 9.2   Curriculum evaluation algorithm

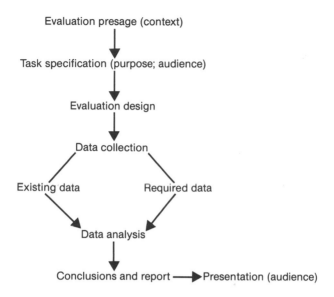

exposed to a wide array of commercially produced and teacher-prepared materials. These vary from a selection of visual and printed materials (such as teacher-prepared overheads and worksheets) to complex, multimedia curriculum packages that may constitute an entire course (as did ASEP, SEMP and MACOS). But how does one select the most appropriate materials? This is particularly important in times of limited school budgets.

The following is a useful procedure for teachers and other educators to evaluate curriculum materials. Such materials may require evaluation for purchase or perhaps for inclusion in a unit of study. In the latter case different materials may already be available and evaluation is required to select the appropriate one from amongst them. The need for instructional materials to be evaluated on criteria other than salespersons' recommendations is particularly important. Unfortunately, few evaluative devices are available. Despite this shortcoming, several general criteria (stated in question form and applying to all types of instructional materials) may be identified. By posing the following questions, a teacher can quickly determine the value of curriculum materials.

Interest

Will the material catch and hold the interest of users? Will it stimulate curiosity? Can it be used to satisfy curiosity?

Authenticity

Is the material factually accurate? Is it up to date? Are author and/or producer well qualified to devise the materials?

Appropriateness

Does the material promote the general educational goals of the school system? Is it in any way objectionable? Is it appropriate (with respect to vocabulary level, difficulty of concepts, methods of development) to the level of instruction intended? If controversial, is the material presented impartially? Is the material basic or supplementary to the curriculum?

Organisation and balance

Is the material well organised and well balanced? Have principles of learning been followed in its development (for example, reinforcement, transfer, application)? Is the material presented logically and clearly? Is the material presented imaginatively (not tritely) when imagination is really needed? Is the quality of narration or dialogue satisfactory (content and delivery)? Do the music and background strengthen the presentation? Are titles, labels or captions appropriate?

Technical quality

Is the technical quality of the material satisfactory? Is the visual imagery satisfactory (in focus, pleasantly and effectively composed, functionally varied in distance and angle)? Is the sound clear and intelligible? Is colour used effectively? Are sound and visual image synchronised satisfactorily?

The above approach was designed to provide a time-efficient, straightforward approach to evaluating the suitability of curriculum materials. However, there are other methods available although they tend to be more detailed and hence more time consuming. Two of the more well-known methods have been developed by Kevin Piper (1976) and Meredith Gall (1981). Piper's checklist comes from his book *Evaluation in the Social Sciences,* while Gall devised the Handbook for Evaluating and Selecting Curriculum Materials.

Summary

- Evaluation is concerned with making value judgments about all sorts of things in our lives. In education, evaluation usually refers to making judgments about student performance and behaviours and the use of that information to enhance both learning/teaching and the curriculum.
- In education we distinguish between product evaluation (student performance) and process evaluation (the learning situation).
- Evaluation in curriculum is useful for:
  — Providing feedback to learners.
  — Determining how well learners achieved the objectives.
  — Providing information to improve curricula.
  — Assisting learners with decision making.
  — Clarifying the stated objectives.
  — Assisting others making decisons about students.
- Evaluation can occur formatively (during the learning experience), summatively (at the end of the learning experience) or diagnostically (to determine deficiencies).
- To make evaluative judgments one needs useful data gathered from assessment and measurement techniques.
- Assessment involves the interpretation of measurement data. It makes sense of the data collected on student performance.
- Assessment may be norm-referenced (related to other learners) or criterion/standards-referenced (related to predetermined criteria/standards).
- Measurement is the collection of data, usually in quantitative terms, of student performance.
- A range of measurement devices is available. Useful techniques include standardised tests, teacher-made tests, oral tests, work samples, systematic observation, interviews, questionnaires, checklists and rating scales, anecdotal records, sociograms and self-reports.
- A curriculum evaluation algorithm involves seven stages:
  — Evaluation presage
  — Task specification
  — Evaluation design
  — Data collection
  — Data analysis
  — Conclusions and recommendations
  — Presentation of report
- Curriculum materials may be evaluated by criteria such as:
  interest, authenticity, organisation and balance, appropriateness, and technical quality.

10 Curriculum application and change

There is nothing more difficult to carry out, nor more doubtful of success, nor more dangerous to handle than to initiate a new order of things. (Machiavelli, *The Prince*)

Change is a phenomenon which we experience continuously. Daily, it seems, features of our society are changing. Indeed, some changes are so frequent and substantial that we may find it difficult to keep abreast with these developments. So it is with schooling and education; substantive and frequent change appears to have become something of a norm, a continuing reality of schools. Curriculum change may be considered as a subset of educational change and as such is affected by the same type of factors affecting change within education in general.

The past few years have witnessed the most significant and sustained period of curriculum change that we have known. Perhaps those driving curriculum change will lessen its pace, though probably not, given the substantially increased politicisation of education in general, and curriculum in particular, over the past decade. In order to cope effectively with curriculum change we must learn to understand more about the concepts and processes involved.

This chapter will address curriculum implementation and curriculum change from two slightly different points of view. First, it will relate the concept of curriculum implementation in the context of the model of curriculum development outlined at the end of chapter 3 in what I have called the curriculum application phase. In so doing it will highlight the integral nature of curriculum implementation in the entire curriculum development process. This will complete the model and thus show how one may approach the task of curriculum development effectively.

Second, this chapter will address the more fundamental, generic issue of implementation in curricula and the consequential curriculum change that occurs. It is important for teachers and curriculum developers to be aware of this feature of modern education, particularly in terms of the accelerated rate of curriculum change. Innovations and change generally besiege our schools, and teachers are in need of greater understanding of the concept of change and how implementation might be undertaken successfully.

Implementation and modification

Towards the end of chapter 3 an algorithmic model of curriculum development was presented as a useful way to construct a curriculum (see figure 3.8). This was essentially a model for the conceptualisation of curriculum development which also provided a set of sequential procedures for devising and developing a curriculum. Three phases were conceptualised in the model—presage, development and application. The earlier chapters have discussed the first two phases and it is now appropriate to examine the final phase. From the algorithmic perspective, the final phase (application) consists of the activities of implementation, modification, monitoring and curriculum evaluation.

Implementation in curriculum involves changing the status quo by accepting and utilising a newly created curriculum or part of a curriculum. That is, taking the curriculum document as devised in the development phase of the model and putting it into practice. If the curriculum is accepted and utilised successfully we say that it has become *institutionalised.*

In the short term any newly implemented curriculum will be expected to experience some difficulties. To a large degree this will reflect the effectiveness of the curriculum developers in meeting the need of the curriculum's clients. Thus implementation is a short-term phenomenon that attempts to integrate the new curriculum into existing practice. To some degree the problems experienced in implementing curricula reside with a lack of systematic implementation procedures. As noted in chapter 3, for any new curriculum to be implemented requires an educational institution to change. This itself is a daunting phenomenon and so a plan or strategy is required to facilitate change to take place.

The nature of change and change strategies will be dealt with more substantially later in this chapter. At this point it is important for teachers to know that a new curriculum (as an example of a curriculum innovation) can be implemented more successfully in a school when cognisance and action are taken of the following points:

1 A deliberate strategy is developed to implement the curriculum in the school.
2 The curriculum is presented in terms of its favourable characteristics.
3 Support is obtained at a systemic level for the innovation.
4 The characteristics of the school are disposed towards the innovation.

In implementing the curriculum it would be expected that some *modification* will be required. If, for example, a curriculum was developed externally to a school and was then implemented within it, one would anticipate some modifications being necessary to take account of differing local contextual factors such as the varying nature of students, differing school resources, differing teachers, parental input variations, community support and so forth. These modifications might be quite minor in nature or quite substantial, depending upon how effectively the curriculum developers have undertaken their task.

What is extremely useful for teachers in schools in recent times is the realisation, acceptance and support by central authorities of individual differences between schools. To claim, even tacitly, that all schools within an educational system are the same, or even substantially similar, is just nonsense. Yet that was the very basis of systemic curriculum development and design in the past. It is simply not possible for curriculum developers, such as those in a centralised organisation, to take into account all variables relating to different schools, particularly as some in one school may be counterproductive to others in another. Similarly, educators and the community cannot expect schooling outcomes to be the same.

Take, for example, a newly constructed history curriculum disseminated by a central curriculum development and assessment agency (such as the NSW Board of Studies, the WA Secondary Education Authority or similar agencies in each state). The assumption is made by those agencies that all schools will treat the curriculum document the same and their students are essentially the same. Yet we all know this is not the case. One school may have a very advanced approach to teaching history, ample teaching–learning resources and students able to cope with the abstract learning involved. Another school may resist history, possess few resources and have students struggling to understand English as a language let alone the subtleties of history. Clearly these schools cannot, nor should they have to, address the history curriculum in identical ways.

Even if a curriculum was initially developed within a school, or by a cluster of local schools, one would expect some adjustments to be made as the curriculum was taken from theory to practice through the implementation process. To a significant degree, then, the success of a curriculum's implementation will reflect the willingness and ability of developers to accommodate changes to their curriculum. This may require changes to curriculum intent, content, learning, activities or evaluation procedures and, in turn, may require developers to revise their situational analysis.

This sub-process within the final phase of the curriculum development model is likely to occur in the short term and may require regular reflection to ensure that the curriculum is achieving its purpose within a school context. Consequently the modification of a curriculum may occur every year or two, though these changes are likely to be minor in nature.

The essential feature of this first part of the model's application phase is that developers have a useful role to play in the implementation of their curricula within schools. As developers they can explain the working of the curriculum in detail. As developers they are in a better place to make modifications, if required, to the curriculum. And as developers involved in implementation they have a stake in making their curriculum work successfully. While these are short-term considerations they are important to the long-term success of the curriculum.

Monitoring and curriculum evaluation

As a rule of thumb, over the long term, a curriculum will require continual monitoring and the provision of substantive feedback to curriculum developers every five to seven years. A decade or so ago we would have said that curricula would require substantial revision every seven to ten years, but in this time of substantial educational and societal change, a seven-year period may be the outer parameter (see Print, 1990).

As the task of curriculum development is such an extensive, resource-demanding activity, it is obvious that constant development or redevelopment of curricula is impractical. However, it is equally obvious that societal and educational conditions are changing constantly and these will need to be reflected in the school curriculum. How are these positions to be resolved?

Within the model (figure 3.8) the long-term aspect of the final phase recommends constant monitoring of the curriculum. This is undertaken as part of the regular activities of classroom teachers through the collection of feedback data on student performance. In addition some group is needed to undertake the task of regularly and systematically monitoring the curriculum. If those implementing and using the curriculum are amenable to also pooling their feedback data, the process of monitoring the curriculum can be achieved relatively painlessly.

As the situation changes with time (due to changed societal circumstances, different types of students, new technology, additional content information and so forth) so the monitoring of the curriculum should report the direction for needed changes. On an annual basis this feedback can be forwarded to the original curriculum development group for consideration and for possible relatively minor changes to the curriculum document.

Experience suggests that constant monitoring of curricula, while desirable, is rarely achieved consistently at school level. After several years of operation, it is highly probable that a curriculum is no longer as appropriate as previously and substantial adjustments may be required. After several years of tinkering with minor changes to the curriculum it is apparent that a substantial revision is required. At this point a *comprehensive curriculum evaluation* is an essential task to be undertaken (figure 3.8).

For example, a decade ago the suburb of Cabramatta, in the mid-western area of Sydney, was populated by peoples essentially from a Southern

European background. A school curriculum for local primary and secondary schools should have taken that variable into account. However, to have maintained that curriculum today would be quite inappropriate as the suburb is now almost entirely populated by people from a Vietnamese background.

An approach for conducting comprehensive curriculum evaluation has been mentioned in the previous chapter and one such method can be seen in Print, (1990) *Curriculum Review of Social Studies and Social Sciences Education.* Many other ways of conducting curriculum evaluations are available as may be seen in the literature (Kemmis & Stake, 1988; Simons, 1987; McLaughlin & Phillips, 1991; Patton, 1986; Stufflebeam, et al., 1972; Parlett & Hamilton, 1972; Davis, 1981; Eisner, 1979).

The essential stages in conducting a curriculum evaluation were discussed in the previous chapter and were outlined in figure 9.2. The algorithm suggests a seven-stage sequential procedure for evaluating a curriculum (such as a school's curriculum or year 11 and 12 history) or a component of a curriculum (such as years 5 and 6 of the primary mathematics syllabus). The same procedure is appropriate for evaluating a component part of a curriculum such as a unit of work (e.g. coastal landforms in year 11 geography) or a sequence of teaching units (Australian History 1850–1990;1901–45;1945–82) as well as for an entire curriculum.

A more comprehensive coverage of curriculum evaluation in an Australian context, with examples, may be found in Davis (1980) *Teachers as Curriculum Evaluators*, Kemmis & Stake (1988) *Evaluating Curriculum* and in Print (1990) *Curriculum Review of Social Studies and Social Sciences Education,* as well as in chapter 9.

Curriculum model

This book has been constructed around the algorithmic model of curriculum development outlined at the end of chapter 3, and it is now complete. The remaining chapters have covered the three phases of that model—presage, development and application—and provided an understanding of the sequential procedure required to undertake curriculum development effectively. What is important for teachers and curriculum developers is to understand the curriculum development process and then apply it to the context for which it has been devised.

Figure 3.8 illustrates the phases of the algorithmic model and the interrelationships between them and their constituent parts. In providing this algorithmic approach of the model, it has been the intention to identify and explain a sequence of procedures whereby one can conduct the process of curriculum development effectively. In schools and other institutions with educational programs, those involved in curriculum development now have a logical, sequential and practical procedure for devising and developing curriculum documents, curriculum materials and curriculum projects.

Dynamics of curriculum change

Curriculum change invariably reflects change in the society at large and education in general. Hence most of what we deal with in curriculum change within the school context addresses ways of implementing change effectively. A specific curriculum innovation may lead society in changing in a particular direction, but usually curriculum change reflects societal change.

Consequently when we consider curriculum change we need to include both the content of that change as well as the process by which that change comes about. By content, we mean the knowledge, skills, concepts, understandings, values and so forth associated with the material concerned, such as a new history syllabus or a primary mathematics syllabus. The change process refers to means by which teachers will be introduced to that content and how they will be convinced to adopt and implement it. This requires the use of appropriate change strategies to convince teachers of the need for the change, the value in participating in the change and importance of developing appropriate perceptions, beliefs and actions that accord with that change.

This is not an easy or straightforward task, nor should it be. An important beginning is for curriculum developers, indeed all participants in the educational process, to be aware of the generic forces of curriculum change if they are to survive effectively. As the fast pace of curriculum change continues apparently unabated, driven by the increased politicisation of curriculum, so those involved in developing and implementing curricula will need to know more about the nature of change and how to deal with it purposefully. To that end the following section will examine the nature of curriculum change, the change process, change strategies, the characteristics of innovations and some concluding comments on effecting change in schools.

Change concepts

Constant and substantial change is a phenomenon of our lives that has become a feature of post-Second World War society. Education has reflected that significant change and will, undoubtedly, continue to do so. Therefore it is important for us to comprehend this phenomenon and see how it may be employed effectively in understanding and implementing curricula at school and system levels. Curriculum, being the essential heart of schooling, has experienced enormous swings with the pendulum of change. As curriculum is concerned with the what, how, when and so what questions in teaching, it also has the scope for multidimensional change. However, before examining the nature of that change, it is useful to distinguish the significant terms employed in the literature.

Change is a generic term used in education to incorporate a number of associated concepts (innovation, adoption) in order to analyse and explain curricula phenomena. Change is, in effect, the process of transformation of phenomena and in analysing that transformation it is useful to consider the dimensions of rate (speed), scale (size), degree (thoroughness), significance (profoundness) and direction (orientation). It usually refers to a general concept which describes what has happened, particularly as the result of the dissemination of an innovation.

Much of curriculum is concerned with *planned change,* which may be defined as: 'a deliberate and collaborative process involving a change agent and a client system which are brought together to solve a problem or, more generally, to plan and attain an improved state of functioning and applying valid knowledge' (Bennis, 1966). Most of what we address in curriculum change is some form of planned change.

Innovation means either an object, idea or practice which is perceived to be *new* and also the process by which that new object, idea or practice becomes adopted. This definition includes the more recent emphasis upon viewing innovations as a *process* as well as particular objects and practices. In particular innovations refer to specific objects, ideas and practices that will result in change.

Diffusion is a process concerned with the spread of a new idea/object/practice from its point of origin to its adopters. The term implies neutral action by the innovation's developers or adopters and, in effect, means the spread of an innovation by natural means such as word of mouth.

Dissemination means a *deliberate* process to spread a new idea/object/practice from its origin to adopters. Dissemination is more specific than diffusion with an emphasis upon deliberate, goal-directed activities carried out by change agents to facilitate the adoption of an innovation.

Change agents are significant individuals and groups involved in the process of facilitating change through establishing communication links between developers and clients. Change agents seek to bring about change through their effective leadership and participation in the change process. They may be termed 'innovators', 'early adopters', 'early majority', 'late majority' or 'laggards', depending upon their role in facilitating change.

Adoption refers to the initial acceptance of an innovation and its rate of acceptance (implementation) within a system. Adoption of an innovation is the second stage in the change process involving the sequence need, adoption, implementation, institutionalisation.

These terms will become useful in any analysis and discussion of the process of curriculum change in general and in relation to any specific curriculum innovation. It should be noted that the past few years has witnessed multifarious curriculum change within Australia and the dissemination of numerous curriculum innovations, not the least of which has been specific subject syllabuses. Other curriculum innovations include many forms of curriculum policy on specific areas such as girls' education, gifted and talented, equity, multiculturalism, curriculum materials, technological developments relating to curriculum and distinctive moves towards a national curriculum within Australia.

Sources of curriculum change

At any one time the curriculum of a school is subjected to considerable pressures to change from its current situation. But where do these pressures come from and what do they mean for teachers? Pressures emerge from what Skilbeck (1984:54–7) considers to be four principal sources, as can be seen in figure 10.1.

Figure 10.1   Sources of curriculum change

1 Changes in society (indirect effects)		3 Changes in education (indirect effects)	
Policy	Practice	Policy	Practice
2 Changes in society (direct effects)		4 Changes in education (direct effects)	
Policy	Practice	Policy	Practice

Source: M. Skilbeck, 1984

In figure 10.1 Skilbeck suggests that changes to the school curriculum reflect four major inputs: changes in society (indirect and direct) and changes in education (indirect and direct).

1 Curriculum change in schools *reflects* changes in *society* at large. Such changes are invariably indirect in nature and the association or linkage between societal and curriculum change is rarely a perfect match. Nevertheless, many societal changes may have significant impact upon the school curriculum. Recent examples of societal change include high levels of youth unemployment, family relationship 'breakdown' and declining birth rate.

One could argue, for example, that the decline of the educational role within the family has placed indirect societal pressure on the school curriculum to accommodate that teaching. The last decade, therefore, has witnessed the inclusion of more health education, moral education, sex education and so forth within school curricula. On a very broad scale one could consider how the school curriculum has changed to reflect the general politico-economic changes in society since the Second World War. These changes may be seen in terms of the fundamental nature of the past four decades.

1950s: conservative yet changing, high economic growth, low levels of accountability

1960s: social revolution, rapid economic growth, very low accountabilty

1970s: consolidation and liberalism, sustained growth, some concern about accountability

1980s: conservatism growing, extremely variable economic growth, growing accountability

1990s: waning conservatism? slow economic growth? high levels of accountability

In terms of the 1980s, did you notice how schools became more conservative over the years of that decade? In the five years between the writing of the first and second editions of this book our society became even more conservative. Greater demands have been expressed for basic competencies, a greater vocational orientation is being pursued, discipline and control have been tackled, higher standards are being pushed, fewer radical ideas are being accepted and above all there exists a general push for greater accountability and significantly enhanced school effectiveness.

2 Skilbeck suggests that the school curriculum responds to '. . . changes in society which explicitly and deliberately enlist curriculum policy and practice as a means of achieving stated goals and ends. These

include, for example, attempts to encourage schools to show greater awareness of industry, or problems of peace and war' (1984:55).

In recent years the school curriculum in Australian schools has changed to accommodate such direct pressures as new standards of literacy, enhanced numeracy skills, environmental studies and peace studies. These examples demonstrate how deliberate changes have occurred in schools as a response to societal change. In the immediate future we shall witness substantial change to the post-compulsory curriculum in our secondary schools as the curriculum and schools react to numerous societal changes manifest in such significant reports as Finn (1991), Mayer (1992) and Carmichael (1992). Can you cite other examples of this *direct* relationship?

3 Within education itself, changes occur which impinge or implicitly challenge existing curriculum practices and policies. While Skilbeck states that these are internally based, they obviously reflect aspects of the outside society. Nevertheless, internally instigated changes (those emanating from within education systems) can have a profound effect upon school curricula. In the 1980s, for example, there have been numerous inquiries into education which have affected curricula in schools (for example, the Beazley Report (WA), Excellence and Equity (NSW), Blackburn Report (VIC), National Commission on Excellence in Education in the US, and Quality of Education in Australia). Other sources of change include educational structural reorganisation, pushes for multicultural and gender equity, and Participation and Equity Program (PEP) initiatives.

4 Skilbeck suggests that changes may be '. . . made or sought in curriculum policy and practice to promote certain ends or achieve particular goals in the education system' (1984:55). Such changes in recent years would include the gifted and talented programs, daily physical fitness, conference writing, Uninterrupted Sustained Silent Reading (USSR), and Year 11 and 12 alternative courses. These are changes which have been designed to have direct effects and specific outcomes upon the curriculum as a whole or some component part of the curriculum.

With an understanding of where curriculum change comes from, teachers and developers are in a position to relate more effectively to changing situations. But how does that change occur?

Curriculum change process

In schools today teachers encounter at least three 'layers' of curriculum change—national, state and school levels. Most recently teachers have been exposed to embryonic changes resulting from a 'national curriculum', a set of national curriculum statements designed to provide direction for curriculum across the states and territories (Kennedy, 1989; 1991). Such curriculum changes are just begining to impact upon classroom teachers, and athough the effect currently is negligible, the degree of that impact is likely to substantially increase over the next few years.

A second and currently more profound degree of impact in curriculum change is the state level of curriculum development. Each state has a curriculum and assessment agency which is responsible for devising, implementing and assessing certain system-level curricula, usually restricted to secondary schools. The state department of education, or the curriculum and assessment agency, also has responsibility for curricula in primary schools and sometimes in TAFE. The process of developing and implementing curricula creates significant curriculum change as a base-line, let alone a range of other curriculum initiatives at the state level (such as gender curriculum issues; gifted and talented education; multicultural education; and so forth).

The third level of curriculum change results from intitiatives at the school level (or perhaps a group of schools), usually resulting from attempts to address the needs of diverse students. Contextual factors, such as language background, numeracy skills, employment opportunities, ethnic background, and so forth, require teachers in schools to reflect upon their curriculum offerings in order to make appropriate changes or to develop more suitable curricula. Consequently another layer of curriculum change must be considered by teachers. However, it should be noted that little evidence exists of significant curriculum initiatives being undertaken by groups or clusters of schools (as in regions, districts or clusters), despite schools being encouraged to seek an individual identity through the creation of a school 'vision' and mission statements.

If teachers and curriculum developers are in a position to understand the nature of the change process, they are also better served to take appropriate action. In particular, teachers can relate to the various problems thrown up by change as it affects their school. Typical questions posed in schools by teachers include:

1 Do we need this change?
2 Why has it arisen?
3 How will it affect us?
4 What ways can we best support/oppose it?
5 Will it improve the quality of learning?
6 How can we ensure the continuance of the change?

Curriculum change, it has been said, reflects the broader changes in education and the social system at large. But how can that change be made to be taken aboard effectively in educational institutions? There has been extensive research in this area and most curriculum writers agree that three (or four as stated here) basic phases of the curriculum change process may be distinguished (Fullan, 1982, 1987; Miles et al., 1987; Smith & Lovat, 1991; Print, 1988).

Figure 10.2 depicts the readily apparent nature of the interaction between the four phases. While these phases have been separated for analysis purposes, in reality they will merge imperceptibly into each other and thus depict more of a continuous process. But what constitutes these four phases and how do they interact with each other?

Need

The beginnings of the curriculum change process lies in expression of concern, dissatisfaction or need with the current curriculum or curriculum practices. Consequently a demand or expressed need is created for a variation in the existing situation. This expressed need may come from a variety of sources such as teachers, students, parents, administrators, employers, educational systems or some combination of these sources.

Change will not occur without this need being present, although not all individuals perceive the same need for change, while others are not aware of the need for change at all. At times persuasive methods to promote change are necessary if change is to succeed. In recent years, for example, all educational systems within Australia have experienced substantial and profound curriculum change. In many cases the need for this change was perceived by a small group of powerful decision-makers who then sought to convince others that the need and direction of proposed curriculum change was indeed appropriate.

With the release of the policy document *Excellence and Equity* (1989), the NSW Minister for Education and his supporters expressed a need for major curriculum change.

> There is widespread community unease with the quality and focus of education currently provided to our young people in schools. Absolutely central to this unease is the perception that many young people are not learning the right things, are not gaining essential skills, and are not sufficiently motivated to exert themselves beyond minimum levels of achievement.
>
> . . . our schools are confronted with a major challenge to which they must respond effectively and speedily. The current curriculum, particularly at the secondary level, is not fully adequate to this challenge. (1989:10)

What is important about this phase, should those associated with the change process wish it to be successful, is the recognition and acceptance of the *need for curriculum change* by a substantial majority of those involved. If classroom teachers, for example, do not recognise and accept the need for a particular curriculum innovation they will become resistant

228   *Curriculum development and design*

Figure 10.2   Educational change process

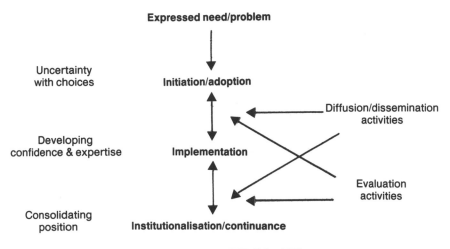

Source: After Fullan, 1982, 1987: Miles, 1987; Print,1988

to it and hence place the success of the curriculum change in jeopardy. Thus the first phase of successful curriculum change may involve those initiating the change in the process of convincing change participants as to its value. To facilitate that process the characteristics of innovations— relative advantage, compatibility, complexity, trialability and communication—should be employed purposively.

In the field of school curriculum there appears, nevertheless, particularly in recent years, to be a constant demand for variation to the status quo. This demand may be generated generally in society or from within the educational system as suggested earlier by Skilbeck (1984: 54–7). Certainly a plethora of educational system and politically inspired curriculum changes have been experienced throughout Australia in the past decade. And as we move into the early 1990s we may be experiencing the most significant curriculum change—the move towards a national curriculum!

If you believe that change is necessary in schools you might pose the following questions to yourself. Should the schools you know stay the same? Are you aware of societal pressures indicating the need for change in schools? What is it about your institution's curriculum that requires change? In answering these questions we have a starting point for the change process.

Adoption

Adoption means the deliberate acceptance of an innovation to resolve an expressed need. After seeking information to resolve the problem, alternatives may be examined and this process serves as a step towards consolidation of change. From amongst the many alternatives available, an attempted resolution or innovation is decided and accepted. At this stage, however, the innovation is by no means secure within the institution.

Dissemination or diffusion of information about the proposed change occurs with varying degrees of success within educational institutions. Significant works in the literature on educational change (Fullan, 1982, 1987; Huberman & Miles, 1984; Miles et al., 1987; Miles, et al., 1988) suggest a number of factors that codetermine adoption rates within institutions. Among the more important factors in accounting for the successful adoption of the change are: access to information of decision-makers; alternative innovations in competition; central administrative support for a particular change; shared vision of the need for change; good quality innovation/change program; funding availability to support implementation; purposeful role and effectiveness of change agents; significant and sustained community pressures and, most importantly state government department position on the proposed change.

These factors will have a significant impact upon how willingly the change is adopted by teachers in schools. The next section on strategies for curriculum change provides specific examples of how the adoption procedure may be deliberately manipulated, particularly by significant change agents, to ensure a high adoption rate and subsequently an effective implementation, leading to successful institutionalisation.

Implementation

The implementation phase may be considered as a continuum, stretching from the adoption of an innovation until its complete acceptance or institutionalisation. In education, implementation begins with the initial attempts by educators to effect the innovation into various schools/institutions. As this phase progresses, participants usually develop confidence and expertise with the innovation and so it has a greater chance of success, as seen in figure 10.2. This is a crucial phase in the change process, for although the innovation has been adopted, few participants or even change agents would guarantee successful implementation to the institutionalisation phase. Indeed the innovation will succeed or fail in large measure by how effectively it is implemented.

It may be, however, for a variety of reasons that this phase is not successful and hence the innovation languishes. Or perhaps the *rate* of acceptance is slow and the subsequent usage rate is low. We should all be aware of innovations that have failed to gain substantial acceptance at the implementation phase. Many curriculum materials such as SEMP and

ASEP achieved only partial implementation and although they were still used in a few schools for many years, they never achieved what could be called near complete acceptance or institutionalisation. Similarly, in the early to mid 1980s many educational systems and schools introduced curriculum innovations to address the needs of gifted and talented students. In large measure these also failed and have mostly disappeared from the curricula of our schools.

Alternatively the innovation could be implemented very successfully. There are several factors which research (Fullan, 1982, 1987; Huberman & Miles, 1984; Miles et al., 1987; Miles, et al., 1988) has indicated will influence the effectiveness of the implementation phase and hence the rate at which the innovation is accepted and used. These may be categorised as:

1 Strategies for enhancing change.
2 Characteristics of the innovation.
3 Internal nature of the organisation.
4 Characteristics of the broader social context.

The first two of the above sets of factors are discussed in the last major sections of this chapter. The last two factors are extremely broad and can be discussed only briefly here. It can be said in summary, however, that the implementation phase of any change process will be enhanced if the internal nature of the receiving organisation and the characteristics of the social context are conducive to change.

The third factor above concerns the internal nature of the organisation undergoing change. Institutions that have an internal means to facilitate change will be in a favourable position to make the implementation phase more effective. Take, for example, a school experiencing difficulty matching student needs with existing curricula. If the school also has a collaborative decision-making procedure for curriculum decision-making and a cooperative administration, the means are available to implement change effectively. At a systemic level, an educational system which has effective lines of communication, strong leadership, adequate support services, significant administrative commitment to the innovation and so forth, then successful implementation can occur.

Similarly, if society at large is desirous of a particular change, or is being pushed towards a changed direction, and there is political support for the change (such as a new curriculum structure as evidenced in the Carrick, Beazley and Blackburn Reports), then effective implementation in the school system will be enhanced. Perhaps society perceives it is time for a change and hence is relatively supportive of curriculum initiatives which will produce substantive change.

This would appear to have been the case in the early 1970s and the mid 1980s when periods of major educational change were initiated through the Commonwealth government. Similarly when the Carrick Report (1989) and Beazley Report (1984) were introduced in New South Wales and Western Australia respectively, extensive public and educational support was received.

Implementation, the third stage in the change process, shows that the innovation is gaining strength but its transformation into the fourth phase cannot yet be guaranteed. In effect, the implementation phase is a testing procedure which will determine the innovation's ultimate fate. Meanwhile, an innovation exists somewhere along an implementation continuum ranging from non-implementation to complete acceptance. Can you cite examples of innovations and their position on this continuum at this moment?

Institutionalisation/continuance

Should the innovation be used continually over time and in the process become interwoven into an organisational structure, then it may be said that institutionalisation has occurred (figure 10.2). This phase must take time and change cannot be considered to have occurred successfully until institutionalisation is evident. Indeed, many innovations appear to succeed in the earlier stages only to flounder when exposed to the broader context for which they were intended.

Many innovations in curriculum receive artificial support in the form of finance, consultants, administrative favour and so forth during the early stages of implementation. An acid test for the success of an innovation is to gauge the effectiveness of the innovation on the removal of those crutches. Should the innovation remain in place then the institutionalisation phase will have occurred and change been effected. All too often in curriculum, however, the removal of these supportive factors leads to the demise of the innovation.

Can you cite examples of successful institutionalised change? What about examples of innovations that failed after the removal of supportive props? In the last decade in Australian schools, there have been many programs initiated and implemented to meet the needs of both intellectually able and disadvantaged pupils. You may be able to cite some. But how many of them are still operating once their supportive props were removed?

Facilitating the achievement of institutionalisation (and by definition the phase of implementation as well) is a major goal of those who would bring about planned educational change (such as change agents in a school). To enhance the achievement of that goal within educational organisations, in relation to curriculum change, teachers and curriculum developers need to consider the following factors (Fullan, 1982, 1987; Huberman & Miles, 1984; Miles, 1983, 1987; Miles, et al., 1988):

— strong administrative commitments;

— positive pressure and support from within the school;
— support activities (in-service, local facilitators);
— resource allocation to fund change;
— removal of competing practices;
— believable evaluation of innovation;
— linked with current classroom practices.

By contrast, schools that are lacking in support and which are essentially destabilised by high staff turnover, inadequate leadership support, low levels of resources, poor support services and constant student mobility, have difficulty institutionalising change. Despite the need for change in these schools, the status quo will undoubtedly remain.

The four phases of the change process may be summarised in terms of a matrix which considers the phases in relation to the typical sorts of activities conducted, factors to enhance that phase and the typical time taken in schools to achieve that phase.

Table 10.1   Curriculum change matrix

Phase	Typical activities	Enhancing factors	Time line
Need	Perceived need; felt problem. Deciding to start; examine similar contexts; needs assessment	Shared vision; active advocate. Local agendas; similar societal needs	Short–medium
Adoption	Launching process; acceptance; building commitment; front-end training for key people	All the above factors, plus: quality innovation; fit local setting; perceived value	Relatively short after-initiation phase
Implementation	Design action plan; setting goals, maintaining active commitment; developing confidence and expertise	Strong leadership commitment; shared control; clear direction; rewards for participants; peer support; quality innovation	Short–long (perhaps incomplete)
Institutionalisation	Building strength; evaluating; changing organisation; integrating into structures; building networks	Strong leadership; institutional support; resource support; in-servicing staff; remove competing activities; evaluation	Medium–long, depending upon effect of implementation

Change strategies

We have come to accept, albeit reluctantly at times, planned educational change within educational circles in general and within curriculum in particular. A significant congruence of ideas exists in the literature about how this change could, and should, occur. A minimum requirement to effect planned change within school curricula is some form of plan or method of procedure. These procedures are called strategies and a wide range is available for change agents and those who would effect change.

Most planned change in schools involves the implementation of specific innovations. As we will discover later in this chapter, innovations are objects, ideas or practices perceived to be new by the receiving audience. The question posed by those who wish to implement the change is: How then can these innovations be adopted, implemented and institutionalised effectively in schools? After more than two decades of educational research, a high degree of consensus exists as to how change strategies may be classified and what they constitute (table 10.2). Three groupings of change strategies are evident according to the many authors (Miles, 1964; Chin, 1967; Sieber, 1968; Zaltman et al., 1972; Bennis, Benne & Chin, 1976) who have contributed to these typologies.

Of these various typologies in table 10.2, the most commonly accepted terminology has been that of Bennis, Benne & Chin (1976). Nevertheless one interesting feature of the table is the high degree of similarity between the change strategies advocated by the various authors. Using Bennis, Benne & Chin as a guide, it is useful to examine these classifications of change strategies as a means for devising planned change in the curriculum. Our basic question then is: How do we facilitate change within the curriculum of a school or group of schools?

Table 10.2   Change strategies

	Rational	Persuasive	Power
Miles (1964)	Problem–process	Relation–attitude	Power–solution
Chin (1967)	Empirical–rational	Normative–re-educative	Power–coercive
Sieber (1968)	'Rational man'	Cooperation	'Powerless participant'
Jones (1969)	Utilitarian	Normative	Coercive
Zaltman (1972)	Facilitative	Pursuasive	Power–re-educative
Bennis Benne & Chin (1976)	Empirical–rational	Normative–re-educative	Power-coercive

Rational-empirical strategies

The basic premise of these strategies is that people are reasonable and will therefore act in a rational manner. Supporters of these strategies argue that, when exposed to an innovation, people will react according to their best interests, that is, when aware of an innovation, seeing its inherent value to themselves, people will adopt it. That, after all, is both rational and logical action and quite a reasonable expectation for people to follow.

Strategies using a logical and rational justification rely upon the active and effective dissemination of knowledge in order to link the innovation with potential users. Those users, acting rationally, will then seek the innovation as a logical solution to their problem and thereby adopt it. In these models the change agent plays an active role, which centres on facilitating dissemination of knowledge about the innovation. Typically in schools, with the implementation of a curriculum innovation, dissemination is achieved through holding numerous workshops, seminars and demonstrations to illustrate the innovation's inherent value. General displays of curriculum materials, perhaps extended by the use of promotional brochures, is a favoured way of providing information to teachers who then, exposed to the innovation, perceive its value and adopt it.

Such strategies are based on a positive, optimistic view of people and have been employed frequently by educational systems in Australia as well as in our schools. Within curricula, examples of innovations adopted using rational approaches include conference writing in primary school English, the use of video-recorders, Uninterrupted Sustained Silent Reading (USSR) or similar reading programs in secondary schools, overhead projectors in classrooms and increasingly the use of computers in classrooms. In these cases the rational message is clear—this innovation is of value to you! Can you cite other examples?

In many instances teachers have realised the inherent advantages of these products and procedures and consequently adopted them. Hoyle (1976) suggested that rational–empirical strategies are appropriate to curriculum where the resource is well supported by expertise (researcher, inspector, specialist) to demonstrate its strength in a largely one-way communication flow. Teachers then adopt the innovation because of its logical value to them.

But equally obviously many teachers do not adopt innovations based upon rational and logical grounds. A major problem is the assumption that there is but one form of logic and one reality for all teachers. This is clearly not the case, though there may be times when the vast majority of teachers may perceive the value of adopting a curriculum innovation (such as vocationally related curricula for post-compulsory students who are not tertiary bound).

However in many situations, such as the 'expert' created curriculum packages in the 1960s and 1970s (such as ASEP, SEMP, BSCS, HSGP), teachers did not perceive the value of such curriculum materials and the subsequent adoption rate was barely moderate, while the implementation rates fell away as well. This is because teachers have differing perceptions of reality, ascribe differing meanings to events and subsequently differing understandings of what is rational and logical. Consequently in the case of most curriculum innovations, some form of persuasion is employed to encourage teachers to adopt and implement curriculum innovations.

Normative-re-educative strategies

Perhaps a rational, logical strategy has been ineffective in achieving planned change in your school. To overcome this problem you will require a strategy that can convince teachers that the planned change should be adopted. The underlying premise for normative–re-educative strategies is concerned with changing people, particularly their perceptions and attitudes, and hence their subsequent behaviour.

The changing of behaviour may be viewed in two ways. First, from the perspective of a change agent who perceives substantial resistance from participants to the proposed change and who consequently seeks to ensure that behaviour is changed in the appropriate direction. And second, from the viewpoint of a change agent (perhaps an internal change agent) who realises that effective change will ensue when participants are re-educated as to the benefits of the proposed change.

The essential differences between these approaches are the degree of perceived opposition and the consequential degree of persuasion needed to change participant behaviour. The former approach would argue for a more forceful persuasion than the latter approach which seeks to encourage participants to perceive the value through educative strategies. Of central importance to these strategies is knowing how clients ascertained their attitudes, values and perceived problems. Once this has been determined then people's attitudes, values and perceptions may be manipulated, to varying degrees, towards the particular innovation. Thus the central feature of normative–re-educative strategies is to encourage through re-education, and even to manipulate, people to act in a manner differently from their current behaviour.

Group-work techniques such as group decision-making, workshops, training/therapy groups and so forth are used as means of re-educating people to see things differently. To achieve this, persuasive communication of various forms are employed. Thus most forms of advertising, which emphasise a transformational approach to attitudes and values, may be considered as normative-re-educative strategies. Advertising is certainly a persuasive means of changing people's attitudes and thus their purchasing behaviour, and education could do well by taking heed of advertising strategies.

The change agent in normative-re-educative strategies is usually an external force working with a group in a collaborative manner. Emphasis is placed upon encouraging clients to recognise, acknowledge and adopt the innovation. According to Bennis, Benne & Chin (1976):

change in a pattern of practice or action, according to this view, will occur only as the persons involved are brought to change their normative orientation to old patterns and develop commitments to new ones. And changes in normative orientations involve changes in attitudes, values, skills and significant relationships, not just changes in knowledge, information or intellectual rationales . . .

Obviously there are times when we change our behaviour and it does not appear logical, rational or even in our best interest to do so. These strategies help explain how that phenomenon may have occurred or, indeed, may be achieved in the future. It is not a mistake then that these strategies are called normative-re-educative because they, as Smith & Lovat point out, '. . . clearly recognize the centrality of beliefs, interests, perceptions and feelings and the re-education by the individuals that are involved, if the change process is to be effective.' (1991:176)

Examples of the normative-re-educative strategies in education include groups such as staff meetings, departmental meetings, in-service groups, working parties, consultants working with staff groups and so forth. Communication is essentially two-way and clients are usually cooperative, at least in the group context. The persuasiveness of the message and the facilitator are also significant elements in explaining the effectiveness of these change strategies.

Within the school curriculum many changes may have occurred as a result of normative-re-educative strategies. Perhaps a new writing program has been introduced into a primary school or a gender equity approach adopted to secondary school subject selection. The genre approach to literature has been largely adopted through normative–re-educative strategies. Perhaps a primary school principal may have used a normative-re-educative strategy to get his or her staff to introduce a new basic skills testing program. In recent times in New South Wales, several schools have employed a combination of rational-empirical and normative–re-educative strategies to encourage staff to adopt curriculum changes for gifted and talented students. Can you cite changes that you have seen resulting from normative–re-educative strategies?

Power-coercive strategies

But what happens to the planned change in our school if we can't persuade participants to alter their behaviour? Or perhaps an educational system, aware of potential opposition, may decide on a more 'frontal' approach to change from the very beginning of the process. The answer to achieving effective change lies with the use of power-coercive strategies.

Sometimes referred to as political-administrative strategies, for they are top-down in nature, this group of change procedures is based upon the control of rewards and punishments as a means of regulating the behaviour of participants. Power is used as the ultimate sanction (that is, people are told to do something such as adopt an innovation, or else!) by someone in authority. If the action is not carried out, then the threat of a sanction is applied. Subsequently the sanction may be applied in order to ensure compliance.

This situation, however, invariably requires significant influence over subordinates by superordinates as well as the perception of a sanction threat held by the subordinate. Thus the essential features of power-coercive strategies for curriculum change are:

1 possessing the power to demand the curriculum be changed; and
2 possessing the power to force, or appearing to force, people to comply with the directed change. Ultimately, those in power who are forcing the planned change will decide if they are willing, and able, to apply the sanction should it be necessary.

With these strategies participants are forced to comply with imposed directions on the curriculum if they want rewards or wish to avoid sanctions. In both cases, although particularly the latter, participants invariably do not relate meaningfully to the innovation and have little consequential intrinsic motivation to ensure the innovation's success.

Change agents using power-coercive strategies within an educational context are usually figures of authority such as senior system managers or senior school administrators. As such, these persons have the power to invoke sanctions and allocate rewards. More likely they would initially employ the threat of a sanction if the curriculum innovation concerned was not being implemented effectively. However, as mentioned above, such authority figures have some power to force participants to comply. Consequently such strategies are not well received by participants. And for many, when the threat of the sanction is lifted, the opportunity is perceived appropriate to revert to previous behaviour.

Power-coercive strategies are usually employed where change agents want a quick response either to achieve institutionalisation of the innovation or if it is a particularly large and complicated innovation, to ensure it is well under way. Similarly, power-coercive strategies are usually used for implementing technical changes to the curriculum, such as new assessment procedures, or a new syllabus document. Innovations that require substantial changes to teachers' perceptions, practices and beliefs are unlikely to be implemented effectively through the use of power-coercive strategies.

In schools, power-coercive strategies are commonly employed to change the curriculum. Where changes apply to the structure of education (rules, procedures, requirements), these strategies are most frequently found. However, imposed curricula or procedures are also examples of situations where power-coercive strategies are employed. Specific instances of this form of curriculum change include the restructuring of curriculum in New South Wales through *Excellence and Equity* (1989), K10 Social Studies Syllabus (Western Australia), Blackburn Report (1985), *Better Schools in WA* (1987), open-area schools, secondary school external examinations and the development of senior colleges. In these instances the change was directed by senior departmental or political figures into schools using power to ensure compliance.

The approach to initiating major curriculum change by educational systems may be described as a process of *cumulative change strategies.* Frequently educational systems have sought to implement a curriculum change, which they initiated upon their perception of its importance, through the use of rational-empirical strategies in the first instance. Should these not work effectively, they are supplemented by normative–re-educative strategies that particularly revolve around in-servicing teachers. And as a last measure, depending upon the level of significance attributed to the curriculum innovation, educational systems will employ power-coercive strategies.

Generally speaking, educational systems are well aware of the need to have positive teacher support in order to enhance innovation acceptance. But there are times when the forces of the system, or pushing the system, demand the implementaion of an innovation. In these situations educational systems may well resort to power coercive strategies as a last resort or even as the initial change strategy.

These, then, represent the main categories of educational change in schools. You can undoubtedly cite many examples of the three alternatives and you should compare them with the examples given. Table 10.3 may assist your understanding of change strategies and their application to schools.

Change agents

The concept of a change agent has been around for some fifty years, since researchers noticed that certain individuals, or groups of people, could make a significant difference to the implementation of innovations. Earlier in this chapter change agents were defined as significant individuals and groups involved in the process of facilitating change through establishing communication links between developers and clients. In this general role the change agent may have a very significant role to play and overall the change agent may make a significant difference in accounting for the successful implementation of an innovation.

Typical curriculum change agents are senior staff of curriculum and assessment agencies, curriculum consultants in those agencies or education systems (e.g. history consultant, primary mathematics consultant), specialist consultants in the same organisations (e.g. gifted and talented

Table 10.3   Change strategies in education

	Rational–empirical	Normative–re-educative	Power–coercive
Features	Rational adopters see personal gain in change; information for teachers to understand innovation.	Manipulates teacher attitudes and values to produce change; use groups and persuasive communication.	Control of rewards and punishments regulates teacher behaviour; ultimate sanction is power.
Examples	Daily physical education; Aussie Sports; USSR.	Gender equity; school effectiveness; collaborative planning; school councils; mainstreaming.	Beazley Report; open-area schools; better schools in WA; Most syllabuses.
Advantages	Commitment of teachers is high; straightforward; consistent with nature of teaching; success rate high.	Commitment of staff; high success within groups.	Speed of change; ordered and relatively easy; relatively inexpensive; uniformity enhanced.
Disadvantages	Time-consuming; haphazard adoption; costly.	Time-consuming; group difficulties; incomplete adoption; costly.	Resistance to innovation; develops internal dissension; lack of commitment by teachers.

consultant, multicultural consultant), primary school principal or deputy principal, director of curriculum in schools, heads of departments in schools and so forth. In some cases the change agent may be an external, independent person such a university staff member or a representative of an organisation (such as the Law Society, environmental organisations, traffic authorities).

The work of Gene Hall and his colleagues (1975, 1979, 1987) has provided a useful set of concepts and instruments to help direct the change agent to become more effective in the change process. The concept of Stages of Concern (SoC) proved valuable in determining teachers' levels of mental arousement about a proposed innovation (Marsh & Stafford, 1988). This may be effectively employed by change agents in attempting to implement an innovation. Similarly the concept of Levels of Use (LoU) was developed by Hall and his colleagues to explain the user's behaviour in relation to an innovation's implementation. The LoU can help explain, at the individual level, why teachers do, or do not, adopt and implement specific innovations.

Change agents may play one of many different roles (and frequently play multiple roles in any single change event), when working to enhance the implementation of an innovation. In examining different change strategies we have seen how change agents may operate. In the following summary (after Havelock, 1979; Miles, et al., 1988; Print, 1988) change agents are discussed in the singular though it should be remembered that a change agent may be a group of people.

- Information disseminator or resource linker: where the change agent makes information about the innovation and appropriate resources available to participants and ensures they have the opportunity to become familiar with that information. A curriculum consultant, for example, may provide information on a new syllabus and resources associated with it.

- Catalyst: where the change agent acts as a conduit and encourager for the participants to change their own behaviour. For example, a university staff member with specific expertise, might act as a motivator and support person for a primary staff to address the curriculum needs of gifted and talented children whose needs have been identified as a priority action for that school.

- Solution giver: where the change agent provides, or suggests, a solution to an identified problem. Usually the provision of this solution is performed without substantial negotiation on the change agent's behalf. A deputy principal, for example, might act as this form of change agent to facilitate the implementation of a new reading program to address the problem of student reading levels.

- Process supporter: where the change agent, after negotiation with the participants, facilitates a change process in which those involved voluntarily seek to change their behaviour. As the process continues, the change agent, acting as a supportive friend, provides feedback and support on the effectiveness of the change process. For example a member of school's staff, or perhaps an external agent, may act as a supportive friend while school staff seek to address the identified problem of gender equity within the school curriculum.

- Policy enforcer, where the change agent acts to apply a curriculum change from an external source or enforce a locally initiated curriculum change. The principal of a school may act as an enforcer of an educational system's demand for curriculum change such as a new structure for the curriculum. Alternatively the principal may enforce a local curriculum initiative of the school executive to ensure student numeracy skills are improved.

The nature of innovations

As seen earlier in this chapter, a subtle difference exists between the concepts 'change' and 'innovation'. Change is a broad generic term incorporating many concepts such as innovation, adoption and implementation. We often think about change as the process resulting from the introduction of an innovation. Change may also be defined as the process of transforming phenomena into something different. It also includes accidental or unintentional movements and shifts, although with curricula we are more concerned with planned change.

Innovation has been defined as an object, idea or practice which is perceived to be new by the participants in the change process and also the process by which that object, idea or practice becomes adopted. Given this definition, it is obvious that schools are constantly besieged by innovations which may, or may not, be adopted and which could hence lead to change. Thus the essential features of an innovation are:

1 Its multidimensional nature—object, idea or practice.
2 Its being perceived as new by its adopters.
3 Its process-oriented emphasis.
4 Its intention of improvement.

It should be emphasised that innovations which are *perceived* as *new* by the great majority of participants are still considered as innovations even if the innovation has been functioning elsewhere. Thus an object, idea or practice may be imported from another location and, because it is perceived to be new, still considered and treated as an innovation. Hoyle (1976) also emphasises the dual nature of innovations as new objects, ideas or practices as well as the process of adoption. He then suggests that the process of adoption may be seen as a continuum, beginning with invention and concluding with adoption, as illustrated in figure 10.3.

In figure 10.3 Hoyle highlights the significant phenomena in the process of an innovation from its embryonic beginnings to its adoption by users. It is suggested here, however, that dissemination is a more appropriate

Figure 10.3   Process of innovation

Source: After E. Hoyle, 1976

concept than diffusion to employ in this model (particularly where planned change is occurring). This is because diffusion is defined as the natural spread of an innovation while dissemination is defined as the deliberate process of facilitating the spread of an innovation (see glossary).

Hoyle (1976) further suggests that the adoption phase encountered in the process of innovation incorporates the concepts of acceptance of the innovation, over time, by adopting units through specific channels of communication, to an educational structure and culture.

Characteristics of innovations

The extent to which innovations are adopted, implemented and even adapted by educators is profoundly influenced by the very nature of those innovations, or the way those innovations may be represented to participants in the situation where change is occurring. In other words, the very characteristics of the new idea, object or practice may well determine how successful it will be put into practice.

A survey of the literature (Nicholls, 1983; Hall, et al., 1975; Hoyle, 1976; Fullan, 1982, 1987; Huberman & Miles, 1984; Miles et al., 1987; Marsh, 1988) has revealed five significant characteristics of innovations which help explain the difference between the varying adoption rates of innovations. Where there is evidence of a high degree of these characteristics present, the innovation has a significant chance of being successfully adopted.

Certainly the literature presents a clear message for change agents and those who would initiate planned educational change. If you want the innovation to be *adopted successfully* in schools, employ innovations which are as consistent as possible with the following characteristics. Or, if that is not possible, modify the innovation so that it represents the following characteristics as closely as possible.

Relative advantage

The extent to which an innovation is perceived to be more advantageous to the user than existing ideas, objects or practices constitutes its relative advantage. That is, if the relative advantage of the innovation is high, its chances of successful implementation are also high. At the level of the individual, such as a classroom teacher, the relative advantage of an innovation is an extremely significant factor in accounting for an adoption/rejection decision. The key factor is the teacher's perception that the innovation will enhance one's teaching or enhance student learning.

The extensive research of Gene Hall and his team (1975, 1979, 1987) in Texas has substantiated this position clearly. In terms of their Levels of Use (LoU) indicator, Hall and his colleagues found that teachers will not rise above the preliminary levels unless a perceived relative advantage exists. The team also developed the concept Stages of Concern (SoC) to explain levels of teachers' feelings as they become involved in the implementation of an innovation.

Indeed, a high relative advantage may be the most significant factor in accounting for the innovation's success or failure. Advantages may be perceived by users in terms of greater efficiency, cost saving, educational enhancement time saving or greater rewards such as enhanced student learning. At the level of the individual teacher relating to a specific curriculum innovation, it is highly unlikely that the teacher would implement an innovation effectively if there was no perceived relative advantage.

Nicholls notes (1983:24) that innovations manifesting this characteristic tend to have high adoption rates and subsequently high rates of institutionalisation. Examples include the use of conference writing in primary schools, introducing reading programs for secondary students, the use of overhead projectors, the four-term school year in most Australian states (introduced from mid-1980s) and four-year training programs for teachers. What other examples can you cite from curricula with which you are familiar? Certainly a lot of audio-visual hardware has been perceived as of high relative advantage for teachers, although interestingly the same could not be said of a lot of software and materials.

The 1990s has already, and will continue, to witness considerable curriculum change as our society attempts to relate to high levels of post-compulsory schooling and high levels of youth unemployment. The outcomes of sustained attempts at resolving these problems (Finn, 1991; Mayer, 1992; Carmichael, 1992) will be implemented in schools in the early–mid 1990s. The result will be a substantial change to the way curriculum experiences are offered to post-compulsory students. Should these attempts be perceived as having low levels of relative advantage to teachers or students, their implementation will be resisted.

Compatibility

Where an innovation or new idea, object or practice is perceived by those involved in the change context to be consistent with existing values, past experiences and present needs, it is said to have high levels of compatibility. In this situation it is also highly likely have a high rate of adoption. Essentially this occurs because the innovation, whilst being new, does not demand substantial changes to behaviour by participants and thus is not perceived as a threat to individuals.

High levels of compatibility, as one would expect, enhance a sense of security within individuals in the change context and hence less risk is required should the innovation be adopted. It also implies that the innovation will not be radically different from existing ideas, objects or practices. Thus innovations that rate highly on compatibility, or at least appear to rate highly, will experience more successful adoption and subsequent implementation.

Conference writing in primary schools appears to be an innovation that is being adopted successfully. Although perceived as new, this procedure certainly has a high compatibility with past writing practices. In many states the adoption of open-area schools was resisted because of the lack of compatibility with existing teaching practices. It is worth noting that recent models of school design have reverted more to traditional concepts. Daily physical education ('daily PE') appears to have a high adoption rate in primary schools as its compatibility is high with existing physical education practices.

Complexity

Should an innovation be perceived to be unduly complex in nature, potential adopters will avoid it. Nicholls defines complexity as 'the degree to which an innovation is perceived as relatively difficult to understand and use' (1983:25). The emphasis again is on the perception held by participants, rather than the actual level of difficulty. Hence those involved in the change process, and particularly change agents, should endeavour to present the innovation as a straightfoward, uncomplicated change.

While this appears obvious and logical, apparently many developers have not been aware that high levels of complexity in an innovation can be a significant factor inhibiting adoption. Major curriculum projects such as MACOS, ASEP, SEMP and so forth were generally perceived to be too complex, especially to use, by teachers. Conversely, conference writing in primary schools is not perceived as too complex in use or understanding. As it has high levels of relative advantage and compatibility as well, it is likely to be a successful innovation.

The introduction of modern computers in schools is an interesting example of a mixed reaction to an innovation by teachers. Some teachers perceive computers as low in complexity, high in relative advantage and reasonably compatible and consequently have implemented them effectively into their teaching. However, quite clearly many teachers have firmly resisted anything to do with computers, particularly as this innovation is perceived as possessing extremely high levels of complexity. In large measure this reaction is age, subject and technology-experience related, where older teachers, particularly those with little experience with modern technology and who do not perceive the need to use computers in their subjects, have resisted using computers both personally and in teaching their area of the curriculum.

Trialability

There is some evidence to suggest that if an innovation can be partially implemented before full-scale adoption is attempted, then it is more likely to succeed. It seems logical to trial an innovation first, receive feedback from participants and then make appropriate revisions before one attempts to implement the innovation generally. Yet many educational innovations do not manifest this characteristic which Nicholls defines as: ' . . . the extent to which an innovation can be tried out on a limited basis' (1983:25).

A relationship certainly exists between trialability and later adoption rates, although it is not always positive. In education, for example, there are instances where curricula and curriculum materials have been tested only to be subsequently rejected by teachers. This may be due as much to the other characteristics influencing the innovation's adoption as to the early exposure factor. Certain curriculum materials, for example, were not tested before complete adoption was attempted and, as changes were not made to meet local needs, the innovations were rejected. Many curriculum packages from the United States in the 1970s were in this category.

On the other hand, the successful adoption of the K10 Social Studies Syllabus in Western Australia was due, in part, to early testing of the prototype material (Marsh & Stafford, 1988). Not only were trial exposures conducted, but several revisions of the tested materials were carried out as well (Marsh & Stafford, 1988). This flexibility gives an innovation additional strength and opportunity to be adopted successfully. What curriculum examples can you cite of successfully adopted innovations that were tested?

Communication

When the features and benefits of an innovation are communicated effectively to others, it is more likely that it will be adopted successfully. Logically this means that others cannot adopt what they do not know about and thus it is incumbent upon change agents and others to ensure that potential adopters are aware of the innovation's existence. While this appears to be obvious and logical, many innovations do not succeed largely because of poor levels of communication. This can certainly be the case in schools.

The communication process is not as straightforward a task as it sounds as there are numerous barriers within schools preventing effective communication. Barriers may be found in bureaucratic educational systems, information blockages in schools, overloaded teachers unable or unwilling to respond, ineffective commercial distributors and so forth. Any change agent planning to implement an innovation should ensure the availability of effective communication channels. Indeed this would one of the first steps undertaken by a change agent seeking to enhance the implementation of an innovation.

There are countless curriculum innovations that teachers know little or nothing about and hence cannot implement. Many curriculum innovations developed by agencies external to the school system fall into this situation. In recent years this includes road safety curriculum materials, environmental studies curriculum packages, health education materials and so forth. In addition the earlier curriculum materials developed in Australia, Britain and the United States, such as ASEP, BSCS, CHEM Study, HSGP, ISIS, SEMP and many others, are largely unknown by the modern generation of teachers.

A final characteristic which might have a bearing on the rate of adoption of innovations is *status;* the importance attached to the innovation (Marsh, 1986:106). Where individuals, such as classroom teachers, ascribe high status to an innovation, its chances of successful implementation are significantly increased. Many major curriculum reports (Carrick, Beazley, Blackburn) received high initial status and hence received extensive support. Can you think of others?

Overall, the above factors suggest strategic actions for would-be change agents and those interested in facilitating the implementation of innovations. And for those involved in developing innovations the message is clear—make your innovation more acceptable, if you wish it to be adopted effectively, according to the above criteria.

Summary

- The final phase of the model of curriculum development outlined in chapter 3 is application. This involves implementing and modifying the curriculum in the short term, as well as long-term monitoring and curriculum evaluation.
- With an examination of the final phase of the curriculum algorithm—application—it is now complete.
- Curriculum change is the process of transformation of phenomena and it has the dimensions of rate, scale, degree, continuity and direction.
- Planned change, particularly appropriate to curriculum, is defined as a deliberate and collaborative process to solve a problem or plan and attain an improved state of functioning.
- Skilbeck has suggested four principal sources of curriculum change—changes in society (indirect and direct effects); change in education (indirect and direct effects).
- When curriculum change occurs, the process involves:
  — Initiation: an initial concern.
  — Adoption: acceptance, but not security.

— Implementation: effecting change into practice.
— Institutionalisation: consolidation of the change into normal practice.

* To facilitate change, a number of strategies are available which can be grouped into:
  a Rational-empirical strategies.
  b Normative-re-educative strategies.
  c Power-coercive strategies.
* Change agents may play a very significant role in enhancing the implementation of an innovation
* Innovations are defined as any object, idea or practice which is perceived as new and also the process whereby that object, idea or practice becomes adopted.
* Innovations that are more readily adopted and implemented are characterised by a high degree of relative advantage, compatibility, effective communication, trialability and low complexity.
* Curriculum developers must be aware of change and how to facilitate it as this is a feature of a successfully implemented curriculum.

Appendix

'The Hobart Declaration on Schooling', April 1989

Common and Agreed National Goals for Schooling in Australia

Ten national goals for Schooling will, for the first time, provide a frame-work for co-operation between Schools, States and Territories and the Commonwealth. The goals are to assist schools and systems to develop specific objectives and strategies, particularly in the areas of curriculum and assessment.

The agreed national goals for schooling include the following aims:

1 To provide an excellent education for all young people, being one which develops their talents and capacities to full potential, and is relevant to the social, cultural and economic needs of the nation.

2 To enable all students to achieve high standards of learning and to develop self-confidence, optimism, high self-esteem, respect for others, and achievement of personal excellence.

3 To promote equality of educational opportunities, and to provide for groups with special learning needs.

4 To respond to the current and emerging economic and social needs of the nation, and to provide those skills which will allow students maximum flexibility and adaptability in their future employment and other aspects of life.

5 To provide a foundation for further education and training, in terms of knowledge and skills, respect for learning and positive attitudes for life-long education.

6 To develop in students:
   - the skills of English literacy, including skills in listening, speaking, reading and writing;

- skills of numeracy, and other mathematical skills;
- skills of analysis and problem solving;
- skills of information processing and computing;
- an understanding of the role of science and technology in society, together with scientific and technological skills;
- a knowledge and appreciation of Australia's historical and geographical contexts;
- a knowledge of languages other than English;
- an appreciation and understanding of, and confidence to participate in, the creative arts;
- an understanding of, and concern for, balanced development and the global environment; and
- a capacity to exercise judgment in matters of morality, ethics and social justice.

7 To develop knowledge, skills, attitudes and values which will enable students to participate as active and informed citizens in our democratic Australian society within an international context.

8 To provide students with an understanding and respect for our cultural heritage including the particular cultural background of Aboriginal and ethnic groups.

9 To provide for the physical development and personal health and fitness of students, and for the creative use of leisure time.

10 To provide appropriate career education and knowledge of the world of work, including an understanding of the nature and place of work in our society.

References

The following references relating to curriculum will be of value to you in your study of curriculum in general and curriculum development in particular.

Anyon, J. (1980) 'Social Class and the hidden curriculum of work', *Journal of Education* , 162, 67–92

Apple, M (1983) *Education and Power* London: Routledge & Kegan Paul

——(1990) *Ideology and Curriculum* 2nd edn, London: Routledge & Kegan Paul

——(1992) 'The text and cultural politics', *Educational Researcher*, 21, 7, 4–11

——(1993) *The Politics of Official Knowledge* New York: Routledge

Australian Education Council (1989) *Common and Agreed National Goals for Schooling in Australia* Hobart: AEC

Ball, D. (1990) 'The mathematical understandings that preservice teachers bring to teacher education', *Elementary School Journal*, 90, 449–66

Barry, K. & King, L. (1988) *Beginning Teaching* Sydney: Social Sciences Press

Beazley, K. (Chair) (1984) *Education in Western Australia* Report of the Committee of Inquiry into Education in Western Australia, Perth

Bennis, W. (1966) *Changing Organizations* New York: McGraw-Hill

Bennis, W., Benne, K. & Chin, R. (1976) *The Planning of Change* New York: Holt, Rinehart & Winston

Beyer, L. & Apple, M. (1988) *The Curriculum: Problems, Politics and Possibilities* Albany, New York: State University of New York

Blackburn, J. (Chair) (1984) *Ministerial Review of Post-compulsory Schooling* Melbourne, Ministry of Education

Bloom, B. S. (1971) *Handbook on Formative and Summative Evaluation of Student Learning* New York: McGraw-Hill

Board of Studies, NSW (1991) *Curriculum Requirements for NSW Schools* North Sydney: BOS

—— (1992) *Curriculum Outcomes*, North Sydney: BOS

Brady, L. (1981) The Relationship Between School Based Curriculum Development and Organizational Climate, PhD thesis, Sydney: Macquarie University

——(1992) *Curriculum Development in Australia* 4th edn, Sydney: Prentice-Hall

Bruner, J . (1965) *The Process of Education* 2nd edn, Cambridge, Massachusetts: Harvard University Press

Caldwell, B. (1985a) 'The Management of Curriculum Development: Shifting the Focus to Leadership' (conference paper) Hobart: SPATE Conference

——(1985b) 'Managing Curriculum Development in Schools: Implications for the Beazley Report' (conference paper) Perth: Western Australian Curriculum Conference

Caldwell, B. & Spinks, J. (1986) *Policy Making and Planning for School Effectiveness* Hobart: Education Department of Tasmania

Carmichael, L. (Chair) (1992) *Australian Vocational Certificate Training System* Employment and Skills Formation Council, Canberra: AGPS, Canberra

Carrick, J. (Chair) (1989) *Report of the Committee of Review of New South Wales Schools* Sydney: NSW Government

Chin, R. (1967) 'Basic Structures and Procedures in Effecting Change' in E. Morphet (ed.) *Educational Organizational and Administration Concepts Practice and Issues* Englewood-Cliffs, New Jersey: Prentice-Hall

Cohen, D. & Harrison, M. (1982) *Curriculum Action Project* Sydney: Macquarie University

Cole, P. & Chan, L. (1987) *Teaching Principles and Practice* Sydney: Prentice-Hall

Curriculum Branch, Education Department of Western Australia (1981) *Social Studies K10 Syllabus* Perth: EDWA

Curriculum Development Centre (1977) *Support Systems for SBCD* Canberra: Study Group of the CDC, AGPS

——(1980) *Core Curriculum for Australian Schools* Canberra: CDC, AGPS

Davis, E. (1980) *Teachers as Curriculum Evaluators* Sydney: George Allen & Unwin

Dawkins, J. (1988) *Strengthening Australia's Schools: A Consideration of the Focus and Content of Schooling* Canberra: AGPS

Deschamp, P. (1983) Planning for teaching—a study of teachers' intentions in planning, PhD thesis, Perth: Murdoch University

Deschamp, P. & Ryan, A. (1986) 'A Model for Teachers' Curriculum Planning: Paradigm or Algorithm?' (conference paper) Perth: Western Australian Curriculum Conference

Dewey, J. (1916) *Democracy and Education* New York: Macmillan

Doll, R. C. (1978) *Curriculum Improvement: Decision making and Process* Boston: Allyn & Bacon

Dunkin, M. and Biddle, B. (1974) *The Study of Teaching* New York: Holt, Rinehart & Winston

Ebel, R. (1972) *Essentials of Educational Measurement* Englewood Cliffs, New Jersey: Prentice Hall

Eisner, E. (1979) *The Educational Imagination: On the Design and Evaluation of School Programs* New York: Macmillan

Eisner, E. W. & Vallance, E. (eds) (1974) *Conflicting Conceptions of Curriculum* Berkeley, California: McCutchan

Feimen-Nemser, S. & Parker, M. (1990) 'Making subject matter part of the conversation in learning to teach' *Journal of Teacher Education* 41, 3, 32–43

Finn, B. (Chair) (1991) *Young People's Participation in Post-Compulsory Education and Training*, Report of the AEC Review Committee, Canberra: AGPS

Fraser, B. & Fisher, D. (1983) *Assessment of Classroom Psychosocial Environment* Perth: WAIT

Freire, P. (1970) *Pedagogy of the Oppressed* New York: Herder & Herder

Fullan, M. (1982) *The Meaning of Educational Change* New York: Teachers' College Press

——(1987) 'Support systems for implementing curriculum in schools' Keynote address, Australian Curriculum Studies Association, Macquarie University, Sydney

Gagne, R. M. (1970) *The Conditions of Learning* New York: Holt, Rinehart & Winston

Gall, M. (1981) *Handbook for Evaluating and Selecting Curriculum Materials* Boston: Allyn & Bacon

Gay, L. (1985) *Educational Evaluation and Measurement* Columbus, Ohio: Charles Merrill

Giroux, H. (1981) *Ideology, Culture and the Process of Schooling* Philadelphia: Temple University Press

Glatthorn, A. (1987) *Curriculum Leadership* Glenview, Illinois: Scott, Foresman

Gress, J. & Purpel, D. (eds) (1988) *Curriculum: An Introduction to the Field* Berkeley, California: McCutchan

Grossman, P., Wilson, S. & Shulman, L. (1989) 'Teachers of substance: the subject matter knowledge of teachers', in M. Reynolds (ed.) *The Knowledge Base for Beginning Teachers* New York: Pergamon

Habermas, J. (1972) *Knowledge and Human Interest* London: Heinemann

Hall, G. et al. (1975) 'Levels of Use of the Innovation' *Journal of Teacher Education* 29, 1, 52–56

Hall, G., George, A. & Rutherford, W. (1979) *Measuring the Stages of Concern about the Innovation* 2nd edn, Austin, Texas: University of Texas

Hall, G. & Hord, S. (1987) *Change in Schools: Facilitating the Process* Albany, New York: State University of New York

Harris, A., Lawn, M. & Prescott, W. (eds) (1978) *Curriculum Innovation* London: Croom Helm

Harrow, A. (1972) *A Taxonomy of the Psychomotor Domain* New York: McKay

Hattie, J. (1992) 'Measuring the effects of schooling' *Australian Journal of Education*, 36, 1, 5–13

Havelock, R. (1979) *The Change Agent's Guide to Innovation in Education* New Jersey: Free Press

Hewitson, M. (1982) *The Hidden Curriculum* St Lucia, Queensland: published by the author

Hirst, P. (1968) 'The contribution of philosophy to the study of curriculum' in J. Kerr (ed.) *Changing the Curriculum* London: University of London Press

——(1974) *Knowledge and the Curriculum* London: Routledge & Kegan Paul

Hirst, P. & Peters, R. (1970) *The Logic of Education* London, Routledge & Kegan Paul

Holt, M. (1978) *The Common Curriculum: Its Structure and Style in the Comprehensive School* London: Routledge & Kegan Paul

Hoyle, E. (1976) *Strategies of Curriculum Change,* Unit 23, Curriculum Design, Milton Keynes: Open University

Huberman, A. & Miles, M. (1984) *Innovation Up Close: How School Improvement Works,* New York: Plenum

Hughes, P. (ed.) (1973) *The Teacher's Role in Curriculum Design* Sydney: Angus & Robertson

Hughes, P. (1990) *A National Curriculum: Promise or Warning,* Canberra: Australian College of Education

Hughes, P. et al. (1979) *Educational Evaluation in Australia: A New Challenge for Teachers,* Teachers as evaluators project, Canberra

Hunkins, F. P. (1980) *Curriculum Development: Program Improvement* Columbus, Ohio: Merrill

Hyman, R. (1973) *Approaches in Curriculum* Englewood Cliffs, New Jersey: Prentice-Hall

Illich, I. (1971) *De-Schooling Society* New York: Harper & Row

Interim Committee for the Australian Schools Commission (Karmel Report) (1973) *Schools in Australia* Canberra: AGPS

Jackson, P. (1968) *Life in Classrooms* New York: Holt, Rineholt & Winston

Joyce, B. & Weil, M. (1992) *Models of Teaching* 4th edn, Englewood Cliffs, New Jersey: Prentice-Hall

Karmel, P. (Chair) (1973) *Schools in Australia* Report of the Interim Committee of the Australian Schools Commission, Canberra: AGPS

Kelly, A. V. (1977) *The Curriculum: Theory and Practice* 2nd edn, London: Harper & Row

Keeves, J. (ed) (1988) *Educational Research, Methodology and Measurement* Oxford, Pergamon

Kemmis, S. (1986) *Curriculum Theorising: Beyond Reproduction Theory* Geelong: Deakin University Press

Kemmis, S. & Stake, R. (1988) *Evaluating Curriculum* Geelong: Deakin University Press

Kennedy, K. (1989) National initiatives in curriculum: the Australian context, *British Journal of Educational Studies,* 37, 2, 11–124

——(1991) National curriculum initiatives as symbolic political action, Paper presented to the annual conference of Australian Association for Research in Education, Gold Coast

Kennedy, M. (1990) *A Survey of Recent Literature on Teachers' Subject Matter Knowledge* Michigan: National Center for Research on Teacher Learning (NCRTL), Michigan State University

Kerlinger, F. (1986) *Foundations of Educational Research* 3rd edn, New York: Holt, Rinehart & Winston

Kirk, J. (1986) *The Core Curriculum* London: Hodder & Stoughton

Kliebard, H. (1970) 'The Tyler rationale', *School Review* 78, 2

Krathwohl, D., Bloom, B. and Masior, B. (1964) *Taxonomy of Education Objectives: Affective Domain* New York: McKay

Lawton, D. (1973) *Social Change, Educational Theory and Curriculum Planning* London: University of London Press

Lawton, D. et al. (1978) *Theory and Practice of Curriculum Studies* London: Routledge & Kegan Paul

Lewy, A. (1977) *Planning the School Curriculum* Paris: UNESCO

Lortie, D. (1975) *School Teacher: A Sociological Study* Chicago: University of Chicago Press

MacDonald, B. and Walker, R. (1976) *Changing the Curriculum* London: Open Books

Macdonald, J. & Purpel, D. (1988) *Curriculum: An Introduction to the Field* 2nd edn, Berkeley, California: McCutchan

McLaughlin, H. & Phillips, D. (eds) (1991) *Evaluation and Education: At Quarter Century*, Chicago: National Society for the Study of Education (NSSE), University of Chicago Press

McNeil, J. D. (1985) *Curriculum: A Comprehensive Introduction* 3rd edn, Boston: Little, Brown

Mager, R. (1962) *Preparing Instructional Objectives* California: Fearon

Marsh, C. (1986) *Curriculum: An Analytical Introduction* Sydney: Novak

Marsh, C. & Print, M. (1975) *The Social Sciences: Skills and Teaching Methods* Perth: Bookland

Marsh, C. & Stafford, K. (1988) *Curriculum: Australian Practices and Issues* 2nd edn, Sydney: McGraw-Hill

Mayer, E. (Chair) (1992) *Employment Related Key Competencies for Post-Compulsory Education and Training* Canberra: AGPS

Miles, M. (1964) *Innovation in Education* New York: Teachers' College Press

——(1983) 'Unravelling the mysteries of institutionalisation' *Educational Leadership*, 41 (3):14–22

Miles, M., Ekholm, M. & Vandenberghe, R. (1987) *Lasting School Improvement: Exploring the Process of Institutionalisation,* Paris: OECD

Miles, M., Saxl, E. & Lieberman, A. (1988) 'What skills do change agents need? An empirical view' *Curriculum Inquiry,* 18, 2, 157–93

Musgrave, P. (1979) *Society and the Curriculum in Australia* Sydney: George Allen & Unwin

Neill, A. S. (1960) *Summerhill* New York: Hart

Nicholls, A. (1983) *Managing Educational Innovations* London: George Allen & Unwin

Nicholls, A. & Nicholls, A. H. (1978) *Developing a Curriculum: A Practical Guide* 2nd edn, London: George Allen & Unwin

NSW Department of School Education (1991) *The Values We Teach* revised edn, Sydney

NSW Ministry of Education and Youth Affairs (1989) *Excellence and Equity: New South Wales Curriculum Reform*, Sydney

Parlett, M. & Hamilton, D. (1972) *Evaluation as Illumination: A New Approach to the Study of Innovatory Programs* Edinburgh: CRES, University of Edinburgh

Patton, M. (1986) *Utilisation-Focussed Evaluation,* 2nd edn, Beverley Hills, California: Sage

——(1988) 'The evaluator's responsibility for utilisation' *Evaluation Practice,* 9 (2), 5–24

Peters, R. (1966) *Ethics and Education* London: Allen & Unwin

Phenix, P. (1964) *Realms of Meaning: A Philosophy of the Curriculum for General Education* New York: McGraw-Hill

Piaget, J. (1963) *Origins of Intelligence in Children* New York: Norton

Pinar, W. (ed.) (1975) *Curriculum Theorizing* Berkeley, California: McCutchan

Piper, K. (1976) *Evaluation in the Social Sciences* Canberra: AGPS

——(1991) 'National curriculum two years on' *Curriculum Perspectives*, 9, 3, 3–7

Pratt, D. (1980) *Curriculum: Design and Development* New York: Harcourt, Brace & Jovanovich

Print, M. (1986) *Curriculum Planning and Management* Perth: WACAE Monograph

——(1988) *Curriculum Development and Design* Sydney: Allen & Unwin

——(1989) 'Evaluation at systemic level', Paper presented at Adelaide conference of the Australian Association for Research in Education

——(1990) *Curriculum Review of Social Studies and Social Sciences* Education Perth: WA Ministry of Education

——(1991) 'A national curriculum initiative in Australia' Paper presented to Australian Association for Research in Education annual conference, Gold Coast

Reynolds, J. and Skilbeck, M. (1976) *Culture and the Classroom* London: Open Books

Reynolds, M. (ed.) (1989) *Knowledge Base for Beginning Teachers* New York: Pergamon

Robitaille, D. & Overgaard, V. (1991) *Third International Mathematics and Science Study* Vancouver: International Association for the Evaluation of Educational Achievement

Rogers, E. (1983) *Diffusion of Innovations* 3rd edn, New York: Free Press

Rogers, E. and Shoemaker, F. (1971) *Communication of Innovations* New York: Free Press

Ruby, A. (1992) *National Schools Strategy* Canberra: DEET

Saylor, J. G., Alexander, W. & Lewis, A. J. (1981) *Curriculum Planning for Better Teaching and Learning,* 4th edn, New York: Holt Rinehart & Winston

Schubert, W. (1986) *Curriculum: Perspective, Paradigm and Possibility* New York: Macmillan

Seddon, T. (1983) 'The hidden curriculum: an overview' *Curriculum Perspectives* 3, 1, pp. 1–6

Shulman, L. (1986) 'Those who understand: knowledge growth in teaching' *Educational Researcher*, 15, 2, 4–14

——(1987) 'Knowledge and teaching: Foundations of the new reform' *Harvard Educational Review*, 57, 1–22

Sieber, S. (1968) 'Organisational Influence on Innovative Roles' in T. Eidell and J. Kitchell (eds) *Knowledge Production and Utilisation in Educational Administration* Oregon: University of Oregon Press

Simons, H. (1987) *Getting to Know Schools in a Democracy: The Politics and Process of Evaluation* London: Falmer Press

Skilbeck, M. (1976) *School-based Curriculum Development and Teacher Education* Mimeograph, OECD

——(1984) *School-Based Curriculum Development* London: Harper & Row

Smith, D. & Lovat (1991) *Curriculum: Action on Reflection,* 2nd edn, Sydney: Social Science Press

Smith, N. (1989) 'The Weiss-Patton debate: Illuminating fundamental concerns' *Evaluation Practice,* 10, 1, 5–13

Sockett, H. (1976) *Designing the Curriculum* London: Open Books

Soliman, I. (ed.) (1981) *A Model for School Based Curriculum Planning* Canberra: Curriculum Development Centre

Stenhouse, L. (1975) *An Introduction to Curriculum Research and Development* London: Heinemann Educational Books

Stufflebeam, D. et al. (1971) *Educational Evaluation and Decision Making* Itasca, Illinois: Peacock

Taba, H. (1962) *Curriculum Development: Theory and Practice* New York: Harcourt, Brace & World

Tanner, D. & Tanner, L. N. (1980) *Curriculum Development: Theory into Practice* 2nd edn, New York: Macmillan

Tom, A. (1973) 'Teacher reaction to a systematic approach to curriculum implementation' *Curriculum Theory Network* 11, pp. 86–93

Toomey, R. (1977) 'Teachers' approaches to curriculum planning' *Curriculum Inquiry* 7.2, pp. 121–9

Tyler, R. W. (1949) *Basic Principles of Curriculum and Instruction* Chicago: University of Chicago Press

van Dalen, D. (1973) *Understanding Educational Research* 3rd edn, New York: McGraw-Hill

Walker, D. F. (1971) 'A naturalistic model for curriculum development' *School Review* 80, 1, pp. 51–65

Walker, J. & Evers, C. (1988) 'The epistemological unity of educational research' in J. Keeves (ed) *Educational Research, Methodology and Measurement* Oxford: Pergamon

Walton, J. and Morgan, R. (eds) (1978) *Some Perspectives on School Based Curriculum Development* Armidale: University of New England

Weiss, C. (1988) 'Evaluation for decisions: Is anybody there? Does anybody care?' *Evaluation Practice,* 9 (1), 5–19

Western Australian Education Department (1981) *Social Studies K10 Syllabus* Perth: EDWA

Wheeler, D. K. (1967) *Curriculum Process* London: University of London Press

Wiles, J. & Bondi, J. (1989) *Curriculum Development* Columbus, Ohio: Merill

Wilson, S. & Wineburg, S. (1988) 'Peering at history from different lenses' *Teachers College Record,* 89, 542–39

Wyatt, T. & Ruby, A. (eds) (1990) *Educational Indicators for Quality, Accountability and Better Practice* Sydney: Australian Conference of Directors General of Education

Young, R (1989) *A Critical Theory of Education: Habermas and our Children's Future* New York: Harvester Wheatsheaf

Zais, R. S. (1976) *Curriculum: Principles and Foundations* New York: Harper & Row

Zaltman, G. et al. (1972) *Creating Social Change* New York: Wiley

——(1976) *Dynamic Educational Change* New York: Wiley

Zumwalt, K. (1989) 'Beginning professional teachers: The need for a curricular vision of teaching' in M. Reynolds *Knowledge Base for Beginning Teachers* New York: Pergamon

Index